To Peter
from Philip
χρονία φιλίας χάριν
Sept. 1984.

The Logic of Tragedy

The Logic of Tragedy

Morals and Integrity
in Aeschylus' *Oresteia*

Philip Vellacott

Duke University Press   Durham, N.C.   1984

Library of Congress Cataloging in Publication Data

Vellacott, Philip.
  The logic of tragedy.

  Bibliography: p.
  Includes index.
  1. Aeschylus. Oresteia.   2. Aeschylus—Religion and
ethics.   3. Ethics in literature.   4. Integrity in
literature.   5. Moral conditions in literature.
I. Title.
PA3825.A6V37   1984   882'.01   84-4057
ISBN 0-8223-0597-6

Contents

IV. Euripides' Commentary on the *Oresteia*

Preface

This book puts forward a radically new interpretation of the principal surviving works of Aeschylus, the first of European dramatists, and arguably second to none. It is concerned chiefly with the Oresteian trilogy; but since the principles I have followed in studying this work apply also to *Seven Against Thebes* and still more to *Suppliants*, an essay on each of these plays is included. Finally, since it seems to me probable that no one has ever understood Aeschylus as clearly as Euripides did, I have added chapters on the three plays in which Euripides deals with the subject matter of the *Oresteia*.

It cannot be surprising if so immodest an announcement induces in some quarters a weary or hostile incredulity. But the number of those, including not a few professional scholars, who have long felt dissatisfied with accepted views of Aeschylus, but through modesty have refrained from attempting more realistic exposition, must be considerable. The intense quality of this poet's work evokes an emotional response to any questioning of comfortably familiar attitudes. But it may be noted that in the first two plays of the *Oresteia* Aeschylus showed little concern for his audience's comfort; and the comfort that Athenians in 458 B.C. derived from *Eumenides*, and rewarded with the first prize, is so contradictory of every moral principle established in the lyrics of *Agamemnon* and in the first and second choral odes of *Eumenides*, that only the impregnable faith of Athenians in the perfection of their democratic system could have succeeded in disguising, under the acceptable robes of "reconciliation" and "a new concept of justice," the poet's profoundly tragic presentation of judicial solemnities stultified by corruption and false logic. The final pages of *Eumenides* express this deluding comfort in poetry whose fervent millennial promise is deeply affecting; and some modern expositors have embraced that comfort in similarly fervent terms, establishing for Aeschylus an image which, in my view, does him little credit. (Evidence of this is Page's famous dictum, which I have quoted in chapter 3.) To disagree so positively with scholars to whom I, like most readers of Aeschylus, am indebted for valued help, should not seem ungracious, since they too sometimes found enrichment in contradicting their predecessors; and it is to be hoped that the process will continue.

The ideas I develop in this book germinated in 1974. Having spent the previous five years in writing a study of Euripides, I settled down to a strict re-reading of the Oresteian trilogy, resolved to see as truthfully as I could what Aeschylus' text told me. I knew that twenty years earlier, when working on the Penguin translation, I had been uneasy about the traditional acceptance of "reconciliation" and the "new concept of justice," but had felt unqualified as yet to undertake a reexamination of such fundamental matters, about which many scholars of repute seemed to be in general agreement. Now, however, Euripides had taught me something both about the poets and about the audiences of Attic tragedy. In due course, with a painful and exhilarating shock of astonishment, I became aware of an overall design in Aeschylus' trilogy substantially different from that which had been so long familiar. The tracing of this design has occupied me ever since.

In October 1975 I read a paper on the *Oresteia* to a number of American Classical departments, including Harvard, Cornell, Stanford, and the University of California at Los Angeles. A condensed version of this paper appeared in the 1977 issue of *Harvard Studies in Classical Philology*. During the next few years I wrote and rewrote further lectures on the *Oresteia*, and delivered them at other American universities, including Brown, Michigan State, Duquesne, University of Minnesota, and several more, where I had already lectured on various topics in Greek drama. My warm thanks are due to more than thirty campuses whose enterprise and generous hospitality encouraged and made possible five extended lecture tours during the seventies. I am personally indebted to a number of scholars for their interest and encouragement, among whom I name with special gratitude Professor Charles Segal and Professor David Porter. In addition, I would like to express my thanks to Professor Jerry Clack for permission to use, in chapters 2 and 12, articles first published in *The Classical World*; and also for giving me, in October 1982, the opportunity of presenting the thesis of this book in six lectures delivered in the Department of Classics, Duquesne University, Pittsburgh.

It is often said—and it is broadly true—that the present generation finds Greek tragedy remote and unreal. To speak of a "generation" in this way may be taken to mean two different things. It may mean the few thousands, or hundreds, in a generation who study the plays in Greek and equip themselves with a background of Greek history and general literature. Or it may mean the larger group of those to whom European drama of the last four centuries, or the modern English and American theater repertoire, are a valued element in ordinary life. Of this larger group, perhaps one in a thousand is familiar with the Oresteian trilogy in translation. This is an absurd state of affairs, when we reflect that in the present-day European theater, from Moscow to Berlin to Paris and elsewhere, Shakespeare is a living element of intellectual experience (and what, we must sometimes wonder, can Shakespeare be like when translated—impossible feat!). To make accessible to this group of the present generation something of the majesty, theatrical excitement, and mental adventure that is to be found in Aeschylus is an urgent task for teachers of literature. But I do not think it can be undertaken as long as the present line of exposition is exclusively offered by the accredited writers to whom the reading public, and theater directors and actors, apply for expert guidance. Aeschylus wrote for an audience that comprised the whole range of human intelligence and obtuseness. The universal and timeless element in his drama is its concern with moral and humane issues. Nowhere is this element more positive, or more pertinent to the present day, than in the *Oresteia*.

The Logic of Tragedy

There is no reason inherent in the conditions of life on this earth that can make us consider ourselves obliged to do good, to be fastidious, to be polite, even. . . . All these obligations which have not their sanction in our present life seem to belong to a different world, one founded upon kindness, scrupulosity, self-sacrifice, a world entirely different from this, which we leave in order to be born into this world, before, perhaps, returning to the other to live once again beneath the sway of those unknown laws which we have obeyed because we bore their precepts in our hearts . . . those laws to which every profound work of the intellect brings us nearer.

Marcel Proust, *Remembrance of Things Past*

A word which has two meanings, the first direct, the second indirect, is the material of poetry and literature, which these arts alone can manipulate and through which they speak to the soul.

Wassily Kandinsky, *Concerning the Spiritual in Art*

I

The Concept of Integrity
in Greek Tragedy

An important part of the study of the Greek tragedies is the search for their timeless validity as documents of human destiny, quality, and experience. The questions involved in such study are not easy to categorize, and so are sometimes overlooked in academic courses. This search is what I am concerned with here. It can be fruitful only if the reader is willing to credit these poets with the kind of integrity, both artistic and moral, that precludes cynicism and superficiality. The authority for such an assumption probably cannot be argued about; the plays themselves either convince the reader or they do not. Further, in studying the plays we must, I am sure, start from the premise that, unless we can believe it possible to reach common ground with these writers on the broadest moral issues, serious assessment of their thought cannot be attempted. What the essential moral questions are with which tragedy deals I shall discuss presently; but there can be little doubt that the elusive quality we call integrity is among the chief of them.

I have been led to the present inquiry by the fact that, in some of the most notable issues arising in the tragedies, I find it hard not to disagree directly with the moral judgment generally approved in learned comment; and if I am right in some of these disagreements, there may have been serious errors of method in the traditional study of Greek tragedy. Integrity is absolute only in the rarest instances; for most of us it is a scale, upon which we endeavor to rise rather than fall; and the standard I would wish to agree upon in discussion with other scholars is that which the poets themselves set for us by the quality of their work.

I take as my starting point a profound and crucial piece of literary criticism, to be found in a book written not about Greek tragedy but about Homer's *Iliad*, from which, more than from any other source, the minds and art of the tragedians drew sustenance. I refer to the late C. H. Whitman's *Homer and the Heroic Tradition*, and to two chapters in particular. In chapter 8, "Homeric

Character and the Tradition," Whitman deals with the primary and secondary persons in the drama of the *Iliad*, other than Achilles, showing how each is related to the norm of the heroic ideal, to other heroes in the story, and to the design of the whole epic. In chapter 9, "Achilles: The Evolution of a Hero," he analyzes in great detail the central position which Achilles occupies in the structure of the poem, and traces the hero's dedication to the absolute in human values, his pursuit of integrity, his experience of grief, and his acceptance of early death as the only reward of heroism, as these elements appear in the successive phases of Achilles' response to the imperfect society of the Greek camp. In this notable exposition Whitman succeeded in an exacting task: to define the concept of personal integrity in terms which are at the same time valid in relation to the heroic world recorded by Homer, and comprehensible and vital in our twentieth century. In the former of those chapters he demonstrates the exactness, subtlety, and individuality of characterization which the epic style, despite its limiting formality, makes possible. In the latter he shows that the story of "The Wrath" is very much more than a swashbuckling tale of overblown egotism in a remote and legendary setting; that it presents, in the conflict of one hero with the society of his lesser peers, and with events that assail his conscious integrity, a statement of the tragic predicament unsurpassed in literature.

I confess that I did not read Whitman's book until 1972, by which time the general direction of my own studies in Greek tragedy was beginning to be clear; but the vision and force of those two chapters confirmed and developed my own method and perceptions with a clarity for which I remain deeply grateful. I hope to show in the following pages how the widely different fields of epic and tragedy have in common this focal concept of integrity, and that an understanding of it is one of the essentials for a true interpretation of fifth-century drama.

Whitman's analyses of the characters of the *Iliad*—of Diomedes, Menelaus, Ajax of Salamis, Nestor, Patroclus, Antilochus, and others, drawn from many passages—treat these creations of Homer as living persons each with his relationship both to those with whom he shares his life in the camp and on the battlefield, and to the undefined but acknowledged ideal of heroic *aretē*. He shows how the contrast between, for example, Diomedes and Ajax further illuminates the individuality of each; how opposite characters imply distinct views of what reality is, so that "Odysseus sees reality as the situation or problem before him; Achilles sees it as something in himself." Homer's people are moved partly by necessities or conventions of their own time, as we are by ours; but more by their own feeling and purpose. Each one must therefore be described on two planes, that of type and that of individuality; and in some cases, notably those of Agamemnon and Achilles, the second plane strongly modifies the first. The less critical listener accepts the type, and misses the individuality that is significant for the understanding of the poem.

It is in his study of Homer's Agamemnon that Whitman shows most clearly the gentle irony with which Homer sets the one plane beside the other, the individuality beside the type, inviting the listener to consider internal rather than external values. "Homer's poem," he writes, "aimed at drawing the significance of the whole epic tradition about Troy into the framework of a single dramatic action." Since the apex of the moral structure is to be Achilles, a warrior from the small town of Phthia, while Agamemnon, as king of the most powerful Greek state, is to remain commander-in-chief, that formal supremacy of Agamemnon must be combined, by poetic art, with an inferior dramatic status. "Homer has handled him [Agamemnon] with the most subtle irony, as a foil to Achilles, using all his traditional eminence as a means of diminishing the man." Nestor pronounces that Agamemnon is greater than Achilles "because he rules over more men." That line is perhaps material for a study of the Homeric idea of kingship; certainly it is part of the poet's ironic portrait of Agamemnon. Agamemnon's dependence on external symbols, his preference of material values to personal, his assumption that Achilles, estranged by insult, can be bought back with gifts; his stubbornness which insists, when he instructs his envoys to Achilles, that he, Agamemnon, is to be acknowledged as "the kinglier"; the unique savagery of his behavior on the battlefield, recounted in the same terms, in the same tone, as the poet employs in relating other men's prowess, but pushed by gruesome detail just beyond the borderline of convention into repugnance—all these unite to present, in Whitman's words, "a magnificently dressed incompetence, without spirit or spiritual concern." "Yet the touch is everywhere light, and Agamemnon is allowed to gain sympathy, if not respect. His very weakness . . . wins him some measure of compassion" (p. 161). Finally (p. 163): "Yet none of this is ever overtly stated. He is always the king, with honorifics ever present."

Homer, then, in composing the multifarious elements of the *Iliad* into their final and morally significant form, accomplished two things. For popular audiences of his own and later centuries he provided a tale of action, defeat, and victory, a perpetual fountain of wit, pathos, and zest, a crowded gallery of living portraits, an iconography of natural religion, a treasury of family histories and valorous ideals. All this could be enjoyed on an everyday level by innumerable listeners old and young, content to deal with the rough and beautiful and unjust world without looking far below its surface. For such listeners Achilles naturally would be the supreme hero, Agamemnon a dull and unattractive figurehead; Achilles a man who spoke truth on all occasions without fear or favor (*Il.* 9.312f.), in contrast to, for example, Odysseus *polytropos*, "of many wiles." Achilles' resistance to unjust authority, his affection for Patroclos and for Briseis, his sternness and tenderness to Priam, all contribute to a heroic and admirable character. But all these are qualities that can be defined and tabulated; they do not in aggregate complete Homer's account of Achilles.

Whitman's study follows the track of something more difficult to describe in words. When, as he expresses it, Achilles "refuses the easy answer of Phoenix, that social obligation must take precedence" over personal integrity (p. 182, *Il.* 9.496ff.), he is not asserting merely the paramount value of warlike eminence or of truthful speaking. Rather Achilles declares that the sense of nobility and honor is a possession which does not depend on the size of one's city, on the outward comparison implied in the word *basileuteros*, "more kingly" (*Il.* 9.160 and 392), but on the personal quality which each man's self-knowledge, such as it is, must claim—if necessary without human support—solely on "the disposal of Zeus" (9.608). This is not to say that the theme of the *Iliad* is an esoteric one, except insofar as all great poetry includes an esoteric element. Achilles was widely admired in the ancient world, but few, probably, could "pluck out the heart of his mystery," which was something deeper than the definable qualities which most listeners would recognize and applaud.

Agamemnon values himself as most men valued him, for his wealth and regal position. Most men valued Achilles for his warlike prowess, beauty, and speed of foot. But such qualities must be related, for their final assessment, to another quality, powerful and unmistakable, yet so elusive that English has no adjective for it, only the noun "integrity"; while the Greek *aretē*, which may include it, includes much more. The word *haplotēs*, "singleness," discussed by Plato in *Hippias Minor* with reference to Homer's Achilles, seems there to mean little more than the forthright speaking referred to so passionately in 9.312f.; it is a relative virtue. To those who look for the quality of integrity, its presence in Achilles is as plain as its absence in Agamemnon. Because it is indefinable, the poet can only say to his audience, "Look, be moved, and understand."

The understanding of Homer which the Attic tragedians possessed must have differed greatly in detail from that which a modern scholar gains through years of study; but it seems reasonable to assume, from the level of thought that we encounter in the surviving dramas, that they recognized in the principal characters of the *Iliad* Homer's appraisal of "what is to be valued in a man." And if, as I believe, we may accept as valid Whitman's tracing of Achilles' quest for absolute integrity, then it is right also to assume that similar appraisals are at work in the *Oresteia*, in *Ajax* and *Oedipus at Colonus*, in *Medea*, *Heracleidae*, and *Orestes*; that contemporary estimates of the characters of Aeschylus' Clytemnestra, Sophocles' Heracles, Euripides' Theseus, Demophon, and Helen, were divided between the majority who discerned only types and the very small minority who recognized the paramount importance, both for life and for dramatic structure, of individual character.

The dramatic poets depended for their life as artists on a community which, while its corporate activity presented many admirable aesthetic achievements, did not attempt to live, in personal matters, by any correspondingly refined or sensitive ethical code. A large proportion of those whose applause may have influenced the award of prizes at the Dionysiac festivals were like the man who voted to ostracize Aristeides, or like Dionysus in *The Frogs* judging Aeschylus and Euripides. The characters and situations presented by the three tragedians conformed, for the most part, to certain types; but they were always given, in the plays that have survived for us, a life and significance developed beyond that of the type, and sometimes this individuality is the decisive element in the drama. Naturally most spectators saw and accepted the conventional type, while the unique treatment was apparent only to a few, perhaps in some cases to none. Theseus must, for the average citizen, always be noble, his son Demophon a hero, Menelaus always a villain, Oedipus and Heracles always magnificent; Helen a whore, Praxithea a heroine, Clytemnestra a criminal. It was inevitable therefore that in the dramatic art of the tragedians irony—the kind of irony Homer employs in presenting Agamemnon—should be a staple method. The fact that no writing survives to tell us how much of their irony was understood is no more surprising than the fact that something like Whitman's exposition of Homer's Achilles was not written in the eighteenth century A.D. or in the third century B.C.

At this point in the argument some critics may take refuge in the proposition that *de moribus non disputandum*, or *alia tempora alii mores*. The differences in social assumption between the fifth century B.C. and our own day, it is said, are great, and hard to define. Questions of sexual relationship, within marriage or outside it, reveal wide divergence; so does the attitude to slavery. The practice of infant exposure, which persisted at least to the fourth century, can be cited as an example of differing values placed on human life; and such differences may invalidate our instinctive judgments on some situations in tragedy. But arguments based on this principle are apt to lead to confusion. For example, K. J. Dover, in "Some Neglected Aspects of Agamemnon's Dilemma," attempts an unreal distinction between Agamemnon's sacrifice of his daughter *as an act* and *as an event*. He supposes that *anankē* in *A.* 218 refers to the pressures that drove Agamemnon to perform the sacrifice, when in fact it refers rather to the inevitable course of subsequent events to which Agamemnon committed himself by his free decision to shed the blood of his own offspring. Dover more than once writes of "Aeschylus and his contemporaries" as if it could be assumed that the moral judgments of the ordinary citizen, or of "a level-headed *exegetes*" (p. 67), were likely to be comparable or even compatible with those of the poet. Arguments of this "level-headed" nature are as irrelevant to the passions of *Agamemnon* and *Choephori* as are Athena's cynicism and Apollo's perversity in *Eumenides*.

Of a different nature is the reasoning used by Whitman in his description of the long encounter between Agamemnon and Achilles. There, petty differences are lost in the broad opposition between meanness and generosity, qualities which—at least in the European context—transcend any shifts in ethical emphasis that have affected our judgment for better or worse during three millennia. For those who see the individual rather than the type, the person rather than his dress, these concepts are as clear and stable as cowardice and courage, treachery and loyalty. Even to the rough-and-ready judgment content with externals, such qualities are enough in evidence all through the *Iliad* to cast a living glow over many episodes. But the goal to which Whitman's study leads is the apprehension of that subtle, supreme quality whose illumination forms the central stream, fed by many tributaries, of the poem's twenty-four books: the integrity of Achilles. This quality is the essence of Achilles' heroic nature. The gradual development of it from the quarrel in Book 1 to the tragic sublimity of Book 24 is the achievement of the world's greatest poem. And the understanding of this concept forms the most important link between Homer and Attic tragedy.

Personal integrity is the essential criterion of the heroic. In its absolute form, displayed by Homer in the Achilles of the final books, it is the rare complete fulfillment of the precept, "Know thyself." For the common run of heroes—there are many in the *Iliad*—self-knowledge means recognition of one's limitations as a mortal, ignorant of the future, knowing only what can be learned or seen, destined to decay and death, weaker than many beasts, helpless before the elements. But it means also—for all in some degree, and centrally for the exceptional hero—recognition of those powers, of that extra dimension of life, which mortality itself alone confers. Some aspects of this dimension are self-evident. No god needs courage; nor loyalty either, if Zeus is absolute and omnipotent on Olympus. Sympathy and grief, as felt by gods, either in Homer or in tragedy, appear as superficial imitations of a mortal reality. The divine sense of humor is unreliable or childish. For all these reasons men can understand gods better than gods can understand men. The hero's self-knowledge tells him that a god may kill him but cannot defeat him; the cosmos thus displays a harmonious balance of immortal and mortal.

But there is a further and more profound aspect of the mortal dimension. For the unheroic mass of mankind the gods have prescribed—through their patronage of cities, institutions, and wise rulers—laws and the respect for law; and most heroes too are content to live with their fellows under such a contract. But no law covers every case, even where no extravagant crime is involved; and there are crimes which, because they ought to be unthinkable (the notable example is, of course, matricide), no city mentions in its code of law; and a law may itself be defective, even if approved by all members of the community but one. Each of these exceptions to the social contract will call to mind one or more of the situations and heroes of Greek tragedy. In each case the hero or heroine finds his own judgment opposed either by political authority or by (presumed) divine command, or by what others regard as his obligation to friends or family or pious prudence. If he acts on his own judgment, ignoring the cost, he has to face the thought that his judgment may be wrong, and overcome his doubt with an absolute faith in his mortal self; and such faith, even if absolute, may be mistaken. (This is a knife-edge division; and Sophocles, I believe, placed his Ajax on one side of it and his Heracles on the other.) If he chooses to set aside his own moral judgment and accept authority and obligation (as Orestes does in *Choephori*), and to call it *ananke*, "necessity," he forfeits the rank of hero. Equally, there are cases (e.g., Creon in *Antigone*, Agamemnon in *Iphigenia in Aulis*, Pentheus in *Bacchae*) where it is plain to the audience that the character concerned has persuaded himself, or hopes to persuade others, that he is acting heroically, when his decision is in fact unheroic and merely calamitous.

The operations of integrity, in a person of fully heroic stature, are like those of genius: they may be prelude to a struggle, but in themselves they are not a struggle, they are inevitable, a part of the organism. Antigone did not weigh alternatives to reach her decision. Ajax, once recovered from insanity, knew without question what he must do. So Clytemnestra, the supreme and decisive figure in this controversy, saw only one possible path, and planned it competently, consulting no god, and relying on her own steadfastness. There was no one else who could or would do what must, in the name of justice, be done. The cries of horror, the charges of bloodthirsty, cynical cruelty, of vindictiveness, sometimes included in scholarly comment on Clytemnestra's role, are as irrelevant to the facts of the case, and may in some instances be as dubious in their unconscious motivation, as those uttered by the Argive Elders or the chorus in *Choephori*. To admit such charges is to accuse Aeschylus of making superb poetry the medium for a *danse macabre*, a melodrama appealing to that appetite for revenge which was characteristic of his audience. If Aeschylus' lines present in Clytemnestra a creature as repulsive as the Elders in the final scene, and some eminent scholars, describe, then the *Oresteia* is neither profound nor a tragedy. But horror performed in integrity is tragic. This quality has been claimed for Orestes' crime; but the claim is invalid because Orestes acts under external pressure, not from inner conviction. Clytemnestra defies human society and divine authority with her solitary indignation, knowing that in the end there can only be defeat. This is tragic integrity. As Aeschylus shows his heroine's position, she could no more have failed to do what she did than a good musician can decide to give a bad performance. When she has acted, the wheels of Necessity turn; her defeat in *Eumenides* is total, and coincides with the defeat of justice. Yet this outcome was universally accepted by the original audience as the victory of "the good," and their judgment has rarely been questioned in modern times.

At this point stage and auditorium merge into one theater. For it is not only the central figure in a drama who is put on trial, but the audience as well, who may on occasion, when they applaud, betray and slander the dramatist by approving some character's unheroic choice, or by joining a corrupt character or a subservient chorus in execration of someone whom the moral pattern of the play presents as a figure of integrity. For to the dramatists integrity was more than a fruitful theme for the plot of a play. I do not believe that any one of them was less able than a modern reader to recognize the truth of Homer's Achilles. The authors of *Agamemnon*, *Oedipus Tyrannus*, and *Orestes* all knew, as Achilles knew, what it was to live courteously in a world which their own thoughts about human life had left far behind. The achievement or expression of integrity at the cost of life, and the neglect of integrity that is due to moral failure, are both proper subjects for tragedy; and the tragedians knew that what they were writing about was of more urgency than anything else in the life of their nation; but they can hardly have hoped for much response to this part of their message. If we reflect upon the accounts in Thucydides of the Athenian Assembly's reaction to political speeches, it soon becomes as clear to us as it was to the tragic poets that the number of those in the audience who were conscious of such issues was small. In Aristophanes' *Frogs*, when Dionysus explains that he has come to Hades to bring back a poet to Athens, Euripides asks (1418), "What do you want a poet for?" and Dionysus replies, "To save the city, so that the tragic festivals can continue." "To save the city" was the duty, and the purpose, to which the tragedians devoted their poetic genius. They offered to their audience images of integrity achieved, and images of attempt and failure; and left it to each listener to decide for himself which was which. Their own integrity demanded that their work embody this essence of their own vision and experience; but, like all artists, in some matters most important to them they worked first for themselves, knowing that they could not count on a receptive audience in their own time or in any foreseeable future.

Let us now briefly consider examples in four plays, beginning with one in which by general consent we may recognize the portrayal of integrity: Sophocles' *Antigone*. Since full integrity is a rare phenomenon, while Creon's ordinariness is a thing familiar to all, I think Kitto is right in saying (*Greek Tragedy*, p. 126) that the play, despite its title, is less concerned with Antigone herself than with the predicament of an ordinary human who is suddenly, having already committed his mistake, confronted with this rare and uncomfortable phenomenon. Yet Antigone is undoubtedly the heroine of the drama; and Creon, whose destiny—pathetic rather than tragic—is to "learn too late," even then learns only the superficial lesson that his attitude did not pay, and misses the essential lesson that there was something wrong in himself.

Integrity implies, first, self-knowledge; next, a confidence in the self that is known; third, in its heroic manifestations it implies a knowledge that self-betrayal is unthinkable, forbidden by an inner law which overrules all other laws. In Antigone's case all three elements appear at the first challenge. When she, in blazing anger, is telling her sister of Creon's edict, she says (32), "He gives this command to me—yes, I tell you, *to me!*" She knows well the source of her resolve because, whereas some achieve integrity by long self-discipline, Antigone has been familiar since infancy with the divinity that was born in her. The Greek awareness of a world filled with the wonder of divinity had already for centuries expressed human perfection and imperfection in terms of super-natural influence; as, in the *Iliad*, Achilles' self-control is Athena pulling him back by the hair, and Agamemnon's folly is a god stealing his wits—but no god stole Achilles' wits or pulled Agamemnon back. So Antigone speaks to Creon not as she speaks to her sister ("Yes, I tell you, *to me!*"), but in the ordinary terms; she tells him that the command she obeyed is an eternal law of gods, to honor family love above all else. But the known and honored principle of blood loyalty came first, and its presentation as a god-given law came after; men did not, in matters of this kind, know gods first, and afterwards listen to the laws these gods made. (This reversed process is seen in the situation Aeschylus presents in the *Oresteia*, where Apollo corrupts Orestes with the command of matricide.) Antigone in her defiant act obeys no known god, but herself alone. This is heroic integrity, which the mass of honest people recognize with awe from the other side of the broad gulf of *anankē* which they know they dare not cross. Antigone does not struggle for integrity, she possesses it; the passion that we witness is not struggle, but the suffering to which integrity leads her. The sometimes disputed passage 904–20, where she says that she would not have incurred death for a husband or child, only for a brother, is surely to be interpreted as the extreme measure of her anguish at the prospect of death. The wild, trapped misery of these lines depicts for us the hour in the cave that was ended by the noose.

This example from Sophocles shows integrity victorious, and paying for victory with death. But an equally tragic situation can be one that involves a genuine struggle for integrity ending in defeat. (A pretended struggle decorating a choice already made is not tragic.) There is an example of this kind in Euripides' *Hippolytus*. Here Phaedra, Theseus, and Hippolytus present a triple tragedy. The woman is tragic because of her perception, the two men because of their blindness. Phaedra carries her resolve to the point where starvation induces delirium, and in her weakened state is assailed by an accomplished persuader who knows how practical it is to disown the appetite for integrity.

Phaedra's half-agreement to try the Nurse's *pharmakon* entangles her in "the bridle of necessity," and integrity is lost. The price is still death. Defeat is followed first by her cruel, but perhaps excusable, harshness to the Nurse, then by an inexcusable vindictive lie. Phaedra's death is far more tragic than that of Hippolytus, which results partly from the honorable refusal to break his oath, partly from an immature masculine folly displaying itself in a pathological hatred of women.

The recognition of integrity or of its absence is, as I have already suggested, an issue not only between opposed characters in a drama, but sometimes also between the dramatist and his audience. This is especially the case in Aeschylus' *Eumenides* 539–41, where the chorus of Erinyes says, "I bid you reverence (*aidesai*) the altar of Justice, and not spurn it with impious foot through sight of gain." To whom do they say this? It is almost unknown for a chorus to address the audience, and this is perhaps the instance that comes nearest to it. Possibly the jurors summoned by Athena are already assembling; but in fact each man in the audience regularly serves as juror in the public courts, and now has witnessed the crime to be judged, and listened to evidence; at the end he will either applaud or censure. Will the citizen's judgment agree with the stage judgment? or with the poet's? Will the case be fairly tried?

The votes will be six for condemnation and five for acquittal—which suggests a healthy independence in the jurors.[1] The casting vote of Athena which secures acquittal will be delivered in a speech whose total irrelevance to every serious issue the case has involved will constitute a direct attack on judicial integrity. Orestes will accept the verdict as his right, and gratefully confirm the political bribe already offered by his advocate. Apollo himself will quietly vanish, thus ensuring that no one points out to him the unsavory nature of the whole performance. The Erinyes now know themselves defeated, and accept the meager and vague compromise Athena offers them. The final hymn of joy reflects no uneasy questioning as to what has happened to that reverence for the altar of Justice, that recognition of the proper place of fear in just government, which both Athena and the Erinyes commended before and during the trial. The audience, most of them experienced in the practicalities of the law courts, seem to have raised no objection on the ground of integrity either to Apollo's arguments or to Athena's reasons for her casting vote. The former harmonized with their own judicial practice, the latter with a chief principle of their domestic and civic life, the universal supremacy of the male. Every later century that has read and revered this work has adopted broadly the same attitude; and the intensive scholastic interest of recent generations has assumed that this was the meaning that the author himself intended his trilogy to convey.

My fourth example is one that may at first seem unfair, because it is taken not from a complete play but from a fragment. However, the very fact of its isolation from a complete dramatic context, and still more the actual historic context of its preservation, make this fragment one of the most important pieces of evidence we possess for the way in which Athenian audiences of the fifth and fourth centuries listened to and interpreted the tragedians. I refer to the speech of Praxithea, from Euripides' *Erechtheus*. Lycurgus quotes it in full in his address to the jury which in 333 B.C. tried Leocrates for treason. To increase their indignation against the accused, Lycurgus speaks feelingly of the virtue of patriotism, and reminds the jurors of the gratitude they owe to Euripides for expressing in these lines the perfection of a woman's heroic devotion to her country.[2]

Whether an intelligent man of affairs like Lycurgus believed that Euripides wrote the speech as an example of such a virtue will never be known; but undoubtedly he trusted the great majority of his hearers (the jury would probably number five hundred and one) to interpret the speech in that light—and it is fascinating to imagine the emotional tones in which he read it to them. For in fact this speech, if separated from the war-fevered atmosphere of the year 422 in which Euripides produced *Erechtheus*, and from the no less fevered political situation of 333 when the trial of Leocrates took place, would more naturally be read as a burlesque than as a tear-jerking inspiration to patriotism. A professional actor can, of course, turn a purple passage to either extreme with equal effect, if he knows the mood of his audience.

Erechtheus, marshaling the Athenian army to repel a Thracian invader, was told by Delphi that he would defeat the enemy if he sacrificed his daughter. He consulted his wife Praxithea, who replied in this speech of enthusiastic consent, pouring out callous platitudes, and eulogies of her own noble self-sacrifice, without a trace, at any point, of even that feeble show of parental feeling which Aeschylus allows to Agamemnon at Aulis. "O my country! would that each soul within you loved you as I do!" Euripides presented to the Athenians of 422 this epitome of inhumanity, gross egotism, and sentimental falsity, knowing from experience (e.g., of the reception of *Heracleidae*) that they would be blind to its irony because the pressure of their "war-mania" (cf. *Suppliants* 484f., *dorimanēs*) destroyed alike their sense of decency and their sense of the absurd. Lycurgus, in the aftermath of Philip of Macedon's victory at Chaeronea, quoted this speech because he was confident that Athenian political passion was still as impervious to Euripides' irony as it had been three generations earlier.

The unique significance of this passage for the study of Greek tragedy is that we have here fifty-five lines which, in any context, will probably strike the sort of reader who reads tragedy as both shameful and absurd; and the reader of Euripides, above all, knows that this dramatist could distinguish true pathos from selfish sentimentality. Yet the circumstances of Lycurgus' oration make it clear that a large audience of citizens could be relied on to miss its irony altogether. This goes far to explain how it is that generations of serious scholars have missed much of the equally powerful irony to be found in other plays of Euripides, in Aeschylus, especially in *Suppliants* and the *Oresteia*, and to a lesser degree in Sophocles (this kind of irony is strongest in *Oedipus at Colonus*). Praxithea's speech provides us with a reminder that our own integrity of judgment must, first, set no limit to the moral sensitiveness we ascribe to the tragedians; and second that it must respond with an equally direct and independent personal judgment of characters and situations as the poets present them to us.

Young classical scholars, in the present supposedly liberal and independent decade, are faced with a daunting disadvantage. By the time they reach the stage of general interpretative work in the field of tragedy they have already studied with proper respect a body of authoritative comment, backed with a weight of formal learning, in which certain moral attitudes to situations presented in the tragedies have remained pretty well unquestioned for twenty-four centuries. Encouragement to think independently is available here and there;[3] but there are radical and far-reaching questions to which alternative answers have hardly been considered by established critics. A modest scholar may well quail before the overwhelming weight of the argument that asks, with polite, or less polite, amusement, "Is it likely that you have perceived what was missed by the best brains of two millennia?" The kind of student who will cheerfully— and truthfully—reply, "Far from unlikely, and entirely possible," is not common, and gets little support from above; and it cannot be denied that scholarly devotion sometimes allows arcane authority and personal mystique to sidle in with the pursuit of truth. When two such different scholars as the late E. R. Dodds[4] and A. P. Burnett[5] both offer a sentimental picture of Orestes that is little removed from Christian sainthood, what inexperienced lecturer dare suggest that Euripides may have designed his homicidal maniac (in *Orestes*) to cudgel some few of his audience into seeing what Aeschylus meant? Irony is not necessarily humorous; but the capacity to recognize and interpret irony seems to grow from the same flexibility of mind as the faculty of humor. I have mentioned that gods in tragedy appear humorless; and the same deficiency that so diminishes Apollo's dignity by two angry outbursts in *Eumenides* 179–97 and 644ff. may also account for the illogical solemnity with which traditional comment explains Athena's outmaneuvering and corruption of the Erinyes as the wisdom of Zeus Agoraios adapting basic morality to modern requirements, and stamping as out-of-date those principles of justice, those laws of cause and effect, which in the *Agamemnon* lyrics sounded timeless and universal.

In interpreting the tragedies, what kind of question ought scholars to consider? Let us turn to Aristotle for a reminder about the qualities he regarded as essential in the material for a tragedy. The story and the situation, he said, must be not trivial but *spoudaios*, "of recognizable value or significance"; and the central figure must be a person whom we acknowledge as fundamentally good, though capable of error. The destruction of a bad man may cause satisfaction but does not make drama; the destruction of an entirely good man is disaster and not tragedy. Thus it is clear that Aristotle regarded the tragic poet as concerned with the distinction between what is serious and what is trivial in human situations, and with the various grades of moral goodness that come between flawless excellence and depravity.

Therefore if a scholar is to understand a play, his judgment as to what actions are good, or what words are honest, must constitute an important part of his study. They must be his own judgments resulting from both instinct and experience; and they must belong to a conviction that the issues involved are simple and timeless issues in which his judgments coincide with those of the poet himself. That is to say, he must assume that a community of understanding is possible between himself and the poet on such concepts as courage, integrity, generosity, or loyalty; without this assumption the criticism of tragedy is a waste of time. Right judgment on such moral questions may from time to time be a guide in the restoration of a corrupt text; and textual work will occasionally confirm, though it is unlikely to modify, a moral judgment. And on such judgments will depend our use of Aristotle's other criterion—the quality of value or significance, or of triviality, in a scene or a character.

It is, I think, possible to be fairly specific in identifying the virtues that belong to "the heroic" in tragedy. Courage must be called essential, simply because no virtue can operate effectually without it; but courage in itself does not confer heroic status. It is an important part of the claim of Ajax in Sophocles, perhaps because after Achilles' death Ajax was unique in this quality; but to his courage was added another virtue he shared with Achilles—and, incidentally, with Clytemnestra and with Antigone: indignation against injustice. That, together with courage, secures his claim. Heracles in *Trachiniae* has supreme courage; but because he shows neither justice nor nobility, and does not "know himself" as a mortal, what Sophocles creates in him is the most tragic of failures as a hero.

Besides courage there are, I think, only two virtues that we need name as important to the heroic ideal. First, integrity, which, as already shown, includes both loyalty and the love of truth. The other is nobility, *to gennaion*, which includes generosity and the capacity to overlook an injury. A play where this quality can be studied is *Oedipus at Colonus*; here Oedipus claims nobility for himself in his first few lines, but later repeatedly refutes, by his acts and words, his own claim to nobility, and even to integrity. Euripides in *Hippolytus* offers a different pattern. Hippolytus can show nobility towards his father as a fellow male of similar self-centeredness, and utterly deny it in his dealing with Phaedra. Phaedra struggles in anguish to preserve integrity, but when lashed by Hippolytus' cruel tongue abandons integrity for revenge. Hippolytus' chastity (the Old Slave in the prologue knows this) is as irrelevant to heroic quality as Artemis' revenge on Adonis is to chastity. Euripides is quietly merciless in presenting want of integrity. His Agamemnon is contemptibly false in *Hecabe*, unforgivably false in *Iphigenia in Aulis*; his Demophon makes even the chorus ashamed of him. Sophocles shows the clearest picture of heroic virtue and its opposite in *Philoctetes*, and the most baffling complexity in the leading figures of *Electra*. But where, in the whole canon, do we find an unflawed hero? An unflawed heroine, perhaps, in *Antigone*; apart from her, I think, nowhere; certainly not in the often-acclaimed Theseus, either of Euripides or of Sophocles. Courage, integrity, and generosity, then, are the basic virtues of tragedy; and about these qualities I believe we can be fairly sure of a common understanding between the tragedians and ourselves.

Few will disagree with Aristotle about the two qualities necessary for the material of a tragedy; but it is interesting to note that Aristotle himself could make a plain error of judgment in a matter of this kind, as when he says (*Poetics* 54a28–29) that Euripides in *Orestes* made Menelaus an "unnecessarily bad" character. This instance is worth examining, since it illustrates one of several processes which may vitiate a critic's judgment.

Orestes, produced for the fiftieth anniversary of the *Oresteia*, and bearing a close relation to *Choephori*, was inevitably interpreted by the audience of 408 B.C. with the same assumptions that had colored the acceptance of Aeschylus' work. For the audience of the *Oresteia* the two shedders of kindred blood, father and son, were noble heroes, the avenger Clytemnestra an execrated monster, the Furies grotesque anachronisms, the proceedings of Athena's solemn court unexceptionable, the verdict a victory for law and reason over hate and violence. This general view, though its relation to Aeschylus' text is, at best, arbitrarily selective, established itself immediately and has prevailed ever since. When Euripides wrote a play on the same theme of matricide, he presented Orestes as unstable and foolish when not insane, and Pylades as a thoroughly depraved and amoral person; yet his play, like the earlier one, greatly pleased its audience with the divinely sponsored escape of the young hero, and became a popular revival. Since Orestes in his second scene, and again towards the end of the play, shouts abuse at Menelaus, Aristotle joins the rest of the audience in accepting the matricide's judgment of his uncle, and does not notice that it is based on nothing to be found in the play, but is presented as a warped judgment made by a vicious character. *Orestes* contains several other instances where the almost universal judgment of critics has, I believe, fallen into similar error based on traditional assumption. (See *Ironic Drama*, chap. 3 passim.)

It is surely one of the primary functions of the scholar to discover what are the moral standards by reference to which the tragedian designs the persons and actions of his play. He need not tell us whether Orestes is right or wrong in abusing Menelaus; but he should not let us assume without good reason that Orestes in Euripides' play bears the same character that he was generally supposed to bear in Aeschylus' play of fifty years earlier. Yet even the most revered scholar may be capable, like Aristotle, of a plain error of moral judgment. The late Karl Reinhardt, in writing of the character of Theseus in *Oedipus at Colonus*, refers to the role of Theseus' son Demophon in *Heracleidae*, and calls him "the great-hearted son of Theseus."[6] In fact Euripides shows Demophon as a shifty coward; though Reinhardt's assumption is the one usually accepted by scholars, with the result of obscuring and distorting the whole play. Judgments of this kind are not unimportant; they affect major issues of tragedy, and they ramify from one play to another. Is Oedipus in *Oedipus at Colonus* the most sublime of all heroes, or is he shown as a hero in decay, defending his loss of integrity by absorption in the numinous? In *Eumenides*, if we draw up a moral balance sheet between Athena on the one hand, and the Erinyes in their first and second stasima and their part in the trial on the other hand, on which side do we find the greater "respect for the altar of Justice" (539–48), or reverence for an oath (709f., 735ff.) or for truth and honest dealing? To these and other such questions most scholars have either attempted no answer, or have given answers that ignore vital and in some cases conspicuous evidence in the text.

Clearly there are a number of reasons for this, historical and personal; but one reason must surely be that tragedy, being different in nature from other kinds of writing, needs a different approach. In the reading of Herodotus, Plato, Theocritus, the scholar feels an obligation to purge his inquiry of all personal or subjective considerations and contemplate his text as an object of art and history. He does not exercise moral judgment either on his author or on any actions the author describes. But in the study of tragedy such an attitude is self-defeating. Morality is the tragedian's constant preoccupation, and unless we discover correctly how he himself judges the acts and persons he presents, we do not know what the drama is about.

I
The Oresteian Trilogy

2

Orestes

It is not known when this trilogy was first called *Oresteia*, "the story of Orestes." The name, however, is appropriate; not because Orestes has any stronger claim than Agamemnon to be the "hero" of the drama, but because it is in Orestes' act of matricide that the two great themes of the trilogy reach their climax—in the circumstances of its performance and in the judicial assessment, and formal cancellation, of its guilt. In this assessment (whether we think the author offers it as valid or false) the two earlier crimes—the first committed, the second suffered, by Agamemnon—take their place as items of comparison: the proceedings of the trial ignore entirely the sacrifice of Iphigenia (except for one cryptic hint in *Eu.* 632), while they condemn the regicide in the strongest terms and deny it any claim to the sanction of justice.

The first of the two great themes is homicide within the bond of blood kinship. Aeschylus seems to assume that the family unit was recognized as constituting the basis of social order not only in the seven centuries from the Trojan war to the battle of Marathon, but in the misty, unrecorded pre-Olympian era; and in *Eumenides* the chorus of Erinyes claim that they received from the Fates at the creation of the world the solemn function of punishing those who shed kindred blood. The growth of cities rivaling each other in commercial and military power was matched by the growing wealth and influence of Delphi as the center of Olympian religion; and in accord with these developments the social structure of cities gave more and more exclusive power to men and less and less freedom to women. Apollo's command of matricide, and Athena's declaration that she is "wholly on the side of the father," suggest a strong ideological alliance between traditional elements in the city that fought for Hellenic freedom at Marathon and the religious institution that temporized with the invading Persians. The confused issues of justice and retribution which arose in the story of the House of Atreus struggle for expression in the encounter between the Erinyes and Apollo in *Eumenides*; and the first two

plays show how the compulsions of a male-dominated society produce successive encroachments, in the interest of the *polis*, upon the sanctity of kindred
blood and the simplest concept of social justice: the contemptuous deception
of a wife and the sacrifice of a daughter, followed by the killing of a husband,
culminate (this is Cassandra's word in *A.* 1283, *thrinkōsōn*) in the murder of a
mother by her son.

Athens had for many generations been civilized enough to possess laws
providing that debts of blood be settled in judicial order and not by personal
revenge. It is in the nature of laws to be broken, and there is little evidence to
show by what stages in the eighth and seventh centuries the practice of resort-
ing to law gained upon the tradition of violence; but since the reforms of
Dracon in 621 B.C. legal redress was accepted as a principle. The second great
theme of the *Oresteia* is the importance of a judicial system and practice in
which reverence for law and truth are paramount. The claim of reverence for
the bond of blood which Orestes acknowledges (*aidesthō*, "Shall I show reverence?" *Ch.* 899) only to reject, when his mother bares her breast before his
sword, is the same that Athena puts forward (*aidoumenous ton horkon*, "with
reverence for your oath," *Eu.* 710) in the impressive words with which she constitutes the holy court of Areopagus. Yet not only does Apollo in his defense of
Orestes repeatedly flout this sanctity, but Athena herself, first by the reasons
she gives for her partial vote, and later by her cynical use of "persuasion" to
coerce the defeated Erinyes, demonstrates that *aidōs*, "reverence," is for her an
empty word to be used when deemed expedient. The poet's portrait of the goddess is his arraignment of his own city.

When Agamemnon set out with his army from Argos, the chorus of Elders
tells us, they were startled by a portent that appeared before them (*A.*
109–20):

> There in full view two eagles ravenously tear
> The body of a pregnant hare
> Big with her burden, now a living prey
> In the last darkness of their unborn day.

The significance of this passage is discussed in an important article (see note 3,
chapter 1) by J. J. Peradotto, entitled "The Omen of the Eagles and the *Ēthos*
of Agamemnon." This writer maintains—in my view, convincingly—that the
character Aeschylus presents in Agamemnon corresponds closely with the
ruthless, predatory image of the eagles who destroyed the hare. I shall give a
summary of this article later, in chapter 4, where it is most relevant. I refer to it
here because in his last few pages the writer turns his attention from father to
son, to Orestes. "In the *Oresteia*," he writes (p. 256), "the idea of inherited
ēthos is a motive of major significance." This is certainly so; but here Peradotto

is referring not to Orestes, but to the predatory *ēthos* Agamemnon inherited from his father Atreus. Orestes, he tells us, does not follow the rule, but, in carrying out the matricide that Apollo commanded, shows "purity of intent and moral sensitivity," and by this quality "earns the protective intervention of Zeus."

Here I regretfully part company with this brilliant essay. I believe that Aeschylus in his portrait of Orestes offers a quite different and more disturbing moral statement. Peradotto contends (p. 258) that these qualities of Orestes are "a new and creative event in the Trilogy," breaking through "the apparently invariable cycle of inherited *ēthos*"; and that they are rewarded by Zeus' intervention on Orestes' behalf. Both these arguments are, I believe, unsound. In the first place, I find in the text of *Choephori* and *Eumenides* no evidence that the poet was conscious of introducing "an unexpected newness" (p. 261), a different moral element, into the dramatic complex. In the second place, to say that Zeus "intervenes" in Orestes' trial is as mistaken as to say that Zeus "commanded" Agamemnon to attack Troy—a common error which Peradotto's article has properly disposed of. Orestes prays to Zeus more than once; Apollo, whose other testimony is dubious at every point, claims Zeus' authority for his oracle; Athena, after alluding to Zeus' thunderbolt, makes the contradictory claim that "Zeus of the law-courts," *Agoraios*, has persuaded the Erinyes to change their minds. But nowhere does Aeschylus tell us that "Zeus intervenes."

The question of Orestes' character is of central importance in our understanding of the trilogy. In *Choephori*, Peradotto says, a conviction emerges "of Orestes' innocence and his parents' guilt—in moral rather than in juridical terms."[1] I find in the text no ground for any such conviction, and no passage that seems to present or imply any such change in the emotional tone, any interruption of "the apparently inevitable cycle of inherited *ēthos*." If the poet had meant to show such a reversal of maxims elaborated by the chorus in *Agamemnon*, he must surely have articulated this dramatic moral event in plain terms. It was, after all, a most acceptable and comforting doctrine. But nowhere in the trilogy does any such passage occur.

Before we begin to study in detail the Orestes Aeschylus presents, it is well to deal with a question sometimes raised by those who defend the traditional view of the trilogy: Did Greeks of the fifth century think of matricide as a crime of ultimate horror, worse than the common category of homicide? Could the tragedian count on his Athenian audience to agree with him in thinking of Orestes as polluted and guilty?

Chapters 3 and 10 will offer cumulative evidence on this point from Aeschylus' text; but we may now consider it on more general grounds. In the first place, whatever opinions might prevail elsewhere, Athenians of Aeschylus' time regarded themselves as a nation with high moral standards. It seems probable that Thucydides, when he composed the funeral speech of Pericles in Book 2, was consciously describing an ideal already visibly threatened; but there can be no doubt of the reality and splendor of the ideal. All organized communities have rules and principles which, as a community, they value and cherish, but which most individuals would transgress at short notice if moved by either passion or interest. The complete domination exercised by the male sex in Greek cities was a traditional privilege more prized than any rule or principle; and while there may not have been a man in the audience who would murder his mother, there were probably few who would not feel that Orestes, in the world of seven centuries earlier, had dared to strike a necessary blow to vindicate an indispensable masculine right. The legend of the Lemnian massacre (see *Ch.* 631ff.) surely reflects an age-old male fear lest woman should question that right and rebel.

In the second place, though legend provides cases of fathers killed by son or daughter, and of children killed by parents (both are instanced in the choral ode just referred to) there is, as far as I know, only one parallel to Orestes' act of matricide, and that is the story of Alcmaeon, who killed his mother Eriphyle on instruction from the Delphic oracle, and found that repeated rites of purification failed to remove his pollution (see R. Graves, *Greek Myths*, p. 384). The ethical sensitivity of Athenians, Thucydides tells us, declined calamitously in the first decade of the Peloponnesian war; yet in 408, in the last play Euripides presented before quitting Athens, the matricide is spoken of in terms of horrified condemnation not only by the chorus, Tyndareos, and Menelaus, but even more emphatically by Orestes and Electra themselves, who mingle remorse with bitter resentment against Apollo for his command. The same attitude is expressed also in *Electra* and *Iphigenia in Tauris*. (See chapters 13–15 of this book.)

In the third place, as I hope to show later in this chapter and the next, the whole of *Choephori* is pervaded by a peculiar sense of dread attending the contemplation and execution of matricide. It is, I conclude, reasonable to interpret the trilogy as assuming in the audience a general acceptance that matricide was a crime of unique horror, beyond ordinary homicide, even within the family; an act to which such expressions as "no cure," "no escape," "no expiation," repeated in all three plays, were fully applicable.

Orestes is mentioned three times in *Agamemnon*. We learn from Clytemnestra (879ff.) that he is, for his own safety, in Phocis; and in the last scene the Elders twice express a wish that Orestes may return from exile to be the killer, *phoneus*, of both Aegisthus and Clytemnestra. But there are also passages in *Agamemnon* where the poet uses imagery to refer with clear implication to the role that Orestes will assume in the second play.

This brings us to a difficulty involved in the view which I am putting forward, one that must be faced fairly at the outset. Some of the most interesting recent work on the trilogy[2] has analyzed the complex fabric of metaphor and allegory which is evident on every page. And it is generally recognized that as the trilogy progresses the imagery develops in character; that what at first was muddied becomes clear, what was diseased becomes healthy, what was dark becomes lighter. All this I accept; but I am also sure that, as a general principle, we should interpret imagery in the light of action and moral situation, and not trim our judgment of action and moral situation to fit our feelings about the imagery. We may conjecture what the poet intended by this development of tone from dark to light; but conclusions must be based on more tangible evidence. And, since the current zeal for the study of imagery has perhaps loaded the argument in favor of Orestes as the hero of the trilogy, my analysis of his role, including both imagery and action, may in some degree restore a balance.

Let us look first at the second choral ode in *Agamemnon*, where the chorus gives us the parable of the harmless lion cub which later showed its hereditary instinct for destruction. Now, Peradotto applies this parable to the nature that Agamemnon inherited from Atreus. But, of the three possible applications of the parable, this is the least apposite. The lion image in its immediate context reflects the Trojans' experience of Helen, whose presence was at first delightful but in time proved disastrous; and of Paris, who in infancy escaped death, but later brought death to his family. The case of Agamemnon shows no transmutation of nature or contrast of effect; what he was at Aulis, what he was ten years later at Troy, he evidently is still when he appears on the stage. His childhood is never mentioned. The person whom the image fits most closely is Orestes. His childhood in Phocis is mentioned not only in *Agamemnon*, but three times in *Choephori* (6ff., 132–36, 250); and his infancy in Argos is made vivid by the Nurse (*Ch.* 744–65). From sucking babe to matricide—a change of that dramatic kind is the chief point of the lion cub parable.

"Ah, but," Peradotto argues, "unlike other criminals, this matricide has moral sensitivity and purity of intent. Orestes' reaction to the unlovely command of the god contrasts sharply with Agamemnon's decision, though superficially they appear alike. His meticulous and agonising struggle . . ." and so on (p. 259). I confess that I see no contrast in the two cases. Here is Agamemnon's struggle:

> Disaster follows if I disobey;
> Surely no less disaster, if I yield
> And slaughter my own child, my home's delight,
> In her young innocence, and stain my hand
> With blasphemous unnatural cruelty,
> Bathed in the blood I fathered! Either way,

> Ruin! Disband the fleet, sail home, and earn
> The deserter's badge—betray the alliance?—Well,
> May all be for the best!

That is, at face value, not less "meticulous and agonising," nor is it any more honest, than Orestes' defense of his resolve to kill his mother—than his recital of Apollo's threats; nor is Orestes' decision at the last moment less abrupt, nor his execution notably less brutal, than Agamemnon's; while to discern "moral delicacy" (p. 259) in either case of kin murder shows in the critic a leniency seldom extended to Clytemnestra or Helen.

A few lines after the lion cub comes a second passage using the imagery of heredity, A. 763–71. This passage, not discussed by Peradotto, seems relevant to the question, How does Aeschylus conceive Orestes' moral attitude? The chorus are talking about *hubris*, arrogance.

> Old arrogance tends to breed, sooner or later, when the due day of birth comes, a young arrogance, together with . . . reckless infatuation—offspring similar to their parents.

The similarity of nature between parents and children is an ever-recurring theme in the imagery of *Choephori*: the eagle's brood, the she-wolf's cubs, the serpent birth; and it appears with undiminished clarity in *Eu.* 534:

> Impiety has a true-born child—arrogance.

Again in *Agamemnon*, just before the passage about the breeding of *hubris*, we find this (758ff.):

> It is the impious deed [i.e., not the mere possession of wealth] that begets further impious deeds similar to its own nature; for when a house practises genuine goodness, fortune always supplies it with noble sons.

There, of course, the Elders are not thinking of Orestes. But if Aeschylus had meant to show that this kind of generalization, this view of the cosmic pattern of cause and effect, this law that like begets like, was in fact now to be challenged by a glorious exception in the case of Orestes, that this fatalism was to be countered in Orestes with a gleam of brilliant hope, then both reason and dramatic logic require that the moment of this revelation, the cause and features of its working, should have been somewhere articulated as the central message of the entire work. It is true that *Choephori* begins with fatalism and *Eumenides* ends apparently with hope; but between the one state and the other there is nowhere expressed, in relation to Agamemnon and his son, any contrast of intent, any opposition of purity to corruption, of delicacy to sordidness. Instead we have the dull pragmatism of Orestes' parting speech (*Eu.* 754–77), which I shall refer to in more detail presently. The almost hysterical assertion by the chorus in *Choephori* that the act of matricide "will drive out all pollution from the hearth with cleansing that banishes disaster" (966ff.) is soon after contradicted by the somber tone of Orestes himself, who knows that his victory brings with it "defilement not redeemed by glory," *axōla miasmata* (1017).

In the first episode of *Choephori* Orestes tells us that he is here in Argos because Apollo has commanded him to kill his mother; and he spends twenty-eight eloquent lines recounting in detail the threats of torment and death with which the god enforced his bidding. That speech is sufficient evidence that we are meant to think of Orestes as recognizing the depth of pollution he must incur by matricide; and this recognition is echoed by the chorus and Electra in the long invocation of Agamemnon's spirit, and is implicit in the brooding tension that pervades the play. Orestes, like his father, undertakes an act that affronts his humane instinct and breaks a natural family bond. Apollo's command is admittedly a weightier authority than the equivocal and unproven word of Calchas; but the crime enjoined is far more heinous. A father's right to dispose of his child's life was a tradition that died hard; and a girl remained a child until she was married. But the horror of pollution incurred by one who destroys the source of his own life is expressed by Orestes in his interpretation of Clytemnestra's dream (*Ch.* 542–50) with a persuasive vividness far more real and dramatically potent than Apollo's genetic theorizing in the trial.

Orestes himself nowhere claims to take a different moral position from his father's, but in his opening speech mentions Agamemnon five times in terms of deepest respect. Later, in his prayer to Zeus (246–63) he takes to himself the eagle imagery already associated with Agamemnon. His expression of the feeling of identity at one point goes unconsciously beyond his intention, betraying in the speaker a guilt that links him with his father's initial crime (255–59):

> Zeus, if you destroy us, the children of one who as a sacrificer honored you greatly, where will you find a hand like this to feast you as is your due?

The rare word *thutēr*, "sacrificer," occurs three times in the *Oresteia*, and three times, with a significance only a little less pointed, in Sophocles' *Trachiniae*. Agamemnon "endured to become his daughter's sacrificer" (*A.* 224); and Iphigenia "cast imploring eyes upon each of her sacrificers" (240). Now Orestes comes, the son of a "sacrificer" (*Ch.* 255), with "a hand like his father's," to pour out before the gods "a third draught of blood" (*Ch.* 578). The death of Iphigenia, and the word "sacrifice," have already been mentioned, almost inadvertently, by Electra (239–42); and those lines point yet again to the one fact which, since Agamemnon's death, everyone refuses to refer to: the crime by which he earned his death.

The opening scene contains also one or two pointers to the way in which Orestes' character will be developed in the course of the action. First, the need he feels for authority is shared by his sister. Electra does not initiate the thought of matricide. The chorus does this, by four stages, in the *stichomythia* 114–21. They avoid naming Clytemnestra, or saying "your mother"; they refer to "those guilty of your father's murder." When Electra suggests "justice" as a motive, the chorus replies: "Put it simply: take life for life." When she asks, "Is this consistent with piety?" they evade the question just as Athena evades it in *Eumenides*, refusing to acknowledge any distinction between homicide and matricide. Orestes too will decline to rely on his own judgment, and instead will seek from others support for the course which, as he says in 298, he is resolved to pursue "even if Apollo's word is not to be trusted." This recognition that the act he contemplates is unspeakable shows indeed a moral awareness; but since he pursues his purpose unflinching, to call it sensitivity or delicacy is surely mistaken.

Orestes chiefly reveals himself in the long speech 269–305; here is his justification, before his sister, the chorus, and the audience, of the act to which he has dedicated himself. Here, as later in 554–84, in speaking of his task Orestes refers either to "the killers" or to Aegisthus alone; so reflecting the desperate self-deception needed for goading himself to an act that both instinct and society condemn.

A notable feature of this speech is that, though it purports to justify the culminating act in a trilogy whose dominant theme is justice, it contains no mention of *dikē*. The wrong suffered by a usurped city, the need to demonstrate that assassination is punished inexorably—these are passed over. The fact that immediately after this speech the chorus launches into a passionate appeal to justice in its most primitive aspect makes Orestes' omission the more remarkable. Instead of the expected claim of justice, we find an admission of terror: the first three-quarters of the speech is devoted to a recital of the supernatural torments with which he says Apollo threatened him, should he fail to obey. The deed is one that only terror could excuse. As far as line 296 he appears to believe Apollo's threats. Are we, then, meant to believe Orestes? Is Aeschylus presenting the Erinyes as divinities who will insist on kin murder and then punish the murderer? Doubtless the majority of the first audience accepted this, as they accepted the many other contradictions contained in the trilogy. But to suppose that this was Aeschylus' own belief is to refuse to take him seriously as a writer of tragedy (see Page, "Introduction," p. xv). In *Eumenides* we learn that the Erinyes insist on punishment—*not* on mere reprisal—for kin murder, as a deterrent necessary to a healthy society. In a formal statement of their primeval, divinely appointed function, they declare (312–15):

We claim that we are strictly just. No anger from us pursues the man whose hands are clean; he lives an unharmed life.

Therefore either Orestes or Apollo is lying; and a scrutiny of the god's role in this play and in *Eumenides* will incline us to judge that it is Apollo. Orestes apparently believes Apollo's threats as he believes his promises (cf., e.g., *Ch.* 1031, *Eu.* 465ff.); and he makes it clear that what he does is against his own judgment and is carried out in obedience to a god who terrifies him. The curious lines which end this speech are worth noticing.

> Am I to put my trust in such oracles? Even if I cannot trust them, yet I must do this deed. Many impulses urge me to one end—the god's command, my deep grief for my father; and in addition I am galled by the loss of my inheritance, without which I cannot save my renowned fellow-citizens . . . from living as slaves to a woman—no, to a pair of women. *His* spirit is womanish; he shall soon know mine.

Surely, at the back of these uneasy lines lurks Orestes' fear that he will himself be called "woman" if he fails to kill the woman everyone hates. This, in fact, is a groundless fear. When, fifty years later, Euripides, in the play he wrote as a tribute to Aeschylus, made Tyndareos explain (*Or.* 500ff.) how Orestes "ought to have taken lawful proceedings, prosecuted his mother for murder, and expelled her from the palace"—that was not a new idea. Aeschylus' Argive Elders tell Clytemnestra (*A.* 1410f.) that

> the heavy hatred of the citizens will drive you from Argos into exile.

It appears, then, that Orestes' honor would have been secured with the blood of Aegisthus and his mother's banishment. Had Orestes been of the same heroic mold as Cassandra, he would have held his pride above his piety and accused the god as Electra accuses him in Euripides, with bitter indignation. But, like his father, he is wanting in heroic pride. He believes Apollo's threats because he needs something to fear—something more tyrannical than his own pliant sense of *aidōs*, which speaks at sight of his mother's breast, only to accept from Pylades contradiction and dismissal. Orestes is a man of weak will looking for authority; and in Greek cities the authority rated next after the Delphic oracle is that tradition which Athena, without a blush, substitutes for justice (*Eu.* 736–41):

> No mother gave me birth; therefore with all my heart I favour the father's claim and male supremacy in all things.

This popular principle, and not justice, is the authority that Aeschylus' Orestes dare not resist.

The long invocation of Agamemnon's spirit begins with the chorus' appeal to primitive justice and the enunciation of the law, *drasanti pathein*, "the doer shall suffer." The purpose of the invocation is to confirm Orestes in his resolve; but he, Electra, and the chorus are all equally oblivious of the simple fact that Orestes intends to be a "doer" in exactly the same sense as Clytemnestra. The same double edge is even more obvious in the chorus' lines 400–4:

> The gods ordain that blood by murder shed
> Cries from the ground for blood to flow again.
> The Furies, sent by anger of the dead,
> Howl for new ruin to tread in ruin's train.

Was the author, as he wrote those lines, unaware how they equate Orestes' vengeance with Clytemnestra's? By far the longest share in the antiphony is given to the chorus; the shortest to Orestes. The chorus stimulate Orestes to action by detailing the wickedness of Clytemnestra and the injustice of the present situation; Orestes' lines express chiefly his emotional identification with his father. The steadily intensifying excitement brings its effect: Orestes is now ready to hear Clytemnestra's dream, to seize on it point by point, and with a fascinated eagerness (526–34, 540–50) to see himself as the son, once nursed at the breast, now grown to be his mother's killer. The connection with the lion cub parable is obvious; but added to it is the deadly power of persuasion as illustrated in this long incantatory interlude. Here we should turn back for brief reflection on another celebrated passage in *Agamemnon*.

The subtlety of Persuasion, the deity *Peithō*, operates at almost every crisis in the trilogy. Fascination is a more powerful persuader than reason, and second only to fear. The *ēthos* of Orestes includes the fascination with which a mind unsure of itself regards the mystery of ultimate wickedness. Matricide equally repels and attracts him: "Even if I cannot believe the oracle, yet I must do this." In the first choral ode of *Agamemnon* the chorus, ostensibly commenting on the sin of Paris in abducting Helen (399–402), describe the inevitable ruin of the man who impiously "tramples on the beauty of holy things." This is what they say (385–89):

> Relentless Persuasion, irresistible child of scheming Ruin, compels him. All remedy is vain; pollution is not concealed, but is evident as a baleful light. . . .

Page comments: "It is hard to see what this has to do with Paris's crime." It certainly is; and while several scholars recently have pointed out that the passage is more applicable to Agamemnon than to Paris, I suggest that it is still more clearly applicable to Orestes. Orestes is relentlessly persuaded by Apollo, by Electra, by the chorus, and Pylades, to incur gross pollution. Whatever purificatory ritual Apollo performed for him (see chap. 3, passim) proves a "vain remedy" (A. 387), since the blood on his hands "is evident" not only to the Priestess (*Eu.* 41f.), but later, in Athens, to the pursuing chorus, from whom his pollution "is not concealed" (*A.* 387), but still marks him as "clear evidence," *ekphanēs tekmar* (*Eu.* 244), and "smiles at them" (253). The fascination with evil becomes especially vivid in the short scene after the invocation, when the chorus leader tells of "the dreams, night-walking terrors, that frightened the godless woman and made her send these gifts." Clytemnestra dreamt that she gave birth to a snake.

> OR. Surely this new-born monster needed food—what food?
> CH. She herself, in her dream, gave it her breast to suck.
> OR. Her nipple surely was wounded by its loathsome fang?
> CH. Yes, with her milk the creature drew forth clots of blood;
> She screamed out in her sleep, and woke in a fit of trembling.

Here the poet illustrates what the *Agamemnon* chorus described—how the potency of Persuasion works. What is Persuasion? She is a goddess, almost one of the characters in the trilogy, with an active part in every play; and one of her most powerful weapons is sinister fascination.

A short digression will not be out of place here, to consider the further import of the passage about Persuasion quoted above (*A.* 385–89). The first line is a paradox: "Persuasion forces him" (*biazei Peithō*). Force and persuasion are opposites; and the political aspect of this antinomy dominated Athenian life throughout Aeschylus' boyhood and youth. The Athenian revolution of 509 B.C. was, among other things, a libertarian movement rejecting the use of autocratic force as the instrument of government and replacing it with the democratic principle of consent won by persuasion. The hostility that continued between democratic and oligarchic states all over Hellas kept this issue alive in the same simplified and sometimes extreme terms for several generations. Aeschylus wrote his *Suppliants* and *Oresteia* less than fifty years after the revolution. In both these works the two opposed principles are constantly displayed, in personal, political, and philosophical terms and contexts.

In *Suppliants* the right and wrong uses of force and persuasion are clearly and simply demonstrated in a series of situations. (See Chapter 11.) In the *Oresteia* the issues are more complex, but the implied political lesson is even clearer. Persuasion is a democratic ideal; but "who will be just if he has nothing to fear?" Force must not be banished, but held in reserve (*Eu.* 698). Yet force is a constant danger, and often operates under the guise of persuasion, relentless (*talaina*) and irresistible (*aphertos*). Thus it appears that one theme of the trilogy is a reminder to Athenians that their political change from tyranny to democracy has not in itself solved any of the fundamental moral issues that complicate community life. Aeschylus illustrates this truth in each of the three plays.

In *Agamemnon* the chorus tells us (198–221) how Agamemnon was persuaded by the pressure of his "alliance" (213) and their "passionate eagerness" (216) that the sacrifice of his daughter could be justified as necessary; so he "reversed his mind" (*metegnō*, 221) from instinctive *aidōs* to an impious and unscrupulous act. In the third episode we see him again "reverse his mind" under the pressure of "relentless persuasion" by his wife; and again he chooses to ignore instinctive *aidōs* (948, cf. 937) and indulge his own ambition and vanity, in walking on the precious embroidered cloth.

In *Choephori* Orestes tells how Apollo persuaded him (cf. *Eu.* 84, where Apollo says, "I persuaded you") that he must kill his mother. But Apollo's persuasion was not, any more than Clytemnestra's, an appeal to reason, or humanity, or justice; it was a "relentless," "irresistible" appeal to terror, a threat of torment and death.

In *Eumenides* Athena, after the acquittal of Orestes, takes upon herself to reconcile the Erinyes to the verdict they had opposed. Her four speeches contain no allusion to any moral issue that has arisen in the drama—to reverence, justice, or truth. They consist of promises, inducements, and compliments—sharpened by one sinister threat which could not be ignored. Persuasion, once again relentless and irresistible, gains its victory—not over force, but over justice.

This provisional summary anticipates a number of points that will be discussed more fully in later chapters; it is enough at the present stage to suggest that Aeschylus throughout the trilogy shows the activity of Persuasion as destructive, as being in no instance allied to that "good" for whose victory we, the audience, presumed that the Elders were praying in the parodos of *Agamemnon*, or to that freedom and purity of life which the Libation Bearers earnestly hope for as the prize of matricide.

We return to Orestes, listening spellbound to the chorus leader's description of Clytemnestra's dream. As persuasion reaches its goal the only voice heard is Orestes' own:

> First, if this snake came forth from the same place as I,
> And, as though human, was then wrapped in infant-clothes,
> Its gaping mouth clutching the breast that once fed me;
> If it then mingled the sweet milk with curds of blood
> And made her shriek with terror—why, it means that she
> Who nursed this obscene beast must die by violence;
> *I* must transmute my nature, be viperous in heart and act!
> The dream commands it: I am her destined murderer.

The chorus' task is complete; they withdraw at once, saying, "Now give your orders to us"; and Orestes takes over. But he still cannot face the next step without pretense; some shreds of compunction remain. Having once uttered the word, "I will kill her," he reverts yet again to what is easier to say, and fills seventeen lines telling how he will deal with Aegisthus. When we come to the trial, and hear Apollo argue that a mother is not the real parent of her child, it will be irrelevant to ask what theories about heredity Athenian lawyers or philosophers were discussing in 458 B.C. Aeschylus shows us Orestes, who is neither a fool nor a coward, recoiling from matricide with an anguish that shatters and destroys him, yet forced to it by persuasion. That is the real answer to Apollo's sophistry. Because matricide is what Orestes knows it to be—moral suicide (cf. *Ch.* 438), when he appears for trial he has become as barren a being as his advocate Apollo. And this barrenness seems to cause a strange obtuseness, shown in his question to the chorus (*Ch.* 517ff.):

> She sends this paltry offering for such a crime?
> Why, if a man poured out his wealth to the last drop
> To atone a single murder, it is labour wasted, they say.

Does he forget that his father's fate illustrated this truth? Does he ask, Then how will matricide be atoned? When *aidōs* goes overboard, logic goes with it; and logic is essential to morality. If the *Agamemnon* chorus was right about piety and justice, Athena's bland answer in *Eumenides* is as foolish as it is immoral.

Orestes knocks at the gate of his own house; and when Clytemnestra appears he conducts the interview with jaunty assurance. The dialogue includes several standard "dramatic ironies"; but there is no ground for imagining any half-conscious recognition on either side. Orestes, as if he wanted to prove that he is unassailable by any pang of obligation to *aidōs* or *eusebeia*, "piety," deliberately uses both those words (665, 704). Clytemnestra believes his story and admits him to the house. He is now, like Paris, a guest of those against whom he plots.

One consideration in the Nurse's scene is relevant to the character of Orestes. Some critics (e.g., W. Whallon, G. Devereux) have drawn unwarranted conclusions from *Ch.* 750, where the Nurse says that she brought up Orestes, "having received him from his mother." In most kinds of society in any age the normal pattern for a royal or wealthy mother would be to nurse her infant herself until she felt disinclined to do so; then she would send for a wet nurse. This is clearly what Aeschylus means by *mētrothen dedegmenē*. But the writers I refer to insist that the Nurse alone suckled Orestes, and that Clytemnestra, having rejected her son, thereby forfeited the claims of motherhood.[3] If this were so, knowledge of it would mitigate somewhat the enormity of Orestes' crime; and, by the same token, it would cancel half of the tragic tension of the play. But in that case it is inconceivable that Orestes himself should never speak of so powerful a factor in his situation; or that the chorus, who rehearse for him every other incitement to revenge, should omit this; or that Orestes, in interpreting the dream, should speak of the snake "clutching the breast that once fed me" (*maston emon threptērion,* 545).

When we next see Orestes, he comes from the palace with Aegisthus' blood on his sword. Clytemnestra, from downstage, faces him. She uses first the tone of authority: "Stay where you are, my son." Orestes advances. She appeals to *aidōs:* "My little child, reverence this breast, where many times you drowsily sucked from me nourishing milk." He turns to Pylades: "Shall I show reverence (*aidesthō*) and not kill my mother?" Pylades in his reply says three things, which are taken by himself and by Orestes to be decisive.

The first is "Where, then, in future are Apollo's oracles?" In other words, you must allow greater importance to the reputation of Delphi than to the primary law of morality. This ignores the more obvious truth, which the Erinyes will point out in *Eu.* 162–72 and 714f., that a command to incur the pollution of matricide can hardly add luster to Apollo's reputation. And is it likely that Aeschylus, who had twice fought for the freedom of Hellas in the years when Delphi gave comfort and encouragement to Persia, considered this argument decisive? The second choral ode of *Eumenides* gives a different answer to almost the same question: "If you Athenians fail to punish such a crime as matricide," say the Erinyes, "decent life in cities will come to an end."

Pylades' second point is "If you fail to kill her, what of the oath you swore?" We do not need to argue that many a man has sworn a foolish or impious oath; for we can turn to Apollo's own words in *Eu.* 621. He is addressing Athenian citizens enrolled in the holy court of Areopagus, men who have taken an oath "to see justice well discerned"; and Apollo tells them, "Remember that not only my oracle, but Zeus himself, is on the side of the accused, requiring a verdict of Not Guilty. No oath is stronger than Zeus." That should dispose of Pylades' second argument.

His third line is "Think all men your enemies, rather than the gods." This reminds us of Apollo's fearsome threats as described by Orestes in the first episode. Does a crime become less criminal because it is enforced by fear? Where is Orestes' pride? Is it not relevant here to recall Cassandra, who, enslaved and helpless, in her innocent integrity chose to defy the god who was her enemy, flinging off Apollo's insignia and trampling them before his face? Orestes confronts two opposed authorities. The authority of Delphi represents the social order established in the cities of Hellas, defended by Apollo in his pleading before the Areopagus, and enunciated by Athena: "I support the male side in all matters." But Orestes is aware of another authority, one that resides in the instinct of all mankind: "My child, reverence this breast." Below the surface of Pylades' words lies a contrary meaning. If Orestes spares his mother, Apollo will be his enemy; if he kills her, all mankind will condemn him. Yet the poet, even while he wrote this, knew that it was too desirable to be true; that despite the even voting, judicial *dikē* would obey Athena, and that the Athenian audience would applaud the success of *Peithō* and Zeus Agoraios (*Eu.* 970–75) in silencing the sole voice that had spoken for the first principle of social morality.

This question and answer, then, show once more that Orestes depends on judgments other than his own; therefore inevitably he accepts an unsound interpretation. And it is for us to judge why Aeschylus so composed the three lines of this momentous reply that none of Pylades' points has clear validity.

So Orestes performs his duty. When he reappears, displaying the robe stained, since seven years ago, with his father's blood, he dwells for twenty-five lines on the vileness of his mother's crime, its nature and its method. Now, as he feels his sanity ebbing, he "proclaims to his friends that he killed her not without justice." He cannot echo the chorus in calling his act a liberation and cleansing of the house, a bright hope for the future. He calls on Apollo for the promised protection. Apollo does not answer; instead the Erinyes crowd upon him, and he flees in terror. At this moment Orestes, betrayed by his authority, wins more sympathy than before. He has acted obediently; and the doer must suffer.

But in *Eumenides* we meet a different Orestes. The sense of horror that made him pray for his own death has left him. His mental and physical suffering has not sharpened his moral sense, but has accustomed him to guilt. He is concerned now not with any moral issue but with legal status, with ritual purity, and with regaining his inheritance. He has no qualms about what he did; only about how to escape punishment for it. In fact, he is now no longer a person, but wholly the creature of Apollo. Our study of his character thus comes to an abrupt end; and all that remains is for us to look at the parting speech he makes after his acquittal. Here he refers to none of the serious issues which have dominated the drama—they all end not with a bang but a whimper. Orestes speaks only of his own restoration. He concludes by confirming the political bargain which Apollo had offered in his name in return for the desired verdict (*Eu.* 670ff.). These words link the end of the trilogy with the beginning. Just as Agamemnon for the sake of his alliance (*A.* 213) had sacrificed his daughter and bought his glory with her blood, so now Orestes with the pledge of an Argive alliance has bought his social and political acceptance. There is no contrast between father and son, no hopeful transmutation of nature. The Elders were right: young *hubris* is like its parent.

To those who find the traditional view of Orestes sympathetic or inspiring, it may seem that my analysis has been merely destructive; that I have taken away a hero and left in his place a failure, substituted for the hopeful pageant of the closing scene a depressing mockery. I reply that nothing matters except understanding, as far as we can, every aspect of the meaning that Aeschylus put into this supreme work. The accepted view tells us that Aeschylus presents as his hero a man afraid to act except under authority and threat, and guilty of the ultimate crime by obedience not to his own vision or judgment but to the same inhumane tradition that had led his father to a similar offense and to the death it merited. This view shows us the young hero justified and acquitted by a casting vote announced in terms that ignore the moral argument of the entire trilogy, which name neither justice nor mercy, but claim simply that a man must be right and a woman wrong. The old view tells us that at the end of his drama the poet forgets the truths of which he convinced us at the beginning: namely, the reality of wickedness, the permanence of pollution; above all, the necessity of justice—and in the lyrics of *Agamemnon* there is no clause assigning justice as an exclusive privilege to the male sex. The tradition implies that Aeschylus allows true pathos and seriousness to give way to the formal and superficial, morality to masculine sentiment, tragedy to complacency. At the close of *Eumenides* the sudden crowd representing the panathenaic procession unites stage and auditorium in fervent rejoicing. Agamemnon's cruelty, Clytemnestra's heroic justice, Orestes' matricide, the abdication of the Erinyes—all have been forgotten, every question answered in Athena's bland principle: I favor the male cause, and am wholly on the side of the father. If by this principle alone Fate and Zeus are to be reconciled, and the city glorified, does not Aeschylus invite us to suspect, behind the jubilant music, a somber tone of tragic irony?

3

Apollo *Katharsios*

At the end of *Choephori* Orestes, knowing himself polluted by his mother's blood and feeling already the onset of the Erinyes, stands ready, equipped with a suppliant's wreath and branches, to go to Delphi, to claim from Apollo the cleansing the god had promised. For an exceptional pollution an exceptional religious authority was needed; and in *Ch.* 1036ff. Orestes describes the special sanctity of "Apollo's ground, the temple at the earth's navel, where, they say, the lamp gleams with undying flame." The chorus too urges him to this pilgrimage. Orestes has told us that Apollo commanded him "to turn to no other hearth" (1038f.); and the chorus' words, *heis soi katharmos* (1059), "that is your one hope of cleansing," show their awareness that his need is not only urgent but unique. For ordinary homicide ritual purification was an everyday affair which could be performed by any man possessing the kind of authority necessary to an *anēr katharsios* (*Eu.* 449); but for kindred blood, in the closest degree of all—a crime rarely paralleled in Greek legend—both Orestes and the chorus accept that no lesser authority than that of Delphi and Apollo could be valid.

And the urgency of Orestes' situation is not something that has recently arisen. Long ago, in *A.* 381–84, the Argive Elders stated with convincing emphasis that *hubris* cannot be pardoned, and later (1019ff.) reminded us (as Apollo will repeat, with a too obvious ambiguity, in *Eu.* 647–50) that murder cannot be undone. The "elder *hubris*" has already met its "appointed day" (*A.* 763–67), and the "younger *hubris*," "resembling its parents" (771) in violence, is now a guilty fugitive.

In setting out for Delphi Orestes trusts that Apollo will not only cleanse him when he arrives there, but will also protect him until the purification has been accomplished. The god has promised that Orestes, if obedient, will be *ektos aitias kakēs*, "immune from evil blame or guilt" (*Ch.* 1031)—a very vague phrase. Since at this moment the chief evil consequence of his act is the torment which the Erinyes are about to inflict on him, it would seem that this is what he hopes to be protected from; and his confident statement in 269, "The oracle of Loxias will not betray me," *outoi prodōsei*, which Apollo himself echoes in the same sense in *Eu.* 64, seems to confirm this. Orestes shows a touching faith in Apollo's promise. The anguish of his exit lines in *Ch.* 1061f. has already continued during his journey to Delphi and will continue, Apollo tells him (75ff.), as his tormentors pursue him over land and sea, "wherever the earth is trodden by wanderers' feet." If we examine the text to discover whether the promise of cleansing was less dubious than the promise of protection, we shall find ourselves confronted with a strange ambiguity, which it is hard to believe was not deliberately woven into the fabric of the trilogy by its author.

Before investigating this ambiguity, it will be relevant to note how the character of Orestes changes from the second play to the third, since this change affects the kind of cleansing he looks for. In *Choephori* Orestes, though coerced by Apollo's threats, is still a person in his own right, engaged in a losing struggle for integrity. In *Eumenides* he has become, by line 276, Apollo's creature; after his brief protest at 85f. he is a colorless cardboard figure.

In *Choephori* Orestes expresses his dependence on Apollo chiefly in two passages. The first is 269–96, where he explains in detail that terror at Apollo's threats is his prime motive for undertaking matricide; though he ends this speech with a show of independence by adding that "even if Apollo's words are not to be believed, still I must do this deed." The second passage is the end of the final scene, 1026–62, where Apollo dominates his thoughts. Besides these, there is a short parenthetic reference to Apollo at 558 ("Lord Apollo, who in the past did not prophesy falsely," *mantis apseudēs to prin;*[1] and there is Pylades' answer to Orestes' hesitation (899ff.), "Where then in future are Apollo's oracles . . . ?" (It is tempting, though perhaps unprofitable, to look for reasons why there is no reference at all to Apollo in the invocation, 306–509.) That Orestes acknowledged the unique horror of his act is shown not only by his emphasis on Delphic authority, but still more by the atmosphere of tense foreboding with which he, rather than Electra or the chorus, fills the first half of *Choephori*, and which reaches its climax in his interpretation of Clytemnestra's dream. There Orestes for the first time dares to put into plain words the truth of his resolve, *kteinō nin*, "I shall kill her" (550)—though even after this he relapses (567–78), still reluctant to look his crime in the face, into his former pretense (see, e.g., 305) that his vengeance has as its object only the legitimate killing of Aegisthus. In *Choephori*, then, Orestes is aware that he incurs no ordinary pollution, but one that will require the utmost authority of Apollo to purify. He even feels at one point (438) that there is no hope except in his own death. So now, his crime accomplished and the penalty already threatening, he sets out, confident in the divine promise, for Delphi.

There, after a long interval, we see him again. A subtle but unmistakable change has taken place. He is still compelled to trust Apollo; but disillusionment shows in his first words. Apollo, if he has not actually wronged Orestes (*Eu.* 85ff.), has failed in his promise of protection. "Learn also not to neglect" (86) is hardly the utterance of a satisfied client. But this is superficial; a more serious change shows itself on Orestes' next appearance, when he sits as a suppliant before Athena's statue in Athens.

Here he makes two speeches, separated by the arrival of the Erinyes hot on his trail; and at a quick reading the second speech seems merely to repeat the first, since in both Orestes calls upon Athena for her favor, and claims to have been duly purified. But there is a difference. At the end of the first speech he says to Athena (243), "I will stay here before your statue and await the decision of justice," or, "the outcome of my trial," *telos dikēs*. This attitude reflects the character Orestes bore in *Choephori*: doomed, driven, and despairing, but on the whole honest, believing in justice, and aware of the dreadfulness of his enterprise—as in his last word to Clytemnestra: "Unholy was your deed, unholy be your punishment" (930). He executed justice, and now in *Eu.* 243 he submits to justice. Then the Erinyes appear, tracking him by the blood on his hands. "We will drain your red blood from your living flesh," they say. Terrified, he utters a second appeal to the absent Athena; and this time he ends, not with submission to justice, but with the open offer of a political bribe. If Athena will aid him against his enemies he will pledge the eternal alliance of himself and his citizens to Athens. (This bargain is offered again by Apollo, 667–73, and confirmed at great length by Orestes after his acquittal, 762–74.) Presently, when Athena arrives in person, his appeal to her includes not only equivocation (445–53) but a bid for favor on private grounds: "You know my father well" (455). Orestes is shedding all pretension to the heroic, and becoming an ordinary Athenian citizen fighting his case by hook or by crook. It is not even his own case: he is defending himself for what Apollo terrorized him into doing (465ff.). He is a pathetic and unheroic figure.

Now we proceed to examine the ambiguity surrounding Orestes' purification by Apollo. Let us specify three questions that must be asked. (1) What kind of cleansing does Aeschylus assume that Orestes needs? and does he show him in fact seeking the appropriate kind of cleansing? (2) Are we to accept the statements by Orestes (237, 282f., 445–52) and by Apollo (578) that appropriate cleansing was effectually carried out? (3) How far do the answers to these questions affect our interpretation of the trilogy as a whole?

1. What kind of cleansing does Orestes need? Orestes himself recognizes in *Choephori* that, as I said at the beginning, he needs an exceptional ritual, the *heis katharmos* which only Apollo can provide, since matricide belongs to a

different category of crime from homicide and is indeed presented, in the image of the serpent in Clytemnestra's dream, as a type of ultimate horror. Now, in *Eumenides*, this simple truth is unobtrusively but persistently attacked and eroded not only by Apollo but also by Orestes and Athena. The mental process by which expediency falsifies truth, already demonstrated in the first two plays (e.g., in *A.* 217, *eu gar eiē*, and *Ch.* 298, *kei mē pepoitha* . . .), in *Eumenides* becomes a main feature of the development.

Apollo had told Orestes (*Ch.* 1034–39) to go as suppliant to Delphi, and "not to turn to any other hearth." The chorus of Libation Bearers had said (1059f.), "There is one sole cleansing for you: Loxias will lay his hand on you and set you free from these torments." There is no reason to suppose that Aeschylus intended these passages to supersede the authoritative insistence of the first stasimon of *Agamemnon* that "there is no hope of rescue for the man who has spurned the great altar of Justice. . . . All cure is vain" (*A.* 381–87). *Ch.* 1059 certainly expresses the opinion of the chorus, and is not the poet's announcement of a theological belief that henceforth mercy is to temper judgment. For Apollo's first speech to Orestes (64–84) is in fact, under its disguise of solemnity, a tacit admission that his promised cure is a vain hope. Orestes has reached Delphi, properly equipped as a suppliant, but still polluted and dripping blood, as the Priestess describes him; and before a minute has passed in which any ritual could take place Apollo is passing him on to a different authority,[2] with not a word said about purification at Delphi (78–83):

> Do not weaken. . . . Go to the city of Pallas; clasp her ancient statue as a suppliant. There we shall have jurors (*dikastas*) to decide this case, and with soothing words we shall find contrivances (*mēchanas heurēsomen*) to deliver you from these troubles.

The sinister implications of *mēchanas* in connection with a law court are obvious, but irrelevant at the moment. The relevant significance of the speech I shall discuss later; we note now that Apollo tells Orestes his one hope is after all not purification but legal acquittal; and he adds that a long period of torment by the Erinyes is still to be expected. He promises "not to forsake him," and to be "harsh to his enemies," calling the Erinyes "detested hags . . . born for evil . . . shunned by all creation, hateful to men and gods"; but all this is of little comfort to Orestes, who replies,

> Lord Apollo, you know what it is not to be unjust; since you know it, learn also not to be neglectful. Your power to help is what I rely on.

Thereupon Apollo sends Orestes off under Hermes' escort to Athens; and the suppliant's hopeful visit to Delphi is over. Aeschylus thus leaves us confused at this point as to what kind of purification Orestes ought to be seeking. We must ask next, What kind is Orestes himself looking for?

After the prologue, Orestes' actual words give a firm indication that what he is looking for is something other than what he had in mind at the end of *Choephori*—the one special cleansing for an exceptional pollution which was to be bestowed in the Delphic temple by the god in person (*Ch.* 1059f.), and nowhere else (1038f.). Now, instead of "one cleansing," he says that he "knows many cleansings" (*Eu.* 276f.); and he relies no longer on the unique temple at the earth's navel and its undying flame, but three times speaks of his faith in those "other houses" (*Eu.* 239, 285, 451f.) which Apollo had forbidden him to turn to (*Ch.* 1038f.). Of the several sources of purification mentioned, only one—the touch of the god himself (*prosthigōn, Ch.* 1059)—seems to offer any hope of escape from his doomed condition; and this possibility has been precisely excluded by what happens and does not happen in his interview with Apollo in *Eu.* 64–93.

It seems, then, that in *Eumenides* Orestes has ceased to regard his pollution as exceptional, or his crime as anything worse than simple homicide. The shedding of kindred blood, which in *Agamemnon* aroused unspeakable horror, and in *Choephori* reduced Orestes himself to agony and despair, now loses its cosmic significance as a religious and moral miasma (cf. *Ch.* 1017), and becomes a situation classifiable as "just" or "unjust" (*Eu.* 468, 610) under a judicial code. Matricide, Orestes now assumes, may be dealt with merely as a homicide expiable by common means. He avoids the open admission of such an attitude until, taken off his guard by the Erinyes, he suddenly blurts it out in 606:

CH. She was not of one blood with the man she killed.
OR. Then am I of one blood with my mother?
CH. Did she not nourish you in her womb, polluted man? Do you disown the closest of all blood-kinship, your mother's?

To this Orestes has no answer, which is not surprising, since having few convictions of his own he lives and acts on external authority and persuasion, unheroic like his father. He asks Apollo, "Did I, in your opinion, act justly?" and from that moment has no more to say until after his acquittal.

In the attempt to have his case considered as one of ordinary homicide Orestes has powerful backing. When the Erinyes in 425 and 427 emphasize the special enormity of matricide, Athena gives no sign that she recognizes this crime as being different from the homicide mentioned in 421; she is untouched by the mortal horror that darkened every page of *Choephori*. In 473ff. she clearly hints, what in the trial she will say explicitly (736ff.), that she is entirely on Orestes' side. She declares that she recognizes him as a suppliant who has come "properly prepared," *katērtukōs nomōi*, already pure and "harmless to her temple," and she "welcomes him as one blameless to the city." She thus accepts without question Orestes' ambiguous and evasive statement in 447–52, in the sense in which Orestes wished her to accept it, namely that he has presented evidence of his effectual purification by Apollo—which is certainly not the case; and this pronouncement that he is *katharos*, "pure," is made after she has just said that she is not qualified to judge the issue herself, and before her special court of Areopagus has been appointed. This perhaps does not imply a prejudgment of the case; but it shows an attitude less than reassuring to those who look for impartiality in the president of a law court.

When the court assembles, she charges the jurors to ensure "that justice be well discerned" (573), but says also that they are to decide "the first trial of blood shed," *haimatos chutou* (682), ignoring the vital difference of matricide, and thus herself committing the impropriety which in 693 ff. she warns her citizens to avoid. Apollo too pursues the same evasion with the specious absurdity of his argument in 657 ff., "A mother is not the true parent of her child"; which says in effect: "The universal abhorrence of matricide ought not rationally to exist." It does exist, and the whole drama of *Choephori* is built upon it.

2. Our second question is, Was the purification appropriate to matricide carried out? The evidence on this point is partly circumstantial; there are also statements by Orestes and by Apollo, each of which we must assess on its merits.

Orestes' first speech (after his three lines of just complaint to Apollo in the prologue, 85 ff.) is his prayer to Athena, 235–43. Here he asserts that he is no longer, as the Priestess described him, "a guilty suppliant with polluted hands." He bases his claim to purity, however, not on any ritual performed at Delphi, but on his contact with "other houses" (239) where, he says, his defilement has been "rubbed off." If he was purified by Apollo at Delphi or anywhere else, why does he not say so in this first speech? He is alone on the stage; there is no one to hear or question his words. But immediately, at 244, his words are not merely questioned but circumstantially refuted. The Erinyes arrive, hot on the scent:

> This is plain evidence of the man. . . . We track him out as a hound tracks a wounded fawn, by the dripping blood. . . . The scent of mortal blood smiles at me.

The chorus, like the Priestess, recognizes pollution infallibly. The blood of his guilt is not, after all, "blunted and rubbed off," as Orestes now knows to his terror. The Erinyes see him, surround him, and promise to "drain the red blood from his living limbs" (264). Is there anything he can say to hold them off, to convince them that he is not ripe for immediate destruction? He does not address the chorus, but in their hearing addresses again the absent Athena. First, however, he speaks four significant lines, evidently to himself, but explaining why in this second speech his tactics are different (276–79):

> Schooled by misfortune, I know many kinds of purification, and I know when it is proper to speak, and likewise when to be silent. And in this case I was instructed by a shrewd teacher to speak.

His earlier speech had told spontaneously what he knew to be the substance of his claim to purity, contact with society. That claim has now been shattered; his plight is urgent. He knows that he needs to be able to say, "Apollo purified me." He dare not say this on his own initiative; so yet again he turns to external authority and speaks as Apollo has bidden him (280–85):

> The pollution of my mother's blood is drowsy and withered from my hand, the stain is washed away. While still fresh it was dispelled at the hearth of divine Phoebus by the ritual of a slaughtered pig.

Having uttered this claim under instruction, he then reverts at once to a repetition of the different claim he made spontaneously in his earlier speech—that he had been found acceptable and harmless in human society (284f.). Then, seeing the Erinyes unmoved, he offers to Athena, in return for help, not justice, but the perpetual alliance of himself and his city, and extols the military glory of Athens. All is of no avail; and the dramatic and poetic power of the Erinyes' "binding song" which follows is in its solemn authority at least equal to the theological lyrics of the Elders in *Agamemnon*.

We have to face the suspicion—incredible but irrepressible—that Orestes' shrewd instructor told him, if hard pressed, to lie boldly and say he had been ritually purified. If 282f. is indeed a lie, what more natural than that he should hasten to cover it with the truth of 284f. and then reinforce his plea for help with promises and high-flown compliments? We will consider this further in due course.

There is one more passage in which Orestes claims to have been purified. In the "preliminary hearing" granted him by Athena he protests for the third time that he is not *prostropaios* and that his hand is free from pollution (445f.). He continues thus:

> I will give you strong evidence (*tekmērion mega*) of this: the law bids a guilty man remain speechless until he be sprinkled with the blood of a suckling beast by a man competent to purify from bloodshed. Long ago these rites were performed for me in other houses. . . . I thus dispel your anxiety on this point.

Strong evidence? Sheer bluff. Could any argument for defense be more confused and inconclusive? What Orestes says could not in any sense be called evidence; it is merely his assertion—which, even if supported by evidence, would still be irrelevant, since it applies to ordinary cases of murder, not to the exceptional case of matricide. And what logic follows from *aphthongon*, "speechless"? None. Most remarkable of all: Orestes, when he sat alone before the dumb image of Athena, was ready to state—"under instruction," as he told us—that Apollo had purified him; but now, face to face with Athena herself, though he skirts around the idea of ritual cleansing, he dare not say the words, "Apollo purified me." Why not, if those words were true? As they stand, these lines 447–53 read like a hurried attempt to say something that sounds like a serious argument, from which the speaker glibly proceeds to his more hopeful line, "You know my father well."

These three speeches of Orestes, with their poignant picture of a reluctant and desperate lie, are a revelation of the subtle sympathy Aeschylus was capable of combining with a stern implication of moral necessity. There is guilt that cannot be expiated. The right solution is for the Erinyes to fulfill their function, exempting the gods (*theōn ateleian*, Eu. 361) from the duty of punishment. The alternative is the familiar social compromise of principle, facilitated by a pliable judicial formality, which will presently parade its humbug in the outrageous trial, and be applauded with the sincere and moving religious fervor of the panathenaic procession that ends the trilogy. The price of this compromise is the cutting of the cosmic root of morality by the corruption of the Erinyes, who yield their primeval function with the venal question (892), "What abode, Athena, do you say we are to have? What honor?" Their former honor, as guardians of basic morality, Apollo has roundly said (no one seems embarrassed by his candor) he "would not receive as a gift" (228). And Athena, comparing their older wisdom with her more modern understanding, will commend self-interest and respect for power in a line (850)—"Zeus endowed me too with no mean intelligence"—whose menace, after the flattery of 849, recalls her mention of the thunderbolt in 828, and confirms the perception of the Elders in A. 182f., that the gods exercise their rule *biaiōs*, by violence.

We turn now to what Apollo has to say about his function as *katharsios*, purifier. Near the end of *Choephori*, at the moment of deepest despair in the whole drama, when the Delphic command in all its horror and dread has been obeyed, and the Erinyes are gathering above their guilty victim, one ray of hope shines out as the chorus say (*Ch.* 1059f.):

> You have one source of cleansing: Loxias will lay his hand upon you
> and set you free from these sufferings.

Apollo himself acknowledges that he, who commanded a polluting crime, has an obligation to deliver Orestes (*Eu.* 83f.). The lines Aeschylus gives to Apollo throughout the play attribute to the god of Delphi an assumption of moral authority, emphasized in his frequent references to Zeus (e.g., as "my father," 649), and especially in his claim that he "never yet uttered from his prophetic throne any word that Zeus had not commanded" (616ff.). While lesser Olympians may flout mortal notions of morality in their own interests, Zeus is always the guardian of oaths, the respecter of suppliants, the judge between guest and host—in a word, the upholder of reverence, *aidōs*. Apollo in *Eumenides* claims for himself in the name of Zeus the moral authority, first to command the crime of matricide (84), then to purify the criminal (578). And by the end of *Choephori* it has become clear that the final crisis has been reached, that the one hope of ending the human proliferation of revengeful crimes lies in some drastic solution imposed by divine agency. In *Eumenides* two such agencies offer themselves: the Erinyes claim the right to destroy Orestes out of hand; but Apollo, Orestes says, promised to purify him and has done so. Thus the purification of this ultimate guilt becomes the act, the supreme moment, towards which the whole drama has been advancing; and now, in *Eu.* 64−93, we watch for the divine deliverance. The polluted man stands before the god in his temple. And the god says, "I will not forsake you; endure your continuing pain, and go to Pallas Athena." We should reflect on this.

A theater audience has no time for reflection. Before the spectator can grasp the magnitude of this shocking anticlimax, the ghost of Clytemnestra, and soon the frightening aspect of the chorus, divert his attention; while Apollo himself, by his glorious appearance, his dignity, his sympathetic tone, his solemn—though muddled—religious reasoning, disguises the fact that he has betrayed his suppliant. He elaborates the disguise with scurrilous abuse of the Erinyes, first to Orestes (67−73), then to the chorus themselves (179−97), in phrases whose violence is pointed by the courteous and rational replies of the Erinyes (198−212). Finally, as if aware that the audience may by now have realized how he has failed to keep his promise, he says (232ff.):

> I will help my suppliant and deliver him; for among gods too, as among mortals, the anger of a guilty suppliant is to be feared, should I deliberately betray him.

Aeschylus did not compose the immense complexity of this work without being confident that, even if it had only one performance, it would be read and reread by those who could reflect at leisure. Therefore we are right to assume that he expected a reader to ask, Why did Apollo not cleanse Orestes at Delphi? and that he knew the answer, which is simply this: that as murder is irrevocable, so pollution may be indelible. *Ch.* 71f. repeats, with a different reference, the same truth that convinced us in *A.* 381−98, and at 1017ff.: "There is no cure." Who should know this better than Apollo? He gave the promise of cleansing to induce Orestes to kill Clytemnestra; why he wished this, I shall discuss later; but it was a promise he surely knew he could not fulfill. This explains the otherwise unaccountable fact that, in a play where purification is expected by characters and audience alike as the crucial event, Apollo himself in his first two appearances does not mention the word, and when later he appears in the trial, refers to it only in an inconclusive parenthesis, 576ff.:

> I came not only as witness—since Orestes is a lawful suppliant at my hearth and I am his purifier of bloodshed—but also to plead for him in person.

After this Apollo does not refer to purification again. This casual, bare statement, if it were true, would surely be a decisive point in Orestes' defense, and would, in the mouth of a god, be unanswerable.

The final evidence that Apollo himself knows Orestes to be still unpurified comes later in the trial when the chorus leader asks Apollo (653–56):

> Shall this man, after pouring out his mother's blood on the ground, still live in his father's house in Argos? How can he officiate at public altars? Shall holy water be allowed him at tribal feasts?

This is the moment when Apollo could have settled the question by saying, "Orestes is purified; I performed the necessary ritual and am here to witness to it." What else could have been implied by his words just quoted from 576ff.? But instead of solemnly describing a ritual which either was never performed, or failed in its effect, Apollo recites the formal theory, directed to Athena as a compliment, which denies the vital relationship between mother and son, thus canceling the dramatic power of the second play, and incidentally reduces the holy contract of marriage—which in 213ff. he accused the Erinyes of dishonoring—to a mere convenience, *xenōi xenē* (660). This failure to confirm purification is Apollo's final betrayal of Orestes; and it points only too clearly to the truth: either Apollo had not attempted to purify his suppliant, knowing it was impossible, or he had tried and failed.

We are now confronted with the inference that Apollo's statement, *egō katharsios*, is an outright lie, from which he diverts attention, aware that the matter is passing from the religious sphere to the practical, where society's capacity for compromise will smooth over spiritual contradictions. Is such an inference credible?

In the first place, we must recognize that for the vast majority of the audience it was never meant to be credible. They were ready to take Apollo's word for the cleansing, to accept his (surely needless) protestation, "Being a prophet I will not lie" (615), as they were prepared to listen to his prevarications, threats, offers of inducement, and other ploys judicially inadmissible. If *egō katharsios* is a lie, it is so for those who will read and reflect. The material they have to reflect on is remarkable.

One of the most memorable moments in *Agamemnon* is Cassandra's cursing of Apollo (1264–76). It is the more vivid because Apollo's statue is visible on the stage. Cassandra is the person in this play who wins warmer sympathy from the audience than anyone else. There are many scenes in tragedy (e.g., Creusa in Euripides' *Ion*, 907–22) where a mortal denounces a god's cruelty—and cruelty is the chief ground of Cassandra's violent words; but in no other play does a priestess of Apollo tear off the sacred emblems of her prophetic office, throw them to the ground, and trample on them with a tirade of execration (*A.* 1267).

What was the poet's purpose in presenting this blasphemous act, which forms the climax of a long scene at the heart of the play? Up to this point Apollo has done nothing to incur the indignation of the audience. They have been told of his cruelty to Cassandra; but while this arouses sympathy, no one really minded about cruelty to a woman—to Cassandra any more than to Iphigenia. The scene could omit this curse (Page ad loc. refers to it as Cassandra's "feeble vengeance") and proceed to its conclusion without causing any sense that something was missing. No: Apollo's role in the trilogy is not his treatment of Cassandra, but the part he plays in the main plot, when he commands Orestes, with threats, to kill his mother. The trampling of his prophetic insignia is a powerful and crucial symbol; and its meaning looks not back but forwards. Cassandra is an unheeded prophetess, but she always speaks the truth. This god of prophecy will, before the next play begins, defile his own shrine with a polluting command—in the words of the Erinyes (*Eu.* 162–67):

> Such are the deeds of the younger gods, who use their power to transgress justice. See, the prophetic throne is bloodstained . . . the earth's navel has taken upon itself a foul bloody pollution.

Cassandra may only partly understand what she is prophesying; she speaks indeed not without satisfaction of the crime that will avenge her death (*A.* 1280ff.); but her words remain, for the reflective reader, a warning that Apollo, when he appears, will stand before us as a god who in his prophetic authority has been challenged and insulted by his own priestess, and has not replied.

Four other passages prepare us for the shock of Apollo's lie at *Eu.* 578. First, Orestes in his long speech *Ch.* 269–305 puts forward, as his principal excuse for undertaking so abhorrent an act as matricide, the blood-chilling threats with which he says Apollo reinforced his command; and he refers again to these in 925 when his mother pleads for her life, and again in 1032f. That the Erinyes could be expected to punish matricide was rational and unquestioned (*Eu.* 210). But a situation where a man could be punished equally for killing his mother and for not killing her is irrational, childish, and repellent; it is grotesque, and has no place in the moral world of tragedy. For those who were too slow to perceive this at *Ch.* 924f., where Orestes uses this absurdity to counter his mother's plea, Aeschylus has spelled the matter out in *Eu.* 310–15, where the Erinyes make a solemn declaration of the office entrusted to them by Fate at the creation of the world:

> We claim to be strictly just: the man who can show clean hands no anger of ours pursues; he lives his life unharmed.

Therefore the threats with which Apollo coerces Orestes are a lie.

The next passage to throw doubt on Apollo's verbal honesty is his interview with Orestes in the prologue, *Eu.* 64–93, which we have discussed already. The third passage is Orestes' curious four lines *Eu.* 276–79, in which he refers to the "shrewd teacher" who told him when to speak and when to be silent; here it seems to be implied (see above, pp. 42–43) that Apollo had instructed him to lie if necessary. Finally there is Apollo's dialogue with the Erinyes, 179–234. The violent abuse with which he begins is no answer to the moral and rational accusations made by the chorus in 149–77. Apollo's words in 203 and 205 are an admission that he had promised Orestes purification. His speech 213–24 ("Then you dishonour the marriage of Hera and Zeus. . . .") is not only a prevarication, but an inept one. Apollo himself, a son of Zeus, was not the fruit of the "pledged love" of that pair (214). As for Aphrodite, "from whom arise men's dearest joys" (216), we may ask, since he is referring to Agamemnon, whether these joys arose from Clytemnestra or Cassandra. Again, if "the sexual union of man and wife is greater than an oath" (218), does not the bond of mother and son (*mētros timas*, 624) have an equal claim to be stronger than any oath Orestes may have sworn to avenge his father? Lastly, in 221, instead of saying, "You are unjust to pursue Orestes"—which is patently untrue, why does he not say the one thing that could make it true, namely, "I have purified him"? Because the audience can see the blood on Orestes' hands; and it will still be there in the next scene, in Athens (244).

I cannot find a single passage which could be adduced to counter the uniform effect of those lines that present Apollo as a proved and probable liar, or that could be held to make it incredible that in 578 the word *katharsios* is uttered with conscious intent to deceive.

If this argument stands, we cannot avoid a further question: Why does Aeschylus show Apollo going to unscrupulous lengths to have Clytemnestra murdered and her murderer vindicated? The answer seems to lie in the fact that, while *Agamemnon* is concerned with the metaphysical background of human passion, in *Choephori* and *Eumenides* the scene, despite the active part played by gods, is in truth not the invisible cosmos but human—especially Athenian—society. This society awarded the first prize to the author of the *Trilogy*; condoned, after a seemly show of sentiment, the sacrifice of Iphigenia, execrated the just revenge of Clytemnestra, supported and applauded the enterprise of Orestes, ignored the unscrupulous behavior of the suave Athena and the devious Apollo, and rejoiced in the defeat of the Erinyes—the sole voice upholding public honor—and in their final corruption by Athena's menacing blandishments. The place allowed to woman by this society is one that makes inevitable the defeat which in the trilogy is inflicted on woman and on justice; and Aeschylus presents Apollo as the eternal embodiment, the symbol and the patron, of this society, of which the poet himself was both a clear-sighted critic and a patriotic and heroic member; a society which, deaf though it might be, remained his only audience. There is no reason to suppose that he admitted the possibility of any change in this feature of Athenian society in the foreseeable future. Such a society dared not permit the rebellion of woman any hope of escape from total defeat. Aeschylus shows this defeat successfully contrived by the two divinities.

3. Finally, in what way do these conclusions affect our interpretation of the trilogy as a whole?

The questions I have asked here and in chapter 2 have often been left unexamined by scholars, some of the facts I find significant have rarely been considered, and my conclusions, if sound, must disturb the whole fabric of interpretation that has been built around this vast work of art. The accepted view has in general recognized that the dramatic pattern is a series of victories and defeats, introduced by the refrain in the *Agamemnon* parodos, *to d'eu nikatō*, "May the good prevail!" and illustrated successively by the triumph of Clytemnestra in the first play, her defeat in the second, and in the third by the conflict between the Erinyes and Apollo, in which Athena has traditionally been regarded as an impartial umpire and the exponent of—a much-favored but, I maintain, meaningless phrase—"a new concept of justice." Some scholars, acknowledging that the male-dominated type of society represented by Apollo was harsh and unjust, have argued that Aeschylus upheld its harshness as the only hope for the survival of Athenian democracy in the fifth-century world. Whether that be so or not, it is indisputable that the victory achieved in *Choephori* and vindicated in *Eumenides* was the victory the Elders were thinking of in A. 121, 139, 159, and not the victory Clytemnestra was thinking of in A. 349, "May the good prevail visibly and unambiguously." What remains disputable is the profound question which at the end of *Agamemnon* is still a question (1560–64):

> Reproach answers reproach; and to judge is a hard struggle. The destroyer is destroyed, the killer pays his debt. This maxim remains while Zeus remains on his throne: the doer suffers. This is the law.

Did the Elders, or did Clytemnestra, rightly identify the cause of "the good"? There was never any doubt that virtually the whole of Aeschylus' audience would agree with the Elders; and the performance at the Dionysia was *their* occasion, their annual celebration of patriotic and religious confidence, and it was for them that the poet wrote. Yet not entirely so: whatever his public aim, the supreme artist in any field works first for himself. In the *Oresteia* Aeschylus makes Apollo chief spokesman for the cause which wins the ultimate obvious victory. If that cause is to be acknowledged as "the good," it is essential that we, the audience, should know that the man (how regrettable that one cannot say "hero") who dared the last fearful encounter and avenged his father has been duly purified, by the god whose command he trusted, from the pollution he felt it was his duty to incur. Readers accepting the traditional view have in the past generally felt satisfied upon this point. But the study I have undertaken in this chapter seems to me to show that we ought not to be satisfied; that Aeschylus does not allow us to think with any confidence of Orestes as cleansed from his pollution, or of Apollo as possessing either the magical or the moral power to purify a matricide.

Finally, I think of Aeschylus' audience, then and now. Those who in his own and following centuries heard, and read and reread and learned by heart, the lines and the scenes, the images and the dramatic strategy of this work, responded with veneration and enhanced vision; and the aesthetic response of modern scholars, though only a faint replica of the original experience, is none the less genuine and, within the small world of scholarship, universal in its nature. But—as this chapter has, I hope, helped to show—the first audience's response was on some levels halted and perverted by the social and political certainties of that unique period, of that hectic strength whose precariousness made its certainties the more blind. The result in our day is that students who on first approaching the work are moved and exalted by its aura of poetic authority sometimes find on closer acquaintance that, after all, its metaphysical concepts are primitive, its values cynical, its theology crude, and its moral conclusions remote alike from its poetic splendor and from the unchangeable realities of life. They are apt to ask, "Did Aeschylus really think that his *Eumenides* celebrated a new and inspiring concept of justice, or that persuasion had led to reconciliation? If he did think so, was not Page right after all in saying that 'the faculty of acute or profound thought is not among his gifts'" ("Introduction," p. xv)? The choice lies between accepting that preposterous dictum and beginning the search for a radical revision of the traditional view.

4

Agamemnon, Justice, and the Heroic Role

The character and role of Aeschylus' Agamemnon present an image of subtle complexity. The poet's starting point must surely have been Homer's portrait of the King of Men in the *Iliad*. A valuable study of this portrait is to be found in C. H. Whitman's *Homer and the Heroic Tradition* (see chapter 1, *ad init.*); and J. J. Peradotto, in a more recent article (which I shall presently summarize), also recognizes the Homeric original in Aeschylus' conception. In the play itself Agamemnon is on stage for less than one-eighth of the action, and himself speaks only eighty-two lines; yet the man, his predicament, and his fate constitute a personal world remarkable in its completeness of detail.

Varied light falls upon Agamemnon from many directions. The Watchman loves his master with uncritical devotion, and longs to grasp his hand in welcome; the king's enemies are his enemies. The Herald is a soldier who identifies himself with the army, its commander, and its cause; he fully accepts the politics of the war, though he is frank about the suffering it cost the ordinary fighter. The Elders are loyal; they have a considerable degree of moral perception, and are not uncritical of the king; but their frankness is the measured frankness of politicians. Politicians are also human, and Aeschylus has used this aspect of the Argive Elders to present, in the parodos, a passionate statement of that one truth about Agamemnon which obsesses Clytemnestra and inspires her with courage to act out her indignation. The king's male subjects see him as the king sees himself: a hero and demigod. His encounter with the queen at first gives him opportunity to display his style as commander-in-chief; then two minutes of dialogue prick his bubble, as his wife, taking control line by line, lays bare his hollow vanity and weakness, and leads him to that visible moral defeat which prefigures his physical defeat behind the closed doors of his palace. Yet another—a fifth—source of illumination completes this helpless and all too human figure, when Cassandra, enslaved and doomed, and cursing Apollo for his cruelty, has no word of blame for the man who burned her city, took her virginity, and massacred her family, but instead identifies herself emotionally with her new master, speaking of "my death and Agamemnon's," reviling his enemy, pitying his end, which shall unite her with him; welcoming the further outrage that shall avenge them both. The total effect is a stereoscopic portrait of proud and pitiful humanity in victory and defeat.

Agamemnon's character has been described, with a force and completeness I cannot attempt to emulate, by J. J. Peradotto in the article already mentioned. His portrait, of which I here give only a meager summary, is based—I believe, rightly—on interpretation of the portent of the eagles and the pregnant hare described by the chorus in *A.* 109–20. I would urge any student of the *Oresteia* to read particularly the first three pages of this article. The principles which he there lays down are those that I have tried to follow in my own study.

The theme of the trilogy, says this writer, is primarily and profoundly moral. It is presented at the opening of *Agamemnon* in the description by the chorus of the omen that appeared to the army and its commander as they set out from Argos: two eagles that tore to pieces a pregnant hare and her unborn young. This image symbolizes three events narrated as important elements in the play: the sacrifice of Iphigenia; the total destruction of Troy; and the murder of Thyestes' children, which though prior in time sounds as a later echo in the play's action. All three events are instances of "the slaughter of innocent youth in the pursuit and exercise of power." The character, *ēthos*, of Agamemnon corresponds closely with this ruthless predatory image. It is this character that rouses the anger of the goddess Artemis, who cherishes all young and innocent life, animal or human. It has often been said (e.g., by Page, in his introduction, pp. xxv–xxviii) that Artemis compelled Agamemnon to sacrifice his daughter. Peradotto insists that Artemis "compels Agamemnon to nothing, but creates a situation in which he may either cancel the war, or else pursue it by inflicting on his own household the kind of slaughter he will perpetrate at Troy." The decision made "depends upon the kind of man Agamemnon is." It is not true that Aeschylus shows him as having no alternative, that to disband the expedition was impossible; still less that Zeus commanded him to sail against Troy. Though he inherited his nature from his father Atreus, he was nonetheless responsible for it and free to indulge or curb it. He was the kind of man who would put his own glory first and the sanctity of kindred blood second. When he sacrificed his daughter he freely "put on the bridle of necessity," and thereafter necessity led him inevitably to his death. The omen of the eagles illuminates Agamemnon's war against Troy as "a demonic perversion of society's extermination of the offender." The aggression of the eagles reported in the opening lyrics is parallel to what we see in the third episode—Agamemnon's *hubris* in walking on the purple cloth; and both passages provide an image of his essential nature. "If Agamemnon is victimized, it is by his own *ēthos*"; and the writer quotes Heracleitus: *ēthos anthrōpōi daimōn*, "A man's character is his god-sent destiny."

Peradotto's article is remarkable not only for its logical and honest treatment of detail, but still more for its grasp of the broad moral design of the play. (I say "of the play" rather than "of the trilogy" for reasons which have already appeared in chapters 2 and 3.) It makes an authoritative clearance of much banal, perverse, and inhumane argument. It lays a foundation for further advance, and ought, in my opinion, to have set a few scholars eagerly to work on a restatement of all the main issues in the trilogy. (Perhaps indeed it has.) There is much in it that my summary omits; but I hope I have given a fair account of his main thesis.

A further point, however, needs to be mentioned: Agamemnon's claim to be regarded as a hero, or as "the hero" of the play. Peradotto writes (p. 258): "Agamemnon is not strictly speaking the hero of the Trilogy. . . . Orestes is its central figure." But Agamemnon has usually been allowed some claim to be the hero of the first play. His external status evidently falls within the limits set by Aristotle—that the hero of a play should be someone of recognized importance, and neither wholly good nor wholly bad. But within these limits finer distinctions are possible, as I have already suggested in my introductory chapter. What qualities Aeschylus would have posited as belonging in general terms to the concept of the heroic we can only surmise; but he has shown nobility in Cassandra, and firmness and courage in both Cassandra and Clytemnestra, while Agamemnon lacks both nobility and firmness, and displays ferocity rather than courage. His quality, his claim to the heroic role, is revealed first in the long speech he makes upon arrival, second in the three actions that plot his progress towards sudden death.

His opening speech begins thus (81off.):

> First it is right to salute Argos and the gods of this land, with whose help I have returned home after exacting just retribution from Priam's city. Claims for justice were made not by mere words but by arms; the gods heard these claims, and cast their votes unanimously for the bloody destruction of Troy and her men. The smoke of the dead city can still be seen from afar; from the ashes of luxurious wealth odours rise on the winds. For this victory our endless thanks are due to the gods, since we have taken revenge for Paris's proud rape; the Argive beast, brood of the horse, our armoured ranks, ground a city to powder for a woman's sake. . . . The man-eating lion leapt their defences and licked its fill of royal blood. Thus to the gods I have prolonged my first address. . . .

In twenty lines he has four times ascribed his success to the gods. Before he leaves the stage he will have given us cause to suspect that he almost believes himself a god; already he forgets that gods give success to mortals upon conditions. Clytemnestra knows the conditions (338ff., 345ff.):

> If they reverence the gods who have temples in the captured city, and spare their altars, the destroyers will not be destroyed in turn. . . .
> If the army reaches home without having offended the gods, the anguish of the dead will yet be wakeful, even if no unexpected calamity occurs.

The Herald is not concerned with theology, only with the dramatic events he has witnessed (527):

> The altars, the temples of gods, are overthrown.

And a more sinister comment (662f.):

> Our ship escaped the storm, not by the steersman's skill, but some god snatched us from death, or begged our deliverance.

Agamemnon has forgotten the conditions; his respect for the gods is a verbal formality.

But he has also forgotten his debt to mortals. "All my fellow chiefs," he says, "were jealous of me and unreliable, except Odysseus." Unlike Clytemnestra, he does not think of "the wakeful anguish of the dead." He does not mention Menelaus, or the thousands who fell in battle; later he makes it clear that Iphigenia too has faded from his memory.

Agamemnon is not a god. He has forgotten his obligation as a mortal. Below sublimity, below humanity, is a baser level, where now, in 821–28, Agamemnon finds appropriate utterance. The status he claims for his achievement is that of the irrational beast, a creature that bites (*dakos*, 824), aptly wombed in a horse, grinding a city to dust; a lion that eats raw flesh and licks blood (827f.). Thus he identifies himself, first with the ferocious Agamemnon depicted by Homer in the *Iliad* (e.g., 6.55–60), and next with the enraged vultures of *A.* 49f., and still more closely with the pitiless eagles of 112–20, whose feast Artemis abhors (138).

He has complained at length of the jealousy of his fellow chiefs; and Page in his note on 841f. asks, "What had Agamemnon to complain of in Nestor, Diomede, and many others?" But this is surely not the point. The querulous digression 832–42 serves to emphasize only one notion: that the great victory was Agamemnon's own unique and personal achievement. Clytemnestra, who sees through him at every line, expresses this attitude of his perfectly in 939:

> Greatness wins hate; unenvied is unenviable.

or, No jealousy, no glory. His mind runs on the state of glorious success (*olbos*, 837; *olbisai*, 928); and Clytemnestra's *olbiois*, 941, finally raises him to a level

above mortality, from which he dare stoop to yield victory to her. Just as at
Aulis he wept (204) at hearing Calchas' "expedient," *mēchar* (199), because he
knew that this, cost what it might, was the way his ambition would take, so
now, as soon as he sees the purple drape, he knows that its splendor will properly celebrate his more than mortal status, and that this is the way he will take.
The excitement such a resolve stirs in him accounts for the violence and re-
petitiveness of his words in 918–30:

> And do not with these soft attentions woman me,
> Nor prostrate like a fawning Persian mouth at me
> Your loud addresses; nor with your spread cloths invite
> Envy of gods, for honours due to gods alone.
> I count it dangerous, being mortal, to set foot
> On rich embroidered silks. . . . The god's best gift
> Is a mind free from folly—

words that he will graciously eat a dozen lines later.

The poet's depiction of Agamemnon's soul is not confined to the words
Agamemnon himself speaks. The lines just quoted show an intense and ill-
controlled irritation which is provoked by successive elements in Clytemnestra's long address: that she has found words to touch his guilt for ten years'
absence—for cruelty in deserting his wife (862), folly in abandoning a discontented city to rebellious agitators (883); that she has flattered his self-esteem
both regal and marital to a degree that mocks his credulity, and still leaves him
no possible answer; that she has found precisely the temptation to which he
knows he will yield, and that in yielding he will demonstrate his weakness and
her strength.

Of the three choices of action made by Agamemnon, two are narrated, the
third presented on stage. The first is his decision to lead the assembled Greek
force against Troy. "The sons of Atreus were sent against Alexandros by almighty Zeus Xenios," states the chorus of Elders. Peradotto's discussion of this
statement (pp. 251ff.) is cogent, and his conclusion that it is "a religious interpretation of the chorus, not an empirical description" seems to me indisputable. When the Elders tell Agamemnon (799–804) that in their judgment this
was a foolish decision, they say nothing about any command of Zeus. It was a
decision whose inevitable consequences in human terms were not yet visible at
that time; so it was possible then to put off considering them. To force him to
consider them (see Peradotto, pp. 247–50) Calchas produces, in the name of
Artemis (201f.), the proposal whose horrifying nature is to be guessed only
(204) from Agamemnon's tears and his scepter striking the ground, as he
faces—or tells himself that he is facing—his second decision.

Why the tears? Because Agamemnon knew instantly that this is what he would do. Had such a proposal (the lines never suggest that it was a command—a *mēchar* is a way of getting what you want) been put before Ajax or Achilles, the heroic temper would have defied the "war-loving chiefs," the thoughtless rank and file, priest, prophecy, the entire pantheon, in defense of laws older than the Olympians, laws authorized by Fate (see *Eu.* 334–59) and ratified in human experience since the first family was founded. Agamemnon knows in his heart the authority of these laws: "To kill my child, to pollute my hands with her blood at an altar, is terrible." It is an inner authority, which only he himself can enforce. There is also another, external, authority—his fellow chiefs, his *xymmachia* (213). To refuse is also terrible: he imagines them shouting at him, "*Liponaus!* Traitor!" They are furiously angry, they insist on the sacrifice (215f.). Who is he, to tell them they are not in the right? The word *themis* (217), with which Agamemnon settles his conscience, will be discussed presently. Its vagueness helps the king to shift responsibility, in his own mind, from himself to his fellow chiefs with a diplomatic phrase; and he follows it with a pious prayer that all may be well.

Agamemnon's third decision is taken in 944:

> Then, since you desire it—let someone loose my sandals.

This is the conclusion of the dozen or so lines in which "relentless persuasion forces him" (*biatai d'ha talaina peithō*, 385), step by step dismantling the heroic and dissolving confidence.

> CL. Tell me this, not contradicting your true opinion—
> AG. My true opinion—I shall certainly not contradict it.

So the two sides are set for battle.

> CL. Would you, in a moment of fear, have vowed to the gods to act thus?
> AG. Yes, if someone with expert knowledge had prescribed such a rite.

Agamemnon knows that to tread on rich embroideries is an act which any mortal should fear (924), that it is sheer folly (927); yet he admits that, in a matter like this which an honest man should decide for himself, he, Agamemnon, would in fact be ready to yield to fear, and then to accept the advice of "an expert." Where is the hero?

> CL. Imagine Priam as conqueror: what would he have done?
> AG. Walked on embroidered cloth, I have no doubt.

How did Clytemnestra guess that Agamemnon envied and admired the king of Troy, in whose presence "barbaric grovellings" were fully in order? The great Priam is dead; but he still lives as yet one more authority to whom Agamemnon defers.

CL. Then, do not respect mortal censure (*mē aidestheis*).
AG. Yet the voice of the people has great power.

A man's integrity is shown by what he respects. At Aulis Agamemnon and his fellow chiefs "did not respect" (229f.) Iphigenia's pleading. He honored first the mortal censure of his alliance. (See chapter 6 in this volume.) A few lines later (948f.) he will declare that his sense of *aidōs*, "shame" or "compunction," which was proof against Iphigenia's tears, is offended by the improper use of household possessions which were "bought with silver." In his opening speech, when he was claiming the role of hero, he promised firm action against dissidents (844–50); now he admits that he must respect popular complaint, in which he recognizes yet another authority. "Let them complain," says Clytemnestra; "their envy is your glory." Again she has touched a sensitive spot; but the mere thought of his own glory makes him undervalue his real enemy, and he is ready to humor this woman who longs for a battle (940):

CL. It becomes greatness also to accept defeat.
AG. Why, here's a battle! What would you not give to win?
CL. Yield! You are victor: give me too my victory.
AG. Then, since such is your pleasure, . . .
    And since I have been thus subdued
  To obey you, I will walk on purple to my palace.

His last words on the stage are *porphuras patōn*, "treading on purple." In 369–72 the Elders were sure that the gods destroy those who tread (the same verb, *patein*) on the beauty of things that should not be touched.

The sudden violent death of a powerful and revered king is pitiful and tragic, however far he may fall short of the heroic. The "godlike man" (1547) struck down by a woman (1453f.) claims tears at the end of the play. His restoration to regal and semidivine dignity, with his crime and his hollowness forgotten, is accomplished in the long invocation in *Choephori*—see especially 345–62, and is confirmed in *Eumenides* (456f., 625f., 637). The rejoicing of the citizens in the panathenaic procession over the formal triumph of the male cause, while all trace of Clytemnestra and Iphigenia vanishes from thought and action, and even the Erinyes yield at last to blandishment and threat—all this was naturally found acceptable by the male patriots of 458 B.C. who canonized the trilogy and its author. The notion that heroic quality, or heroic status, could be assigned to Clytemnestra was to them, it can hardly be doubted, an impossibility which no weight of evidence in the text could credibly suggest. We need, of course, to remember that our view of a Greek tragedy is colored by the fact that only the text remains to us; while for the ancient audience the words were one element among six or seven—the costumes, the choreography, the music, individual renderings by known performers, and so forth. But the text was what the poets' admirers learned and treasured in memory; and each poet knew that it was the only part of his work that had a chance of surviving.

The completeness of the victory of Agamemnon's cause—so long assumed to be that victory of "the good" which the Elders prayed for—presents a contradiction which interpreters of Aeschylus must face. Attempts to refute the view put forward in this book may include some insistence on the changes in social standards that have occurred between the fifth century B.C. and our own time. But it may be thought no less remarkable that opinions on the moral interpretation of the trilogy have remained, in this central issue, virtually unchanged for 2500 years; so that modern critics as widely different as Fraenkel and Kitto can embrace the simple faith of the first audience, Fraenkel honoring Agamemnon as "a great gentleman" (in his note on ll. 940ff., p. 414), while Kitto writes (*Greek Tragedy*, p. 92) of the radiance, beauty, and purity of Apollo in *Eumenides*. The recognition of irony in ancient dramatists is a principle not to be recklessly applied; but without it, rational understanding of the *Oresteia* is halted by insoluble contradictions.

Central to the whole trilogy is the theme of justice. The idea of *dikē* appears first in the opening phrase of the parodos of *Agamemnon* (40f.): *Priamou megas antidikos Menelaos*—"legal adversary"; and the passage proceeds to describe the standard syndrome associated with the operations of justice—robbery, resistance, anger that is quelled only by revenge. The Herald celebrates the outcome of this syndrome, Agamemnon's victory, as a light in darkness (522). Agamemnon claims that the justice of his victory was assured by divine judgment (812f.). In *Choephori* the chorus emphasizes justice as the motive for matricide—and it is disconcerting to note that Orestes himself in his eloquent apologia 269–96, with one bare allusion to justice (301), concentrates on his fear of Apollo's threats. In *Eu.* 609, after the dialogue that opens the trial, Orestes, despairing of argument, appeals to Apollo to deliver his opinion whether the matricide was just or unjust. The Erinyes, when they insist that Orestes must be punished with death, claim to be "scrupulously just" (*euthudikaioi*, 312); but Athena, having induced them to reverse their attitude, says that her city will be similarly just, *orthodikaion* (994), in honoring them. Aeschylus' allusions to *dikē* are so various and, in the context of the events they refer to, so contradictory, that Kitto, commenting on the exchange between Clytemnestra and Orestes in *Ch.* 904–30, says, "Nothing could more forcibly express the bankruptcy of the cosmic and social system of Justice which we have been contemplating hitherto" (*Greek Tragedy*, p. 86). Unfortunately he proceeds to confound confusion by describing Athena's solution of Orestes' "impossible dilemma" as a "new dispensation" based on reason and mercy, and embodying "*dikē* in its widest sense." (Mercy is not mentioned anywhere in the trilogy.) This is of course the view most generally held by readers and scholars in both the ancient and the modern world. My reasons for rejecting it are set forth at length in all the chapters of this book.

The complex moral questions raised in the trilogy are somewhat simplified when we recognize that the notion of "justice" is in fact a negative one, definable only in terms of its opposite, "injustice" or "injury." No one could say whether it was "just" that a Greek army should attack Troy; many would dispute Clytemnestra's "justice" in killing Agamemnon, Orestes' "justice" in killing his mother; but the theft of a host's wife, the sacrifice of a daughter, the murder of a husband, of a mother—all these were by common consent outrageous injuries. Justice is the correction of injustice. It is a thing always to be sought, and not to be defined until it is found. For this reason indignation against wrong is a primary virtue, perhaps the seed and motive of all morality. The *Iliad* opens with this word, *menin*; its successive episodes record the search for justice, and Book 24 reveals, at the end of the search, not the definition of justice, but a vision that transcends any definable quality. Indignation against wrong is an element of the heroic which in tragedy unites persons as different as Sophocles' Antigone and Ajax, Euripides' Medea, and Aeschylus' Clytemnestra. The Erinyes are the supernatural embodiment of this "cry for justice," as their name *Arai* (*Eu.* 417) indicates (see Kitto, *Form and Meaning in Drama*, p. 60). Their two choral odes, and their pleading before the Areopagus, show the dignity which Aeschylus assigns to their essential function in human society, while their repellent appearance and grotesque action in the early scenes (up to 275) represent the debased conception by which, inevitably, popular childish belief would recognize them. Their role is more fully discussed in chapter 10.

The word *dikē* covers a wide range of meaning, from exact "justice" to that which is "right" or "proper"—as the Elders say in 259 that it is "right" for them to give royal honor to the queen in the king's absence, or as Agamemnon says (811) that it is "right" for him to salute first Argos and the city's gods. A similar range of meaning can be covered by the word, or the name, *themis*. As a proper noun this can mean Justice personified (not necessarily so in *Eu.* 2); as a common noun it means chiefly "that which is established by custom," and so "right" or "proper"; and from this meaning it is a short step to "obligatory." In this sense it is used significantly at 217, as the last and decisive word in Agamemnon's narrated pondering of the question whether he should sacrifice Iphigenia. His fellow chiefs, he says, "crave with a furious passion the sacrifice which will change the wind, a virgin's blood—and that they should crave it is *themis*." He may mean that to sacrifice a king's daughter in the cause of victory "has precedent" (as, e.g., in Euripides' *Erechtheus*); or that the attack on Troy is "just"; or that military expedience is more valid than family sentiment. The important thing for the reader to notice is that it is Agamemnon, and not Aeschylus, who says that the chiefs' demand is *themis*. Page's devious note on this passage expounds Page's introduction to the play rather than Aeschylus' text, which here, and in the comprehensive condemnation expressed immediately after in 218–30, presents Agamemnon's decision as an irrevocable (*anankas edu lepadnon*, "he put on the bridle of necessity," 218) abdication from the heroic role. A hero accepts no bridle.

Is the structure of *Agamemnon*, then, hollow at the center—a tragedy without a hero? The answer which the next chapter will offer to this question is, I believe, the answer Aeschylus would have given to any inquirer he could trust to listen with an open mind. That open minds could be a rarity in the city and century of Anaxagoras and Socrates seems to contradict the usual notion of Athens as a center of intellectual ferment. But a handful of philosophers could not provide for a dramatist that audience without whose favor no man could be known as a dramatist. What Aeschylus has done is to present Agamemnon as one who superficially satisfies the requirements in dignity, power, and reason, so that the popular audience can accept him in his traditional heroic role; while the text itself is everywhere loaded with details that contradict this picture, showing the king as vain, cruel, foolish, self-deceiving, lacking in firmness and integrity—in a word, as unheroic.

A common response to a statement of this view is the incredulous question: How is it that in all these centuries such an interpretation has apparently not been put forward? Several answers can be offered.

The first is that Aeschylus did not labor to conceal his meaning; it is all there to be seen. And I believe that it was fully understood, in the second half of the fifth century, by Euripides, who was in his early twenties when the *Oresteia* was produced. I shall discuss in chapters 13, 14, and 15 the three plays in which Euripides takes Orestes' matricide as his theme. In these plays he emphasizes the same view of the Atreid crimes that I maintain Aeschylus put forward in the *Oresteia*. Besides these, we have the remnants of *Erechtheus* already mentioned, in which I venture the guess that Euripides offers his Praxithea to average Athenians as a sarcastic picture of the kind of woman, the kind of mother, Clytemnestra ought to have been, to win their approval.

For a second answer, we may remind ourselves that the life of European nations still today embodies two primary assumptions which already governed community life in the time of Agamemnon, in the time of Aeschylus, and in every following century: the priority of military interests over all others; and its corollary, the virtually complete ascendancy of the male over the female. Aeschylus recognized these two assumptions as immovable and inescapable, and illumined them as the twin roots of tragedy. Among the masses of today's European population (to say nothing of the rest of the world) these two as-

sumptions remain as unassailable as they were in Aeschylus' audience; and in
the sheltered life of universities (where almost all serious study of Greek tragedy is done) the professional quest for new perceptions has been no less reluctant to imperil stability by throwing doubt upon the soundness of these assumptions. Scholars have therefore with notable exceptions—tended to see
in the *Oresteia* what the fifth-century audience saw, and to miss the possibility
that the poet's vision reached beyond the scope of his contemporaries. Certainly the vast literature of puzzled comment on this work suggests that accepted interpretations have not been finally satisfactory. The view here offered
is self-consistent, and will, I hope, appear to gather strength as the drama progresses to its close.

Meanwhile the poet has not ignored the heroic idea. Cassandra has always
been recognized as possessing heroic quality; and both Agamemnon and Orestes are diminished by contrast with her integrity. But her quality, like her role,
is limited and not central. For the heroic center of *Agamemnon* we must look
where Athenian citizens, veterans of Marathon and Salamis, saw only execra-
ble vileness. To recognize integrity in an enemy is never easy. Aeschylus was not
concerned, in this case, to make his meaning either obscure or obvious, as
Clytemnestra—no less surely than the Spartan three hundred at Thermopy-
lae—acts out her passionate faith with open eyes, in the certainty of ultimate
defeat and violent death.

5

Clytemnestra

One of the most triumphant contrasts in Greek tragedy is Aeschylus' transition from the sad, anxious, uncertain end of the long parodos in *Agamemnon* to the sudden blaze of Clytemnestra's presence, and the beacon speech. The Argive Elders, defiantly committed to one side of a conflict, have three times spoken of the struggle between the evil they have known and the good they hope for:

> Lament, lament; yet may the good prevail!

The change from night to morning, from apprehension to hope, from doubt to resolution, heralds not only Agamemnon's triumph but Clytemnestra's. In the battle of good and evil a choice is, from the beginning, opened before us, the audience; how, in the end, are we to recognize "the good," its victory, or its defeat? It is true that by "the good" the Elders mean several things—victory over Troy, the king's safe return, the defeat of Clytemnestra's suspected schemes; but there is ample evidence that the phrase bears also a general moral meaning, which extends the scope of the Elders' thoughts.[1] Before the scene ends Clytemnestra too will pray "that the good may prevail visibly and unambiguously." The Elders find their position embarrassing, and at first are almost ready to admit as much. The sacrifice at Aulis, they know, was evil and must lead to more evil. But they hate Clytemnestra, who mocks and shames them. They lack the firmness to prevent her revenge; but when she accomplishes it they will turn upon her as the prime enemy, and—except in one passage of grudging honesty, quickly abandoned (1560–64)—forget the crime she justly punished.

The confrontation between Clytemnestra and the Elders may remind us of two often-quoted lines from W. B. Yeats:

> The best lack all conviction, while the worst
> Are full of passionate intensity.

Almost all comment on the *Oresteia* has designated Clytemnestra as "the worst"; and many scholars of repute leave the impression that they accept the general attitude of the Elders as expressing the mind of Aeschylus—as representing, if not "the best," at least an acceptable idea of "the good." Certainly a lack of conviction is included in the Elders' claim to such a role; they present a picture of self-deception, irresolution, and want of courage to act either on their beliefs or on the evidence of their eyes and ears.[2] They have celebrated the principle of just retribution (40–67), and recognized the "late-punishing Erinys" (59) as Zeus' agent. They have mentioned as a sure provocation of vengeance the stealing of young birds from their nest (50–54)—an image more closely analogous to Agamemnon's crime than to Paris'. They have described the sacrifice of Iphigenia as an act in itself horrifying, impious, unholy, unscrupulous, shameful, and insane (219–24), and likely to provoke revenge (150–55). Yet in spite of all this their firm loyalty is towards the perpetrator of that crime, and their fixed hostility is towards its surviving victim, Clytemnestra. Their hope "that all may be well in the immediate future" (255), since they themselves will take no measures to ensure this, reflects a want of moral conviction in their attitude to the events and persons they have to deal with.

In contrast to this weakness is the passionate intensity of everything that Clytemnestra says or does. Whether she is mocking the staid gentlemen of the chorus, or picturing the scene in Troy, or kindling the chain of beacons, or contemplating the grim justice of her purpose (346), the heat of her utterance never cools. "What swift messenger could come from Troy in one night?" the chorus leader asks; and she replies, "Hephaestus." The fire that lights the dawn of her day of victory is the god himself, little concerned with guilt or punishment, but manifested in splendor, speed, and power. The poet illumines Clytemnestra's first appearance in a paean of beacons symbolizing both intensity and magnificence.

Some valuable recent criticism of the trilogy is flawed by the assumption that Aeschylus presents Clytemnestra to his audience as one whom they should hate and condemn, a vicious, unnatural woman, bloodthirsty, power-hungry, and justly punished for her crime. The choruses of the first two plays, Cassandra, Orestes and Electra, and finally Apollo, all exemplify the same hostility. This is fair, since they are persons in the drama; but it is not for the critic to step onto the stage. It would be possible to collect, from a score of scholarly books and articles, enough vituperation of Clytemnestra to fill a chapter.[3] To adopt this attitude is to distort the whole moral design of this great work. It leads to confusion in each moral issue as it arises, and in particular inhibits any clear judgment of Orestes, both before and after the matricide that forms the fulcrum of the entire action. It is not enough to acknowledge Clytemnestra's courage and competence and then accept with relief her total defeat. The trilogy is about justice; and the usual assumption that it shows the victory of the good is hardly supported by what actually happens in the last play. Clytemnestra is shown as practicing one of the few positive virtues on which a stable society is based: indignation against wrong. We may recall that Sophocles, in *Ajax*, offers this same virtue—which is, in fact, one aspect of integrity—as the decisive claim of another unrepentant regicide to heroic status. So we should clear our minds of traditional postures, and look at the central figure of the *Oresteia* simply as the poet unfolds his creation from scene to scene.

We first hear of Clytemnestra in the opening speech of the Watchman on the palace roof. What is the key line in this famous speech? Most people would say, his description of the queen in line 11: "A woman's heart that looks to the future with a man's resolve." We must remember that a drama is not a treatise. In a drama, what one character says of another describes also the speaker. This Watchman dare not sleep because he is afraid. In this he is not alone; the chorus too are afraid of Clytemnestra. Later the king will come, and will not be afraid of her—and by that we shall know him for a fool. The Watchman, and the Elders, know that a man should not be afraid of a woman. So they find an excuse: Clytemnestra, they say, is abnormal, an anomaly, a mannish woman. Clearly, for the past ten years, the queen has had to exercise some of the authority, the *kratos*, of the absent king; and the chorus acknowledge that this is right, *dikē* (259). Anyone who wields authority competently must be feared, as Athena will remind us in *Eu.* 698ff. But in *Agamemnon* there is little to suggest that Clytemnestra's nature craves mastery, as many scholars have asserted. Fate has given her a weak, vain, and cruel husband, and a set of councillors whose timid old age clings to tradition; while she herself is a person of intelligence, resolution, and wit. That she is unusual is self-evident; heroic quality is always unusual. That is very different from being an anomaly, a masculine woman. Such a judgment belongs to men like the Watchman and the Elders, and diverts attention from the real, dramatic issue, which is a moral one, not a psychological one. The abnormal person in this play is Agamemnon; he is abnormal alike in his bloodthirsty cruelty and in his infatuated blindness. To call Clytemnestra abnormal invites in the reader a feeling of hostility towards her which the poet gives no indication of sharing.

Clytemnestra's motive throughout the play is something other than the craving for power; and Aeschylus devotes two hundred lines at the opening of the play to telling us what it is. In this long lyric narrative he undertakes what he must know is an almost impossible task: to arouse in his audience some real sense of the helpless suffering that men could inflict on women. All three dramatists make this attempt constantly; and it has nothing to do with what we call feminism, and everything to do with what we know as humanity. The tragic poets addressed an audience in which callous indifference, especially to unmarried daughters, was a notable feature.

In the chorus' recital of events at Argos—the setting out of the army—and at Aulis—the sacrifice of Iphigenia—in that recital Clytemnestra is not named. Is she present on stage for all, or part, of the parodos? The point has been much discussed; and the arguments generally held to be relevant are set forth by O. Taplin in *The Stagecraft of Aeschylus*, pp. 280ff. These arguments are sound, but not, I think, conclusive. Taplin's conclusion, that Clytemnestra is present for only part of the time, may be correct; but Clytemnestra's presence during the narrative is not hard to make visually credible, nor is it uncharacteristic of Aeschylus. When the Elders first enter the orchestra they are full of excitement at the beacon, and the memories it has stirred; they fail to notice that above them the stage is not empty. When their tone quiets down into reflection on their own age and feebleness, they are ready to look around them; and they see, beside the effigies of Zeus, Hermes, and Apollo, the silent queen. But there are also more cogent considerations.

I am not aware of any critic who has commented on the potential significance of Clytemnestra's presence during this recital. The two narratives, of the portent of the eagles, and the sacrifice, spread over 150 lines. For the Elders, those events are an ominous memory, but there is nothing they can do about it. For Agamemnon, those events have virtually ceased to exist; he will make it clear, when he comes, how completely he has erased from his mind the unpleasant past. There is only one person to whom the whole story is of immediate and passionate concern, and that is the surviving victim of Agamemnon's treacherous cruelty and ambitious weakness, Clytemnestra. If she is not present, the Elders' words are merely a tale of long ago. But if she is there, refusing to speak, preoccupied with sacrifice, the Elders' opening phrase, "This is the tenth year since . . . ," now relates not only verbally to Agamemnon and Menelaus, but visually to Clytemnestra and her very different memory of that time— a memory which is to engage our emotions for the next twenty minutes of the play. We can never know what postures Aeschylus, as director, may have prescribed for her while the parodos was performed; but he may well have made it theatrically clear, as it can be intellectually clear to a reader, that the Elders are unconsciously telling *on her behalf* the story which she herself cannot yet speak of, which has haunted her for ten years; that they are putting her case irresistibly before us at the outset, and thus enabling us to be aware, in every line which later she will speak to the chorus, or the Herald, or Agamemnon—to be aware of her chosen function as priestess of Justice, Doom, and *Erinys* (1432f.). This interpretation of her part in the parodos not only accounts for the unique length, prominence, and poignancy of what is being said, but provides a logical connection between the parodos and the final scene, where Clytemnestra reminds the Elders four separate times of the story they told when the play opened. The queen's long silence, absorbed with sacrifice, past, present, and soon to come, represents on the stage her ten years' nursing of indignation and resolve.

Clytemnestra turns, and in response to the chorus leader's question delivers her news: "Troy has fallen." They stammer their unbelief, joyful yet grudging. Their questions are not tactful: "What is your proof? Have you been dreaming, or listening to rumours?" With five successive replies she mocks and tantalizes them; then launches into the beacon speech—the midnight torch race, the leaping lightning, the heather blazing like molten gold, the message sent "from my husband, from Troy, to me."

The Elders, spellbound for the moment, ask her to speak again; and Clytemnestra pictures for them what is happening in Troy as they listen—the streets echoing two discordant sounds, despair and jubilation. She speaks to an audience that knows battle and death and brutal pillage. Page in his edition says that she gloats over the sufferings of the conquered; to me her picture seems more objective than his account of it. The sinister tone is heard only when she speaks of the journey home, and its hazards. The victors may have plundered temples; the anguish of the dead may be aroused against them; and other, unexpected, disasters may lie in wait. And she ends with, "May the good prevail, visible and unambiguous."

That phrase is addressed directly to the Elders, who will presently see with their own eyes the answer to her prayer. The good she prays for is not wealth, as the chorus in *Choephori* will insist. Still less has her motive, as Aeschylus shows it, anything to do with Aegisthus, who is not mentioned until the play is two-thirds through. What we are shown is her resolve that unpardonable cruelty, and the violation of kindred blood, shall not be rewarded with flattery and glory but with just retribution. This is a moral resolve; and Clytemnestra claims to be a priestess of Justice. When she stands over Agamemnon's body, she has the right to expect the Elders to recognize, in the blood they gaze at, the corroboration of everything they solemnly stated in their choral odes about the rule of Zeus, cause and effect, the breeding of *hubris* from *hubris*, the permanence of pollution, the finality of murder, the recklessness of the unjust man, and his inevitable downfall. But the Elders recognize none of this; they remember only their hatred for the woman who mocks their indecision and shames their servility. For them, as for Athena in *Eumenides*, the human race is men; and they pray (1646ff., 1667) for the ultimate pollution of matricide. It is the chorus who are ambiguous in their morality. Agamemnon can punish Troy, Orestes can punish Clytemnestra, and both with the excuse of divine sanction. Only Clytemnestra dares to punish the crime that the chorus describes as "an insanity, prime cause of misery." Though Agamemnon is burdened also with

multiple guilt for the massacre of Troy, Clytemnestra has no divine mandate,
no popular approval; only her own indignation and courage. Her one ally,
Aegisthus, is so far below her in stature that his help derogates nothing from
the heroism of her enterprise.

Now Agamemnon's Herald arrives from the harbor. His first speech, giving
thanks to the gods for his safe return, tells us also—but still more tells Clytemnestra—that in the sack of Troy altars and temples were demolished; the king
comes home bearing yet deeper guilt. The Elders now confess that they were
wrong to doubt the evidence of Clytemnestra's beacons; but their brief apology does not save them from her mockery:

> I hailed this victory long ago, when first the beacon
> Blazed out its message. Someone then took me to task:
> 'Beacons! So you believe them? Troy, you think, is taken?
> Typical female hopefulness!' Remarks like these
> Exposed my folly.

She tells the Herald to go back and meet the king with this message:

> Let him come quickly; Argos longs for him; and he
> Will find at home a wife as faithful as he left,
> A watch-dog at his door; knowing one loyalty;
> To enemies implacable; in all ways unchanged.

In these and the following lines she humiliates the Elders and shakes their
nerve. She knows that they know that she means the opposite of what she says,
and by showing them that she knows she paralyzes their will to reveal what
they know. She knows that the Elders call her *kuōn*, "bitch"; so she calls herself *kuna*, "watch-dog" (607). She has "broken no seal" of her husband's,
"known no pleasure or scandal" with another man, any more than she under-
stands "the dipping of bronze." As Page points out, bronze is not hardened by
dipping in water; Clytemnestra means blood. In her last two lines,

> This boastful speech of mine, brimful
> Of truth, is no disgrace for a royal wife to utter,

she picks up, word by word, what the chorus are muttering in their hearts, and
flings it back to silence them.

The picture of a woman planning to murder her husband is not a pleasant
one; many critics, like the Elders, find this speech unforgivable. They have reason; but her reason, which is stronger, was put before us by the Elders themselves in the parodos; and they have forgotten the emotion of half an hour ago.
In a society where direct revenge is honored as Apollo honors it in *Eumenides*,
Clytemnestra's words are a fitting "prologue to the swelling act" of a fundamentally moral theme. The way she chooses is disastrous and comparable in

evil with the crime it repays; but to her lonely integrity no other way is open, and her revenge is more noble than submission. At the end of her speech the Elders show their discomfiture by two lines of embarrassed apology to the Herald, after which they quickly change the subject with

> Now, Herald, tell us about Menelaus. . . .

The queen's iron nerve is too much for them. After the murder they will be almost brought to recognize that the king's fate is just: "It is a hard struggle to decide," they will say (1561). But their resentment will undertake this struggle, and win it against their reason, their theology, and their sense of justice.

From the Herald's third speech we learn that Menelaus' ship is lost: the king returns home with few followers. All is now ready for Agamemnon's entry. There are two different ways in which we may watch the coming scene. We may perhaps recall a few lines from the parodos, the story of Iphigenia's death:

> A prayer was said. Her father gave the word.
> Limp in her flowing dress
> The priest's attendants held her high
> Above the altar, as men hold a kid.
> Her father spoke again, to bid
> One bring a gag, and press
> Her sweet mouth tightly with a cord,
> Lest Atreus' house be cursed by some ill-omened cry.

Then we shall observe the priestess of Justice, whose memory of wrong we have shared, as she approaches the solemn and perilous task she has prepared for during ten years. On the other hand we may watch this scene in the way more often favored by critics—as the unsuspecting advance of a victorious, if misguided, hero to his pitiful death at the hands of a female monster. Aeschylus has provided the verbal material for both views. My purpose is to assert the validity of the former, and generally neglected, aspect of the drama and its central figure.

When Agamemnon arrives, the chorus know well what they fear, and what reason they have for fearing it. It is their duty to warn the king urgently; yet they confine their warning to vague hints of political discontent, showing that they fear Clytemnestra more. Whereupon she mocks them further by including in her speech of welcome every tactless and impious allusion which could wake uneasiness and resentment. Time, she says, has taught her to be without fear. She proclaims the "outrageous evil," *ekpaglon kakon*, inflicted by her husband in abandoning her for ten years. She speaks of Agamemnon's wounds, his death, his grave; words of death, suicide, disaster, treachery, revolt, pour out in a continuous stream. "This is the reason," she says, "why your child, the pledge of our faithful vows, does not stand here at my side, as would be right"

—giving him time, if he will, to recall Iphigenia, before she adds, "Orestes." She speaks of her "nights spent in weeping—because of you"; and leaves him to mistake what she was weeping for. Then come fulsome compliment, extravagant comparison. As Fraenkel points out in his commentary, every image Clytemnestra uses refers to the king as preserver and protector of his household; but Fraenkel seems as unaware of her bitter irony as Agamemnon himself. Finally Clytemnestra invites him to walk to his palace on the costly purple cloth she has prepared for his ceremonial entry.

This superb performance has elicited from some writers eloquent censure of Clytemnestra's lies and deception. So the Trojans complained of the wooden horse. Let us compare her case with her son's. Orestes was instructed by Apollo to use deceit, and did so with competence, though with less brilliance than his mother showed. It is not usual for critics to upbraid Orestes as a liar, any more than, in *Choephori*, they censure the chorus for inducing the Nurse to alter her message to Aegisthus. True, they usually condemn Agamemnon for deceiving his wife about their daughter's marriage; but, like the Elders, tend to forget this when Agamemnon is punished for it. In recent years critical attitudes have broadened somewhat, and it is even conceded now and then that Clytemnestra had some excuse for the duplicity of her words to Agamemnon. What is seldom forgiven is a later passage, which it is convenient to discuss now, since it expresses the same certainty of attitude as the speech we have just considered.

When Agamemnon lies dead at her feet, Clytemnestra thus describes her own feelings at the moment of victory (1388–93):

> So falling he belched forth his life; with cough and retch
> There spurted from him bloody foam in a fierce jet,
> Which, spreading, spattered me with drops of crimson rain;
> While I exulted, as the sown cornfield exults
> Drenched with the dew of heaven when buds burst forth in spring.

Most listeners and readers apparently feel sure that in those lines Aeschylus presents to us an unpardonable and hateful criminal. I believe that they are wrong; that the force of such vivid words reveals something quite different— something that the social climate of Athens made it hard, almost impossible, for the citizen to imagine; something outside a man's experience, that could hardly happen to a man in his male world—the reality of that shadowy world that existed everywhere side by side with the citizen's life, and interwoven with it, yet for ever unknown to the citizen: the world of women (see *Ironic Drama*, chap. 6 passim). Only a poet, whose gift it is to see things as they are, and whose function is to tell what he sees, can know and tell what happens in that world, and know that it is as real as the citizen's world. In both worlds the claims of *aidōs* are unconditional. Clytemnestra's exultant joy in the success of her deception, and the spattering of blood on her dress, are the valid measure of her faith in, and dedication to, the moral principle of *aidōs*, "natural reverence," violated at Aulis by her husband, and now vindicated as the law of Zeus Teleios.

In the first place, we must remember that Clytemnestra is speaking to men and soldiers, both in the chorus and in the audience, on a matter which men claim as their exclusive province, the act of killing. She bursts triumphantly into their world, whose barriers her courage has stormed. The Elders are embarrassed; and they have earned their embarrassment. The queen's flattery was treacherous? What then? Few battles are won without deception, which, as she knows ("How else . . . ?" A. 1374ff.), is an essential part of a soldier's capability. As for the business of shedding blood, this is for the Elders now no longer a male mystique, a secret item in the weaponry of oppression. What a soldier learns among comrades, under the compulsion of tradition and discipline, this woman learned alone, fired by a passionate sense of wrong.

Second, the sacrifice, performed by a king in the presence of his army, was more than an individual crime. It was a public and national assertion that the *aidōs* which guards the institution of family love may be set aside when personal ambition or military interest demands an "expedient" (*mēchar*, A. 199) for success.

Third, the king's pretext of compulsion was false. It was not a question of his "obedience" (*pithesthai*, 206), since there was no command, but of accepting or rejecting evil advice. The powerful emotional hold that such a barbaric performance could, with its sexual, sadistic, occult, and sentimental overtones, exert upon an idle mass of discontented soldiers is spelled out by Euripides in *Hecabe*. Agamemnon's position of command was threatened, and the sacrifice was his best hope.

Fourth, there existed no alternative means whereby the trampling of sanctities, the savagery symbolized in the omen of the eagles, could be condemned "without ambiguity" (*ou dichorropōs*, 349). If Clytemnestra shirked her duty as priestess of Justice (1432f.), Agamemnon would, like his father Atreus, attain an honored old age in wealth and security, his crime condoned or forgotten, the gods slandered as indifferent (cf. 372).

It may seem tedious to argue at length what should be obvious; but the point is not merely important, it is crucial. If in lines 1388–92 the poet wrote his condemnation of the speaker, then we may have to accept the forced and illogical "reconciliation" at the close of *Eumenides*, and feel only a vague surprise at the chain of apparent ineptitudes and contradictions that leads to it. But if in those lines Clytemnestra expresses the depth of the poet's feeling about the crime she has avenged, then we can study the trilogy as a unified work of art, timeless in its morality, and with a logical significance in every puzzling contradiction.

Now, at Clytemnestra's word, her maids have unrolled the dark embroidered cloth; a river the color of blood streams from the palace door to Agamemnon's feet. The fantastic notion does not occur to Agamemnon, that this might be his daughter's blood, shed by his hand (see Lebeck, pp. 85f.). To the queen's flattery the king responds with abrasive rebuke. He is disconcerted to find his wife not at all put down, but ready to engage in gentle dispute. Her every line is loaded:

> Do not feel respect for mortal men's criticism.

Her word is *mē aidesthēis*. Agamemnon the god should be above *aidōs*—as he had been when he raised the knife at Aulis. There, mortal criticism had been his guide; and the Elders have damned the decision he took then. Battle and victory dominate the end of the dialogue:

> AG. It does not suit a woman to be combative.
> CL. Yet it suits greatness also to accept defeat.
> AG. Why, here's a battle! What would you not give to win?
> CL. Yield! You are victor; give me too my victory.

We watch Agamemnon accept defeat; and in his vanity and weakness it is hard to recognize any moral quality that could uphold his character as heroic, or his cause as that of "the good."

The king is still standing in his chariot. A slave has removed his sandals; and Clytemnestra places herself directly before him, as he says,

> I will go into my house treading on crimson.

The word "tread" or "trample," *patein*, rings out repeatedly all through the trilogy to denote ruthless disregard for what should be treated with reverence. Clytemnestra replies:

> There is the sea—who shall exhaust the sea?—which teems
> With purple dye costly as silver, a dark stream
> For staining of fine stuffs, unceasingly renewed. . . .
> Had oracles prescribed it, I would have dedicated
> Twenty such cloths to trampling, if by care and cost
> I might ensure safe journey's end for this one life.

The poetic passion of these and the following lines, their elusive and ominous symbolism, their ironic edge, are unsurpassed in Greek tragedy. With them the poet clothes his heroine in magnificence that dwarfs the puppet king, and ratifies the claim of her courage, wit, and sense of justice, to the central heroic role.

Now Clytemnestra makes way for the king, who in silence steps down upon

the purple cloth. As he does so, she startles the theater with her victory shout—
"as if at the turning-point of battle," says Cassandra later—while the Elders
assume that she acclaims the king's homecoming. Agamemnon walks to his
palace door and disappears. Clytemnestra turns to the statue of Zeus:

> Zeus, Zeus, Fulfiller! Now fulfil these prayers of mine;
> And let thy care accomplish all that is thy will!

The completion of a ritual, the fulfillment of destiny, the paying of a due: all
three meanings of the word *telos* are clear to the chorus, who now, being eyewit-
nesses of the incredible obvious, can only pray, "May there be no fulfillment!"

Since what we are engaged upon is, above all, literary criticism, we may
pause briefly at this point to consider the relation between poetry and drama.
The scene we have just studied is supreme in both fields. The poet's central figure everywhere speaks lines of poetic power and invests her thoughts with imagery of varied beauty. It is proper to ask, Could this have been so, if Aeschylus
had conceived his heroine as either abnormal or merely criminal, and her story
as a tale of ambitious malice spurred by adulterous guilt, pursued with cynical
cruelty, and eventually punished by justifiable matricide? This, or something
near to it, has been a fairly common view of Clytemnestra's role. Yet to accept
such a view surely denies that subtle point of contact between the aesthetic and
the moral that gives life to literary studies. If Clytemnestra were indeed what
such critics maintain, she would be an instance unique in ancient tragedy.
Whatever her ethical status, she has no touch of the sordid. Her quality is heroic, and her role tragic.

In the first two plays the tragic sense is dominant, even oppressive. In *Eumenides*, many readers have felt that it recedes and vanishes, and that the dramatist compensates for this by spectacle and variety. I offer another explanation.
The sense of tragedy vanishes only if we assume that Agamemnon and Orestes,
the two shedders of kindred blood, are presented as the heroes of the drama.
Certainly the first audience so accepted them; certainly Aeschylus knew that
they would; and no less certainly his Clytemnestra eclipses both father and son
alike in moral integrity and in personal splendor. Her integrity, though passionate, is also flawed—which is true of almost every hero in the extant plays;
her alliance with Aegisthus necessarily involves her in injustice to Orestes and
Electra. But her tragic stature, and the magnificence of her presentation, are
both supreme. She is the poet's most complete creation, which we should accept in all its fierce humanity. In the first two plays she is victorious, then defeated. In the third play the full depth of her tragedy is opened, as her heroic
act is slandered, her just motive ignored, her killer justified, and her cause finally betrayed.

When the third choral ode ends, on a note of foreboding, a short and unexpected scene supplies vital clues to Clytemnestra's role. She reappears to call Cassandra indoors. This is a strange action for a queen; why does she not send a servant? Then, her first speech lashes Cassandra three times with the name of slave; this too demeans the confident dignity the queen has shown hitherto. Cassandra ignores the summons. The chorus gently advise her to comply, and she ignores them too. Clytemnestra is disconcerted, calls the captive mad, and after vague threats of violence quits the stage on the word "dishonored." This curious passage tell us two things.

First, Clytemnestra's self-control is proof against every assault save one: she cannot overcome that sexual jealousy which ages of subjection had fixed as characteristic of women. Having gained a victory of will over her husband, she covets a victory of will over the woman who possesses what she no longer wants—Agamemnon's love. Had her nature been masculine, she would have scoffed at Cassandra; but she is a woman—a mother robbed, and a wife slighted. In both aspects she is passionately normal. This quality completes in her the formal role of the tragic hero. With superb courage she performs her sacrifice to Justice; then stains its sanctity with innocent blood.

Second, this tense encounter, coming just before the stroke of victory, is ominous. It foreshadows the heroine's ultimate defeat. In the final scene of this play she already knows that the victory of justice is transitory; that she herself will be defeated in the second play, and justice in the third. Victory will remain with Athenian male democracy, represented by Athena, Apollo, and Zeus Agoraios, god of the law courts (*Eu.* 973). Clytemnestra's fate, even in the theater, will be mere oblivion.

Cassandra vanishes. The chorus, certain now of disaster, hear the king's death cry. While they debate the doors open. Clytemnestra is revealed standing above her victims. She speaks:

> I said, not long since, many things to match the time;
> All which, that time past, without shame I now unsay. . . .
> A great while I have pondered on this trial of strength;
> At long last the pitched battle came, and victory.

She seems cool; she is logical. Earlier, winning her battle of words with Agamemnon, she said,

> Yield! You are victor; give me now my victory.

Now she describes her victory in terms that echo his. Zeus cast over Troy a net from which none could escape; she has cast over the king a net from which he could not escape. She has tested her courage in act. She goes over again the horror of killing a man, knowing that she did not shrink:

> Here where I struck I stand, and see my task achieved.

For twenty lines and more she holds her cool tone, allowing the heat and wild pulse of action to subside, before she permits herself a few lines of dreadful exultation:

> And then I struck him, twice. Twice he cried out and groaned;
> And then fell limp. . . .

The Elders had foreseen this death, and knew that both human passion and divine law made it inevitable. Now that their eyes witness the proof of their own philosophy, they instantly, in their fear and hatred, forget their perception of the rule of Zeus. They abuse her as brutal and insane, and promise her banishment by public outcry. So Clytemnestra at last expresses the emotion she had to keep hidden till her ordeal was over. She recalls to them their own words:

> Yes! Now you righteously award *me* banishment,
> Threaten with public curses, roars of civic hate.
> Why, once before, did you not dare oppose this man?—
> Who with as slight compunction as men butcher sheep,
> When his own fields were white with flocks, must sacrifice
> His child, and my own darling, whom my pain brought forth—
> He killed her for a charm to stop the Thracian wind!
> He was the one you should have driven from Argos; he,
> Marked with his daughter's blood, was ripe for punishment.

Three times more she proclaims her justice. Finally:

> No mourning procession from the palace shall attend his funeral; but his daughter Iphigenia, as is fitting, shall meet her father by the river of grief, and welcome him, and throw her arms around him and kiss him.

This final thrust shakes the Elders a little from their refusal, kept up for 160 lines, to acknowledge the truth. "It is a hard struggle to decide," they say. The queen responds to this admission with a conciliatory tone; then Aegisthus enters. The chorus revert at once to their intransigence, and Clytemnestra's fourfold arraignment of her daughter's killer goes still unanswered. It forms a dramatic balance to the parodos narrative, where the Elders spoke, and she was absent or silent. Unless we recognize this design, the play is near to the macabre, and the theme of justice a theoretical exercise.

When we meet Clytemnestra in *Choephori*, she has for six or seven years ruled, by force, with a consort as bitterly hated as herself, a city where expectation is concentrated on the exiled son who will return to avenge his father. For more than half of the play she is the unseen focus of thought and speech, feared and execrated, her death prayed for. She is isolated, Aegisthus her sole ally. Her victory can lead nowhere; the next act can only be defeat. The Nurse believes that she plotted her son's death; but there is nothing in the text to warrant that suspicion. It was natural for Clytemnestra to fear the grown Orestes, who had sworn to avenge his father; but Aeschylus gives us no reason to assume that her maternal feeling for her son was less strong than towards Iphigenia. The struggle between fear and instinctive affection exactly accounts for the ambiguity of her expression when first told of her son's death.

The failure of fifth-century Athenian society to achieve a fruitful adjustment between the roles of the two sexes produced an endemic malaise to which, a generation later, Euripides devoted much of his creative life. Aeschylus understood his countrymen, and why they found it impossible to see anything but evil in either of Tyndareos' daughters. In Clytemnestra he depicts the defeat of woman in her struggle for dignity and the right to justice. The choruses of the first two plays, and the panathenaic assemblage which crowds the final scene, all represent truly the climate of the city he knew. Its citizens, like Athena, "are wholly on the side of the father." For them, "the good" is the cause of Agamemnon and Orestes, right or wrong. The final rejoicing is their victory song: Zeus and Fate have reached agreement—and woman is not included. The applause that from the first canonized this trilogy showed that the poet's supreme powers had failed to win for his central figure, and for his moral truth and humanity, a sympathetic hearing. Athens chose Orestes for her hero, and named the trilogy after him.

The reception of the *Oresteia* shows that already in 458 B.C. the canon of the heroic that Athens recognized was, like Athena's judgment in *Eumenides*, superficial and inadequate. So in that play the defeat of Clytemnestra becomes final. Her ghost does not retain even a trace of her old vision of justice, only a fixed resentment of the cruelty done to her by her son. This, with the total oblivion that ensues, marks the culmination of tragedy in the last play. The jubilant antiphony of the processional hymn finds hope in the future only by ignoring and distorting the past in the name of *Peithō*, Persuasion, and Zeus Agoraios, god of the law courts. The tragic heroine is forgotten; and the exultant audience, identifying "the good" with success, and applauding its victory, enacts the tragedy of Athens.

6

"Respect" and "Insult" in the *Oresteia*

It has become apparent already in earlier chapters that the verb *aideisthai*, "to feel shame or respect," and its cognates *aidōs* and *aidoios*, and the verbs *patein*, "to tread upon," and *laktizein*, "to spurn," and their cognates, are used frequently in the *Oresteia* to connote two opposite mental attitudes. This chapter explores the proposition that these terms embody the poet's fundamental concept of the attitudes that underlie and produce right conduct and wrong conduct—that they represent an important part, if not the basis, of his moral thinking; and, further, that the study of his use of these words leads, by a logic both dramatic and moral, towards that radical reinterpretation of the whole work which begins to emerge from our study of four principal characters.

Aeschylus describes what he holds to be the appropriate attitude towards things "untouchable" or "holy" (*athikta, A.* 371) as "respect," an attitude of *aidōs* or *sebas* (the former refers rather to moral feeling, the latter to outward behavior). The opposite to this attitude is that of "insult," of treading upon, or of spurning, what is holy. The antithesis of these two concepts is shown, by both imagery and dramatic design, as central to the poet's moral assumptions. He uses the idea of "reverence" or "respect" in carefully selected contexts; and his deployment of the image of "treading upon" or "spurning" constitutes a decisive feature in the pattern of the trilogy.

Our inquiry will entail in particular an examination of three passages, one in each play: *A.* 905–57, where Clytemnestra persuades her husband to tread on embroidered purple; *Ch.* 896–903, where Orestes confronts his mother; and *Eu.* 566–753, Athena's conduct of the trial of Orestes.

In *Agamemnon* the "carpet scene" has always been recognized as of central importance (see, e.g., Taplin, p. 311). As an illustration of Agamemnon's arrogance it parallels the impious excess he showed in victory, destroying a nation for the sake of a woman (*A.* 225, 448), and violating altars of the gods; and it sets him in the ranks of the impious by whom "the beauty of holy things is trampled" (370ff.). Agamemnon accepts Clytemnestra's suggestion (933, 963) that the act of using precious cloth as a carpet is a sacrifice; while the dyed cloth itself is a symbol akin not only to the hunting net of Zeus (358–61) and to the voluminous robe (1382) used as a weapon by Clytemnestra, but also to the stream of crimson blood that flowed upon the altar where the king sacrificed his daughter. The power of this pervasive image is fully expounded in Lebeck's book (chap. 2, note 2). Agamemnon is clearly aware that to tread on costly cloth in the hour of triumph is an act of folly (*kakōs phronein*, 927); yet because he desires to flatter himself with this gesture, he rejects what he himself calls "the gods' greatest gift" (928), which is freedom from folly. The scene contains two allusions to the sacrifice of Iphigenia; one, made unconsciously by Agamemnon—"Yes, if some expert had prescribed such a ritual" (934); and one made by Clytemnestra with conscious relevance both to that line and to the deed at Aulis—"If such a trampling had been enjoined upon our house by an oracle" (963f.). Agamemnon's part in the scene displays dramatically the lack of heroic quality that negates his claim to the leading role; for his decision is not the obstinacy of the great but a yielding to the self-conceit of the small. And he preludes this symbolic folly, as he preluded his act at Aulis, with a feeble prayer for what he knows to be unlikely, if not impossible: then it was "May it be well" (217); now it is "May no envy strike me, watching from afar" (947). As the Elders have already reminded us, *ouk askopoi theoi*, "The gods do not fail to watch."

A sentence of prime significance is 948f., where, for the only time in this play, the noun *aidōs* is used:

> To squander the treasure of one's house (*dōmatophthorein*), by spoiling with one's feet costly cloth bought with silver, is *pollē aidōs*—a great cause of shame or compunction; or, a violation of natural respect.

When persuading Agamemnon to this act Clytemnestra says (937):

> Do not feel respect for mortal censure (*mē aidestheis*).

At Aulis Agamemnon had feared mortal censure on both sides of his dilemma: the censure of his allied chiefs (213) on the one hand, and the censure of sober people like the Elders on the other. The chorus recall their own censure in emphatic terms in 219–27, where they describe the sacrifice as "impious, impure, unholy, unscrupulous, shameful"; and now, even after ten years, they have expressed it firmly to the king in 799–804: "We considered you most unwise." Because Agamemnon and his allies were ready to throw responsibility onto Calchas, and to employ without further reflection the *mēchar*, the "expedient" (199) that the priest offered, Agamemnon's choice was similar to that which Orestes faced (*Ch.* 902) when his mother knelt before him and bared her breast—a choice between the authority of an oracle and the inner prompting of *aidōs*, of the feeling common to "all mankind" (*hapantas*, 902). Agamemnon made the same decision his son was to make years later. When, in the matter of the embroidered purple, he feels "strong compunction," he in his folly overcomes this proper feeling, and "enters his house treading on purple" (957); just as at Aulis he had felt compunction (207–10) and had overcome it. But the "treasure of his house" (*domōn agalma*, 208) that he destroyed at Aulis was more precious than the "woven stuff bought with silver" (949) which Clytemnestra spread before him, and a greater cause for *aidōs*. Agamemnon's last words on the stage, "treading on purple," thus recall exactly the red "streams of a maiden's blood" (209f.) which "stained his hands, a father's hands" at Aulis, and the "inexhaustible sea" full of "costly purple" which Clytemnestra spoke of in 958ff. And now, about to enter his palace for ritual cleansing at the family altar (1056), he is once again, as at Aulis, *pelas bōmou*, "near to the altar" (210); but at this altar he will be the victim.

His last word, *patōn*, "treading," connects him with a series of similar phrases used in all three plays to imply moral offense that is neither relative nor venial but absolute and indelible. The image occurs first in the passage already quoted, *A.* 369–73:

> It has been said that gods disdain to concern themselves with those mortals by whom the beauty of holy things is trampled. But that was an impious assertion.

Here the chorus are, ostensibly, talking about Paris' violation of the law of hospitality (363, 399–402, cf. 701); but many phrases in this part of the ode (cf., e.g., 385ff. with 222f.) suggest no less aptly that other crime, Agamemnon's violation of respect for kindred blood, and his rejection of natural pity (228–47), to which the chorus has already devoted a long and memorable narrative. At the end of the first strophe the same image is repeated (381–84):

> For a man cannot hope to find wealth a safeguard against [his own] excess (*pros koron*) when he has once spurned into oblivion the great altar of Justice.

This last phrase has a close echo in *Eu.* 538–42, where the chorus, just before the jurors assemble to try Orestes, addresses the audience who will be, as it were, assessors to the Areopagites, warning them of the consequences of allowing crime to evade just punishment:

> In general terms I bid you reverence the altar of Justice (*bōmon aidesai Dikas*) and not spurn it with impious foot, having your eye on advantage. Punishment will follow.

There is only one passage in the trilogy where this image is used in a particular rather than a general reference: *Ch.* 642. Here the chorus of Libation Bearers, enslaved and embittered, obsessed with revenge, are eagerly expecting the act of matricide "in the name of Justice"; and they say that justice was "trampled under foot" when Clytemnestra killed her husband. But with equal right Clytemnestra claimed (*A.* 1432) that her act was a sacrifice to Justice; and in the passage just quoted the warning of punishment can only refer to the possibility that the matricide will be acquitted.

So now in this central scene of *Agamemnon* both the act of treading on something precious and the words leading to that act tell us that Agamemnon in his encounter with Clytemnestra is fighting two battles at once. As he stands waiting in his chariot, two courses of action are offered him, two opposed forces are at work. One is his craving for excess, for *koros*, for glory beyond that of a mortal—a craving in which the "relentless persuasion" of Clytemnestra urges him on. The other is the claim of that "strong compunction" (*pollē aidōs*, 948), which, had Agamemnon heeded it, would have robbed Clytemnestra of her victory of will. Agamemnon yields to persuasion, against his better judgment. This is the battle for his wisdom, and it is lost. So he enters his second battle, the battle for his life, already a defeated man. But Agamemnon's "dilemma" at this moment is in fact no more a dilemma than was the choice he faced at Aulis; Aeschylus makes it clear that in both cases the king decided at once to follow ambition and pride, and forget piety and the status of a mortal (see Page's perceptive note on 931ff.). Here, as ten years earlier, as seven years later, the attitude of shame, pity, respect, is defeated, and the act of trampling is victorious; and I maintain that equally in the trial of Orestes the good is defeated, as the numerous appeals for *aidōs* voiced in the second half of *Eumenides* are ignored. For whatever the Elders, or Agamemnon, or Clytemnestra, meant by "the good," the poet leaves little doubt that for him "the good" was the hoped-for result of action inspired by reverence, which alone can forbid men to "trample upon the grace of what is holy."

The defeat of reverence is even more emphatically presented in *Choephori*. Here Aeschylus uses *aideisthai* in only two passages: in 106 and 108, where it has no special significance, and in a short passage whose significance is central to the whole trilogy (896–903). Orestes has gained entrance to the palace and has killed Aegisthus. Now he faces his mother.

> CL. Stay still, my son. And, my child, reverence (*aidesai*) this breast, at which you many times drowsily sucked from me nourishing milk.
> OR. Pylades, what shall I do? Shall reverence forbid me (*aidesthō*) to kill my mother?
> PY. Where then in future are Loxias' oracles, or men's trustworthy oaths? Regard all men as enemies rather than the gods.
> OR. I judge your argument to be the stronger; the advice you give me is good.

Up to this point Orestes is still fully a man—though a weak one, prone to seek guidance and authority; he is not yet "thoroughly viperized" (*ekdrakon-tōtheis*, 549; cf. Euripides *Ba.* 922, *tetaurōsai*); but at this moment he takes the irrevocable step by which he forfeits his human nature. He has already in 438 acknowledged that after an act so self-destructive his own life will be crushed: "When I have killed, then let me perish." After the murder, at first he is conscious, even before the Erinyes appear, of the change in himself—he tells the chorus, "My wits chafe at the rein under my weakened grip and carry me off course" (*Ch.* 1021–26); but the change was precipitated by Pylades, who is in the play chiefly for this purpose. It has nearly always been assumed that Pylades' three lines are a conclusive threefold statement of the importance of piety; and the fact that they contain nothing about morality—about the victory or defeat of "the good"—has received little attention. Doubtless Aeschylus knew that to his audience Pylades' pronouncement would seem impressive; if he himself took the same view, it is strange that the three arguments offered should be so dubious both in logic and in morals. If Pylades is to be taken as demolishing the immemorial sanctity of parenthood (see *Eu.* 508–16), the poet could surely have made him more convincing.

The three points made by Pylades in his reply to Orestes have already been discussed in chapter 2, and shown to be as invalid and ambiguous as the arguments of Apollo which will gain his discharge in the trial. Pylades' words are another example of that "ruthless Persuasion, child of scheming Ruin" (*A.* 385f.) which drives to his doom the man who tramples upon holy things. Orestes accepts this advice in the sense in which he wishes to accept it, and the sacred bond of family love is spurned underfoot, as it was by his father many years earlier.

Before passing on to *Eumenides* we should note briefly two other passages in *Agamemnon*, where the imagery of trampling on sanctities is used somewhat differently. First, Cassandra, in 1264ff., throws to the ground her prophetic garlands, her staff, and other insignia of her priesthood, crying, "Go to destruction; now you are fallen, thus I take revenge on you"—which seems to indicate trampling. The objects trampled are sacred; but Cassandra asserts by her action that, where the irrational holy conflicts with the rational moral, the latter is absolute. Cassandra is heroic because she dares to defy her enemy Apollo, to reverence humanity as no less sacred than divinity. Agamemnon and Orestes are unheroic because they fail to make this judgment. Thus Cassandra's trampling of Apollo's discredited sanctities completes the meaning of the image.

The other passage is Aegisthus' description of the feast of Thyestes. Thyestes was a guest, so his host's table was sacred; but because it ministered an atrocity, Thyestes kicked it over (*laktisma*, 1601), making a judgment similar to Cassandra's.

One further use of *aideisthai* may be noted here, though it occurs in Orestes' parting speech in *Eu*. 760. Bidding a grateful farewell to Athens, Orestes says that Zeus, "showing respect for (*aidestheis*) my father's death, has delivered me, seeing (*horōn*, 761) these my mother's advocates." This is the *aidōs* that should be stirred, in a person less directly involved, by the knowledge of someone else's impiety or cruelty. The same idea occurs also in *Eu*. 640, 739, expressed by the verb *protimō*.

We come now to *Eumenides*, where a different sanctity is at stake—that which above all the young idealism of democratic Athens had reverenced in the constitution set up in 509 B.C.: the sanctity of law and the integrity of judicial procedure. The importance of this idea is expressed by repeated statement: Athena uses *aideisthai* of the juror's oath in 483, 710; *aidoios* of the court of Areopagus in 704, *sebas* in 690, 700; the Erinyes use *aideisthai* of the altar of Justice in 539, and of the juror's oath in 680.

Athenians knew what principles of procedure demanded their reverence. As Athena lays down in 582ff., the prosecutor speaks first and defines precisely what charge the court is to consider. The juror should not be exposed either to offers of reward or to intimidation by any external authority. It seems reasonable to require some explanation of the fact that the trial of Orestes as Aeschylus has designed it shows these sacrosanct principles not reverenced but ignored.

Even in the preliminary hearing Athena makes us uneasy by the unguarded welcome she gives Orestes. We may accept that ritual purification by Apollo, if proved to have been properly carried out, would qualify Orestes to submit his case to Athena's court. But even in the text of the trial, taken at face value, such proof is conspicuously lacking; while careful scrutiny, as I have already shown in chapter 3, offers a strong presumption that, in Aeschylus' view, no ritual purification by Apollo has taken place, or could have been effectual if performed. When the formal proceedings begin in 566, the Erinyes have already stated their case in full, for the benefit of the audience, in the first two choral odes; so they are able to make their charge "summarily" (585) by a simple questioning of the accused. They define the charge as matricide in 587, and underline the point in 606ff. But this charge is barely considered. Orestes soon finds (609) that he cannot answer it, and turns his case over to Apollo, who in his first three speeches ignores it. He substitutes the charge of homicide; but will not admit that, in doing so, he puts Orestes' crime on the same level as the crime which it claimed to avenge. Apollo contends that the life of a woman—he does not say "a mother"—is "not at all the same thing" as that of a revered and powerful king; and he argues that a child's true parent is the father, while the mother is merely a nurse, the soil in which the seed is sown. Apollo not only ignores the fact that matricide is universally regarded with instinctive abhorrence; he also fails to see (though it would be rash to assume that Aeschylus did not see) that, if Agamemnon was the sole true parent of Iphigenia, his crime was the more outrageous, Clytemnestra's vengeance the more justified, and Orestes' act therefore the more unjust.

Apollo's first and last speeches in the trial add to the list of his offenses two more infringements of judicial integrity, of the *aidōs* that Athena assiduously recommends to the court. In 614–21 he seeks to intimidate the jurors by invoking the authority of Zeus. His last speech ends by offering to Athens (667–73), in return for the desired verdict, political greatness and the permanent alliance of Argos—an offer that Orestes later confirms (762ff.).

Athena, in her solemn address to the jurors and to "the Athenian nation" (681), first recalls how in the time of Theseus the Amazons here sacrificed to Ares. The court of "Ares' Hill," she tells them, will be a place where sternness represses evildoing. Twice she speaks of the "awe" that its justice will inspire (*sebas*, 690, 700); three times she speaks of the "fear" which must recognize that law is inexorable (691, 698f., 700). But she has already slipped in, with her first sentence, an implicit warning that the court is to ignore the real charge of matricide, by announcing that they are about to try a case of "bloodshed" (682). She bids them take care that the pure spring of justice not be turned bitter, or polluted, by the citizens through want of vigilance; while "a righteous fear" is present the court will remain "a bulwark of the land such as no other nation possesses," "a council untouched by bribery, revered, sensitive to wrong, a wakeful guardian of Attica." Then she bids them vote and "decide justice with reverence for your oath."[1]

When the eleven jurors have voted, Athena rises (734–42):

> This is my function, to determine the final judgement; and I shall place this vote in favour of Orestes. No mother gave me birth; I support the male cause in all matters (save that of accepting marriage) with all my heart, and am strongly on the side of the father. Thus I shall not attach prior importance to the death of a woman, one who killed her husband, the guardian of his home. So, even if the votes are equally divided, Orestes wins his case.

The final battle is over. Has the good prevailed? In this statement Athena specifically and gratuitously denies what she said in constituting the court (573): that the purpose of the trial is "to discern justice." Her verdict has no connection even with the substituted charge of homicide, still less with the actual charge of matricide. The whole substance of that charge, the bond of blood, the immemorial sanctity of motherhood, are of as little concern to her as justice or injustice, guilt or innocence. The defendant, she says, is a man, his victim was a guilty woman; nothing else counts. She judges not Orestes but Clytemnestra, whom she deprives of her just defense by describing as "guardian of his home" the man who killed his eldest child. The awe of judicial integrity and the fear of inexorable and impartial justice, which Athena herself urged her hearers never to remove from their civic life (698f.), she has at one stroke removed. "Who will be just, if he has nothing to fear?" Athens is now a city where a polluted criminal may hope for acquittal, if he can engage an advocate as unscrupulous as Apollo or Athena.

A word should be said about the logistics of this trial as Aeschylus has presented them. Dispute about the process of voting has generally concluded that there are eleven human jurors, and Athena is the twelfth. In that case it seems fair to infer that Aeschylus, while allowing that there is something to be said on either side, gives the Athenian democratic system due credit for showing a majority of one in favor of condemnation, of recognizing that there are crimes beyond pardon or redemption. It may be said that Athena's vote, which cancels this majority and secures acquittal, was only one of twelve, and not the entire basis for the decision. But this is to ignore the formal pattern of the scene, in which the eleven jurors are mute figures, while Athena is not merely a strongly featured individual, but a goddess, unquestionably representing what most patriotic citizens would claim to be the ideal character of the city they proudly worshipped. Her announcement that justice applies only to the male half of the Athenian community sounds to the audience as a whole so axiomatic that they do not notice how it stultifies not only Athena's exhortations to *aidōs*, but the entire moral argument of the trilogy. It is true that Apollo in 749 commends reverence for arithmetic in counting the votes; but the cause that moves his anxiety is not the establishment of justice, but the survival of the royal house (751). The falsity of the smooth judicial process is hidden beneath the splendor of pageantry and authoritative eloquence. *Peithō* is exalted and becomes *Zeus Agoraios*.

> Hold fast this upright fear of the law's sanctity,
> And you will have a bulwark of your city's strength
> Such as no other race possesses. . . .
> I here establish you a court inviolable,
> Holy, and quick to anger. . . .

When the first audience heard Athena speak these words, they were aware of the same two-sided reaction that is familiar to us today: the words represented an ideal which they knew had faded, probably beyond recall; but they did not want to relinquish the comfortable illusion that this ideal still had life and meaning. Perhaps they were right; it may be better to cherish a dead ideal than to pretend that you never had one. The sanctity of law, the integrity of judicial procedure, are precious things which it is good to possess; if you don't possess them, it still is good simply to wish for them. In the trial of Orestes Aeschylus shows this precious ideal trampled on; the citizens watch and listen, and few among them feel the stir of indignation. The word *patein*, to trample, is not used here; but in 541 we have *lax atiseis*, "dishonor by spurning underfoot," and twice the Erinyes describe the action of Athena and Apollo by the verb *kathippazein*, "to ride roughshod over" (150, 774). Orestes is discharged; the Erinyes are defeated. The fact that, as far as is known, no voice in contemporary Athens was heard to protest, "But this is not justice," indicates that Athenians in general accepted as satisfactory for practical life the superficial and corrupt standards of Athena and Apollo; the serious reflections about justice, truth, and integrity to be found in the choral odes of *Agamemnon* and *Eumenides* could be admired as poetry, and their meaning forgotten.

It is time to summarize. The central scene in *Agamemnon*—the purple cloth spread by Clytemnestra—establishes the imagery of either respecting, or treading upon, what is precious or beautiful or holy, as representing the polarities of a fundamental principle of moral behavior. The connection of this imagery, and of its key words, with the sacrifice of Iphigenia and with the murder of Clytemnestra implies unqualified condemnation of both those crimes. Aeschylus uses neither this imagery nor its key words in connection with Clytemnestra's killing of Agamemnon. This imagery and these words are repeatedly used in connection with the founding of the Areopagus, which clearly stands as a symbol of the principles which, ideally, guided the operation of the Athenian system of democratic justice. In the conduct of Orestes' trial the uninhibited flouting of principles for which an attitude of reverence has been urged suggests that Aeschylus consciously wrote into the trilogy a significance opposite to that which he knew the audience would attribute to it; that he presented matricide as the ultimate rejection of *aidōs*, the basic element of moral feeling—as a crime for which no purification could be effectual and no pardon admissible; that he offered to the more perceptive (cf. *mathousin*, A. 39) a criticism of his countrymen's moral judgment, and an appeal to keep alive the sense of reverence as the soul of all morality.

7

Cassandra

Cassandra tells her story to the Elders in two passages of her long scene. Here is the more specific part of her narrative (in a deliberately prosaic, but otherwise accurate, version)—1202–13:

> CASS. The prophet Apollo appointed me to this office [of prophecy].
> CH. Did this occur when he, though a god, was smitten with desire for you?
> CASS. Formerly I felt embarrassment at speaking of this.
> CH. Everyone is more reserved in time of prosperity.
> CASS. Apollo was urgent, strongly protesting his love for me.
> CH. Did you lie with him and bear him a child?
> CASS. I agreed to this; then broke my promise to Loxias.
> CH. When you had already received the divine skill?
> CASS. I was already revealing to the Trojans all that would happen to them.
> CH. Surely Loxias was angry? Did he not punish you?
> CASS. After I had thus offended, no one believed a word I said.
> CH. Yet to us your prophetic words seem convincing.
> [At this point Cassandra cries out wildly in "the anguish of true prophecy."]

The other passage is 1270–74. Cassandra has stripped off the insignia of her prophetic office and thrown them to the ground.

> CASS. [Apollo] who formerly looked on while I, even in these vestments, was jeered at by friends and enemies alike; abused as an itinerant quack, a wretched starveling beggar—all this I endured.

There is much here that is not explained; in particular, Cassandra gives no hint as to her reason for refusing Apollo's love. When Agamemnon captured and desired her, since the king had not the god's pride, the choice was now not Cassandra's. She sailed in the king's ship as his slave and concubine.

The next development in the story is not given prominence, is indeed unexpected, yet is clearly presented. Cassandra takes her place unequivocally on one side of the central dividing issue which the trilogy works out to its conclusion. She is at Agamemnon's side, emotionally identified with him; and her enemy is Clytemnestra. She feels herself defeated, and shares defeat with Agamemnon; and she prophesies that ultimate wickedness of matricide which is destined to avenge both him and her. She makes the same powerful appeal to our sympathy as Iphigenia—and makes it not through narrative but in person. Yet she herself, a princess slaughtered in her innocence, totally ignores the fate of that other royal victim of human and divine cruelty, Iphigenia, whose innocent suffering had led directly to her own. It is this curious fact that removes Cassandra from the focus of the whole design, and makes her rather shed reflected light on other figures, on Apollo, on Agamemnon, and on Clytemnestra.

It is clear, then, that her story as Aeschylus tells it is second to none in tragic potentiality. Yet, in the long list of dramas known to have been composed by the three great Athenian poets, not one bears the title *Cassandra*. Apart from her momentous appearance in *Agamemnon*, she has a short early scene in Euripides' *Women of Troy*, and is mentioned in *Andromache* and in *Hecabe*; Sophocles does not name her. The *Agamemnon* scene includes virtually all the information given in later references, and Euripides evidently could assume that his audience would be familiar with the fate of Cassandra from their knowledge of Aeschylus' play.

The *Agamemnon* scene is generally accepted as a theatrical and poetic *tour de force* enhancing the audience's apprehension of the murder in which the play culminates. All through the stately arrival of the king, the bitter speeches exchanged between him and Clytemnestra, and the dialogue in which he yields to his wife and consents to walk on purple to his palace door, Cassandra sits silent and unregarded in the second chariot. The king vanishes through the doors of the palace. Later the queen comes out again and orders Cassandra to get down from the chariot and go indoors. Cassandra still sits silent, and Clytemnestra, after some talk with the chorus, goes back into the palace defeated. Alone with the Elders, Cassandra demonstrates her own supernatural knowledge of past and future; she prophesies the murder of Agamemnon, and her own death by the same weapon. She rouses powerfully in the audience the two tragic emotions, pity and fear; but, though she heightens the tension, the plot would apparently be complete without her. For this reason Cassandra often receives less attention than is due to her. In fact Aeschylus relates her with remarkable exactness to the overall pattern of his drama.

When she first breaks silence, Cassandra calls on Apollo. In an earlier scene we heard the Herald call on Apollo. He said, "Apollo, during ten years of the war you destroyed us; do not now destroy us a second time." Now Cassandra says that Apollo has destroyed her, first by his gift of prophecy, then a second time, by bringing her to a house conscious of guilt and pollution by kindred blood. The chorus says,

> She is like a keen-scented hound, tracing the blood of those whose blood she will find.

What blood is meant? Iphigenia's? The chorus themselves told us of that ritual slaughter—told it in horrified detail at the opening of the play. Now the shedder of his daughter's blood has come home in triumph, and been welcomed in sinister phrases by Clytemnestra. The Elders know, but dare not admit to themselves, that the queen is plotting to kill Agamemnon; and they know why. But they have failed to give the king any effective warning; and it is already too late. Naturally they would rather not be reminded at this moment of Iphigenia. But Cassandra is not thinking—she refuses to think—of Iphigenia. She looks further into the past, and sees other evidence:

> Two infants weeping for their cruel death, for the roasted flesh on which their father fed. . . .

To the Elders it is a relief that the prophetess is treading on less dangerous ground. Yet Thyestes' banquet is only a little less dangerous; for the surviving brother of those two infants, Aegisthus, burdened with the duty of revenge, is in the palace, and has supplanted the king in the queen's bed. The Elders' relief is short-lived, for Cassandra proceeds at once to the first of her clear statements that Clytemnestra will kill Agamemnon. It now becomes evident on which side of the central issue the prophetess stands.

Cassandra, born a princess, is today a slave, her father and brothers dead, her home a heap of ashes, her own life at the threshold of death. Whom does she blame for this? Agamemnon led the Greeks to Troy and sacked her city. Agamemnon forced her virginity and brought her as a slave to his wife's house. Cassandra, in two hundred lines, speaks not one word of reproach against Agamemnon. For her, he is "the commander of ships, overthrower of Ilion," shamefully overthrown in his turn by "a lioness mated with a wolf." Cassandra in four separate passages (1139, 1260ff., 1313f., 1324f.) identifies herself, in pity and indignation, with Agamemnon. The treachery (*mēdetai . . . mēdetai*, 1100–02) that destroys him is "an intolerable evil," it is unspeakable (1109). Four successive stanzas reiterate with mounting horror the killing that will occur within the half-hour. And not once does Cassandra speak of the cruel act of ambition by which Agamemnon earned this death. Are we to suppose that Cassandra's supernatural vision is weaker even than the obedient memory of the Elders? The revulsion which her prophecy of the murder evokes is not more painful than that evoked by the chorus one hour earlier, when they described how, before the altar at Aulis, Agamemnon told his men to stop Iphigenia's mouth with a gag and lift her high "without hesitation" (233) for the ritual throat-cutting. Cassandra is not indifferent to the idea of justice; the death that will unite her with Agamemnon will be avenged—this she foresees with horror, but not without satisfaction (1279–89). Yet she banishes from her thought the notion that Agamemnon's death is, "in the judgment of gods" (1289), deserved by any more immediate and personal cause than his destruction of Troy.

This refusal to admit any moral charge against Agamemnon is an attitude in which Aeschylus links Cassandra with another strongly featured element in the trilogy. The chorus of captives in *Choephori*, who encourage Orestes to matricide and rejoice wildly in his success, are as deeply devoted to Agamemnon as Cassandra. Agamemnon, as they tell us in their opening song, destroyed their homes and condemned them to exile and slavery. Yet they, like Cassandra, worship him as a god, and hate the woman who dared to punish his cruelty. (See chapter 9.)

Because Apollo is a *dramatis persona* from as early as the Herald's first speech (*A.* 509f.), the question of how Aeschylus means us to conceive the relationship of Cassandra with Apollo is fundamentally involved with our interpretation of the trilogy. Cruelty is, in Greek terms, an acceptable, even a necessary, attribute of divinity. But Cassandra's royal pride will not accept Apollo's cruelty. Conscious of her own divine knowledge, and of her integrity, she asserts her mortal virtue of compassion in defiance of immortal harshness. She throws back to Apollo the holy emblems of his priesthood (1264ff.):

> This robe—why should I wear what mocks me? Why still keep
> This sceptre, these prophetic garlands round my neck?
> Before I die I'll make an end of you . . . and you . . .
> Go, with my curse, go! Thus I pay my debt to you!
> Go, make some other woman rich in misery!
> See, thus Apollo's hand strips from me his oracular
> Robing. . . .

This violent symbolic action is the visible climax of Cassandra's scene. (It is curious that Page, in his long comment, pp. 164–66, does not even mention it.) Its significance for our understanding of Apollo has already been pointed out in chapter 3. Its significance for Cassandra is no less clear. It sets her side by side with Iphigenia and Clytemnestra, who should be her natural allies, though in the dramatic conflict she is in their enemy's camp. It confirms her heroic integrity: she defies alike the cruelty of the mortal world and the cruelty of gods, and her courage eclipses her error in refusing knowledge of Iphigenia. It contrasts her with Orestes, who accepted Pylades' warning, and did not dare to "make a god his enemy." Cassandra rates human values (*broteia pragmata, A.*

1327–30), even when defeated, above the power of a god. When she has ended her speech the chorus leader says to her,

> O woman deep in wisdom as in suffering. . . .

Cassandra's self-liberation from Apollo is unanswerable.

In the first choral ode the phrase, "trampling on holy things," was used to describe sin that gods will not pardon. When we see Agamemnon treading the crimson cloth, we know that his prayer to escape divine resentment is useless. Why does Aeschylus make Cassandra, like Agamemnon, prelude her death with a trampling of holy things? Surely, so that we may consider how the two acts, superficially similar, are essentially different. Agamemnon's act was a yielding to folly. Cassandra's act is an heroic defiance, an assertion that, for her, human values take precedence over divine claims.

An heroic gesture is of no effect unless it is witnessed. The Elders are timid old men; but they will survive Cassandra, and can witness to what she has said and done. This she claims from them, and from the audience, by the sacred right of a stranger in their midst who is about to die (1300). And because she has witnesses she accepts her death in full knowledge of its finality. The victory of a mortal over the immortal is near to the core of tragic heroism. Before one reality, death, Apollo's power and wisdom melt and vanish. When Troy dies, Apollo must quit the city he built; as, in Euripides, he must leave the house of Admetus when Alcestis dies. The knowledge and acceptance of death gives to human life a dimension, a perspective, which is incomprehensible to gods, for whom such qualities as courage, loyalty, integrity, are meaningless. Thus Cassandra in her despair defeats Apollo.

No two scenes from any tragic poet could present a clearer contrast of the profound with the superficial than Cassandra's words in the last seventy lines of her scene, and Apollo's four speeches in the trial of Orestes. *Sympathy* for Cassandra has never been wanting; but she asked for more than that—for witnesses to her integrity and to her victory. The mortal attains sublimity, the immortal a hollow mediocrity. That is Cassandra's triumph, vindicating her refusal of Apollo's love; and the poet himself is her witness.

Cassandra's second and most obvious relationship is with her captor and master, Agamemnon. Here the forced concubine fulfills the approved feminine role which the wife, under brutal provocation, has rejected. The position she adopts in part reflects quite clearly a personal attachment to Agamemnon; but beyond that it expresses also a social belief. Cassandra believes that a man's nature and right is arbitrary domination, while a woman's role is unquestioning acceptance of man's will. This was the creed of virtually the entire audience. Cassandra condemns Clytemnestra for Agamemnon's murder not because it was unjust but because it was in her view an offense against nature. This makes her forget—as the whole passage 1100–29 makes evident—that it was also the necessary punishment of an offense against nature. Here are Cassandra's words (1231–35):

> Female shall murder male: what kind of brazenness
> Is that? What loathsome beast lends apt comparison?
> A basilisk? Or Scylla's breed, living in rocks
> To drown men in their ships—a raging shark of hell,
> Dreaming of deadly steel thrust at her husband's flesh?

Cassandra rejects Apollo for his cruelty; but she accepts fully the male-dominated world of which Apollo is the religious symbol, in which justice belongs only to men. A daughter killed by a father, a mother by a son, does not stir Cassandra to indignation. Can we doubt that Aeschylus had clearer vision than the prophetess he created?

For Cassandra, then, as for the chorus of the next play, the enemy is a woman, Clytemnestra; and the hero is their master, whose godlike person makes his ethical status irrelevant—which of course is correct theology. But Cassandra knows a closer bond than that of slave to master. She never alludes to the equality that sexual union creates, but she expresses this equality in her knowledge that she and the man who has chosen her will die together. Five times she speaks of "my fate and Agamemnon's" (1313f.):

> Why, Apollo, have you brought me here? Surely that I may die with him (1139). We shall not die unavenged (1279). May the hand that avenges the king avenge also the slave, so easy to kill! (1324ff.). (See also 1261ff.)

This brings us to the third relationship in which Aeschylus has characterized Cassandra. After the murder, Clytemnestra calls Cassandra Agamemnon's "lover" (*philētōr*). Her jealousy is as irresistible as her other emotions; and its part in the dramatic design has already been considered in chapter 5. Because Cassandra's womanhood has succeeded where hers failed, Clytemnestra stains her justice with *hubris*, and in avenging cruelty is herself guilty of the same fault.

And in a curiously similar way Cassandra too weakens the claim of her own cause. The vituperation that she heaps on Clytemnestra matches in ferocity the expressions of hatred that fill the scenes of *Choephori*, especially Orestes' speech after the matricide. But it may also be not over-subtle to hear in Cassandra's passionate vilifications an echo of the abuse which, as she tells us, was showered upon her by her own people in Troy, resentful of the prophet whom no one would believe. Here too Cassandra shares with her enemy the universal fate of woman, which the chorus in *Choephori* describe thus (*Ch.* 635ff.):

> So to this day
> By gods detested, our whole sex is cursed,
> By men disfranchised, scorned, and portionless.

(This passage will be discussed more fully in chapter 9.) When Cassandra joins in execration of Clytemnestra, she reveals the poignant paradox of her position. For Clytemnestra's ultimate enemy is the same as Cassandra's, namely Apollo, whose victorious cause is the full and unanswerable supremacy of man organized as a political group, and committed to oppress and dominate the opposed cause, that of the family, in which man and woman play complementary honorable parts, and in which a first principle is reverence for kindred blood; a cause protected since long before the Olympian era by those primitive powers known as the Erinyes, or Eumenides.

Cassandra is integrated with every other element in the play. The unheroic Elders acknowledge her heroism. She is one with Iphigenia as a helpless victim. She is one with Clytemnestra as a proud woman rebelling against Apollo and weakened only by feminine passion. She is one with Orestes as the dupe and tool of Apollo. She is one with Agamemnon because Fate has linked them in life and in death. Above all Aeschylus presents Cassandra as a symbol of human suffering and heroic integrity. Probably many of the audience, even though deeply moved at the time of the performance, would in their memory simply label her as a prophetess. But Aeschylus, though he does not rationalize Cassandra's prophetic vision, does seem to suggest that such powers are no more astonishing than the capacity of most men and women for knowing only what they choose to know. This theme, that knowledge is an act of the will, is the central theme of Sophocles' *Oedipus Tyrannus*, a play even more closely concerned with prophecy. In *Agamemnon*, the choral lyrics in page after page state in plain words what the Elders know must and will happen; they know it because they know what already has happened. But since they wish that it should not happen, and are afraid of it, and equally afraid of taking any risk to prevent it, they decide not to know that it will happen. Therefore they give the king no warning; and it happens. It is almost as if Aeschylus were saying, "Prophecy is as simple as that." But he does not say it; he uses to the full the theatrical force of Cassandra's superhuman faculties.

Nonetheless, when we come home from the theater, purged, elevated, and eager for close reflection, we have every right to ask, What does the poet say or imply about the nature of prophecy? What qualities in men and women lead this one to see the future in the present, that one to see nothing? There are some 250 lines at the center of this play that we have not yet considered; lines which, even if Apollo had not bestowed his gift, would have inspired Agamemnon's captive to prophecy.

When Cassandra first enters the stage she hears the carefully phrased greet-

ing with which the representatives of the city of Argos welcome the victorious
king. It is not the kind of greeting she would have heard offered to the king of
Troy. The tone is questioning rather than positive; the voice is aware not only
of listening gods but of listening citizens.

> King! Heir of Atreus! Conqueror of Troy!
> What greeting shall we bring? . . .
>> Some harsh embittered faces, forced
> Into a seemly smile, will welcome you,
>> And hide the hearts of traitors
>> Beneath their feigned rejoicing. . . .
> Now this I will not hide: ten years ago
> When you led Greece to war for Helen's sake,
>> You were set down as sailing
>> Far off the course of wisdom. . . .
> Those times are past; you have come victorious home;
> Now from our open hearts we wish you well.
>> Time and your own enquiries
>> Will show, among your people,
> Who has been loyal, who has played you false.

All is not well in Argos. These men know there are traitors, tongues that criticize, hearts that resent; but they dare not tell anything. Agamemnon's answer
is too easy to be reassuring. He has returned home from the most celebrated
victory of his time; conquest has been carried out with ruthless violence. For
their advice, he notes it. He is familiar with jealousy, with two-faced malcon-
tents. At Troy there was only one man he could trust; dealing with dissidents at
home will not be difficult. Victory is his symbol, his nature, his god-given right.

Then Cassandra becomes aware of Clytemnestra—such a voice as she has
never heard before.

> Elders and citizens of Argos! In your presence now
> I will speak, unashamed, a wife's love for her husband.

It is a long speech; and not one of the Elders, and few in Argos or in the Athenian audience, could have missed the resolute controlled hatred that fills every
phrase. As the speaker well knew, only one man could fail to interpret that
speech: Agamemnon himself. To Cassandra, her every sense sharpened by the
apprehension of suffering, Clytemnestra's mind is an open page. (If it is doubted
whether Aeschylus' mind worked in this way as he composed Cassandra's
lines, any serious dramatist will confirm it.) Cassandra hears the king instruct
his wife to receive his concubine in her house. She hears the shrill prolonged
cry, the triumphant *ololugmos*, with which Clytemnestra startles the whole
theater as Agamemnon's foot touches the embroidered purple. When the king
has vanished indoors, she hears the last two lines of the scene:

Zeus, Zeus, Fulfiller! Now fulfil these prayers of mine!
And let thy care accomplish all that is thy will.

After all this, Cassandra hears the chorus perform the third lyric ode. Both compulsive reason, they say, and irrational foreboding, tell them that, perhaps within minutes, blood will flow. They cling to childish hope: "May prophecy vanish, and fulfillment fail!" And immediately after, they remind us that, though wealth and pride may be atoned for,

Yet when, from flesh born mortal,
Man's blood on earth lies fallen,
A dark, unfading stain,
Who then by incantations
Can bid blood live again?

Cassandra did not need Apollo's gift; she had the rational perception Agamemnon should have had, and the courage the Elders should have had. It seems possible that those two qualities were, for Aeschylus, the essence of prophecy.

For, in fact, Cassandra is, even more than Clytemnestra, the poet's full expression of the tragic view of the world, of the human condition. Near the end of her scene she says (1286ff.):

Why then should I lament? Am I so pitiable?
I have seen Troy endure the fate that she endured;
Her captor now, by Heaven's decree, reaches this end.
I will begin the rite, and go to meet my death.
O gates of the dark world, I greet you as I come!

The chorus say to her:

Courage and destiny in you are proudly matched.

She replies:

The happy never hear such praise.

Part of the tragedy is that she shares the heroic plane only with Clytemnestra; and each regards the other with a total hatred. Cassandra ends with these words:

Alas for human destiny! Man's happiest hours
Are pictures drawn in shadow. Then ill fortune comes,
And with two strokes the wet sponge wipes the drawing out.
And grief itself is not more pitiable than joy.

She is the only person in the play who speaks in large terms of human destiny. Clytemnestra's wisdom is limited in scope to the house of Atreus; that of the chorus confines itself to the theme of crime and punishment. Cassandra's tragic view embraces humanity's happiness and misery. The same somber climate prevails throughout *Agamemnon* and the second play, *Choephori*. In *Eumenides* we are aware of a change; the presence of gods invites us for a time to step outside this tragic and passionate complex and review the situation more dispassionately. We are exhorted to respect the sanctity of law and accept a divine wisdom transcending the tragic perceptions of Cassandra and Clytemnestra. The court of Areopagus is solemnly inaugurated. We are shown a formal legal process in which the quality of integrity, personal or judicial, is several times mentioned, never displayed except in the actual casting of the eleven votes, and finally contradicted in plain terms by Athena as president. As the result of all this, the climate changes from tragedy to joy. Hymns of thanksgiving burst forth. The grim necessities of justice lay aside their terror. Zeus and Fate are reconciled. The future brightens with blessing and prosperity. Cruelty, ambition, sacrifice, revenge, the pollution of kindred blood—all are forgotten. Athens, with the Argive matricide as her bought ally, towers over all in glory. This is a different view of the world from Cassandra's. Aeschylus has offered for our choice both views, but has not told us which he regards as the more valid. When we reach the end of the trilogy, is it no longer the case that "man's happiest hours are pictures drawn in shadow"? that "grief itself is not more pitiable than joy"? When we watched Cassandra vanish into the palace, we knew, as did the chorus, that she had spoken the unchangeable truth. Have we been persuaded by Athena and Apollo that we were wrong? Does Aeschylus contradict himself? To answer these questions is outside the scope of this chapter; but to ask them is the essential conclusion of a proper study of Aeschylus' Cassandra.

II

The Three Choruses

8

The Argive Elders

In the first thirty lines of the parodos the chief function of this chorus is to recount the events forming the background of the plot; but they express also, in 60–71, their general comment on the war that has left their city half-empty for the last ten years. It has been a calamitous time "for Greeks and Trojans alike"; and both sides, they feel, deserve censure. The ostensible cause for which the sons of Atreus organized ten years of bloodshed was a trivial and unworthy one—a promiscuous wife; while Paris' contempt for the laws of hospitality was an offense against Zeus for which no burnt sacrifice, no libation, could be expected to win pardon.

The Elders then present their self-portrait. Ten years ago they were already too old to join the army, and now their weakness is like that of children (though at the end of the play, 1650ff., they will draw weapons). The sacrifices which, at Clytemnestra's command, now blaze all over Argos fill them with a painful conflict of fear and hope. To their question, What message has come? they get no response from Clytemnestra (who may, or may not, be present on stage; see chapter 5). They recall watching the two kings set out from the gate of Argos; and the portent of the eagles and their prey dominates every other thought until 159, and persists as background to the resumed narrative from 184 on. The omen was a good one, but mixed with foreboding of evil (156f.). The wanton destruction of young life is something that appalls the Elders; and their refrain,

> Cry Sorrow, sorrow—yet let good prevail!

though evoked at first by the portent of the ravaged hare, in its repetitions points also to the misery and death that the youth of Argos will both suffer and inflict. The Elders' religious sense tells them that if Zeus is god, then everything happens by his will. Violent revenge is observable as a permanent principle of life: on this principle the war was begun; on this principle they can see its results unfolding in more and worse wickedness, with anger (*mēnis*) as its universal motive (151–55). This is how Zeus governs the world; he may even be the author of this cruel principle. Their dilemma is plain: they cannot call this principle good, yet good is what they long and pray for. Zeus is a name they reverence; but who is he (160)?

This is not the place for an exposition of the famous three stanzas which painfully explore Olympian myth and theology (160–83); but one thing must here be stated, because it is crucial in establishing that the Elders are alive to the true sense of tragedy. The reading of 182f. is in almost all editions given as a statement; it should, I believe, be a question. The reasons for this, both technical and intellectual, have been set forth with great clarity by M. W. M. Pope, in an article published in 1974 (see References). The two versions of the text attribute to the Elders two opposite beliefs about the fundamental nature of the world. If the sentence is a statement, they believe that the behavior of gods to men contains some element of *charis*, kindness. If it is a question, they deny that it is any use to look for kindness from gods:

> As for gods, where is their kindness?—since they occupy their august seat by violence.

In the three choral odes the Elders will have much to say about the nature of the world in which man has to struggle with the tragedy of life. In the action they will witness what seems to them the defeat of the good; and in their own attitudes they will illustrate the same defeat. It is therefore essential to the understanding of the play that we attribute to the chorus from the outset the broad view of the world that Aeschylus meant them to represent.

They know that it is useless to look for kindness from gods, because gods occupy their seat of government "violently" (*biaiōs*, 182). Agamemnon, they tell us, felt that the gods forced him to sacrifice his daughter and incur gross pollution; and excused his yielding to their force by the feeble optimism of his prayer, "May good result after all" (*eu gar eiē*, 217). His act of violence in the sacrifice was a foreshadowing symbol of his impious violence in the sack of Troy—both imaged in the portent of the eagles and the hare. The Elders recognize in this sequence the tragic nature of the world as governed by Zeus, who is "cause and doer of all" (1485f.). On this principle, again, though they know Agamemnon's act was evil, they will be ready to excuse him when he comes home, especially since he returns successful (799–806). They imply that, if the end does not justify the means, at least it justifies them in taking a lenient view of the means.

But this politic, accommodating attitude is clearly at variance with both their theology and their experience. The first choral ode, which will be discussed presently, expresses their conviction that Zeus' government is not accommodating but vindictive (369–98). In the parodos they recalled Calchas' prediction that one sacrifice might lead to another (151ff.). At the end of this play they will acknowledge that the cause of the king's death is not the adultery of Helen (1455ff.), not the *daimōn* of the house (1468ff.), but the justice of almighty Zeus (1485ff.). Yet this perception so confuses them that a little later (1646) they express their passionate hope that Orestes will return and kill his mother. The Elders are not, I think, to be heavily censured for inconsistency. Their position is common enough: they can judge honestly a particular action, and they can relate it to an abstract pattern of morality in which they believe; but they cannot themselves use their perceptions and beliefs for their own guidance to wise action. They are old, weary, prejudiced, and timid. We shall see this illustrated in successive scenes; but first we must look at their long narrative in more detail.

Beginning at line 104 they recount two events of ten years ago: the omen of the eagles, and the sacrifice; but the former foreshadows and includes the latter, so that the whole narrative portion (excluding the theological interlude 160–83) is obsessed with one thought—the pity, and the cruelty, of the sacrifice. The Elders' judgment is unequivocal: they condemn with every expression at their command both the act and its perpetrator as impious, unholy, unscrupulous. They quote Agamemnon's self-excuse in 211–17, but themselves offer no excuse for his want of pity. The word *aidōs* is not used; but when we come to consider the third episode, and the powerful central symbol of Iphigenia's blood presented in the purple drape flowing from the palace door (see Lebeck, chaps. 7 and 8), we find *aidōs* used with exact significance. (See chapter 6 of this book.) Agamemnon, persuaded by his wife to "enter the palace treading on purple" (957), declares that "it is *pollē aidōs*, a great cause of shame or compunction, to despoil my house by sullying with my feet cloth that was bought with silver" (948f.). And when he destroyed the "treasure of his house" (208) which no silver could buy, Agamemnon similarly obeyed, not *aidōs*, but his own pride. The Elders understand this perfectly; but the king's living presence will make them condone his offense (805), and his pitiful death will make them forget it altogether.

The ten lines in which the chorus conclude their lyric parodos are worth study. Page's note on 249ff. (p. 92) states their attitude succinctly: "The chorus are reluctant to express their forebodings." When they say, "What Calchas prophesies will certainly be fulfilled," they plainly mean, "Troy will eventually fall"; but Calchas, they have told us, spoke also of "a spirit of wrath waiting at home to avenge a child's death" (155). When they say, "The scale of Justice turns, and men learn by suffering," they plainly think of Paris' offense; but Calchas spoke also of "another sacrifice, lawless, maker of hatreds, and having no fear of a man"—and the chorus will show in their first ode (367–98) that in their minds the crimes of Paris and of Agamemnon are easily confused. When they say, "As for the future—better to hear about it when it happens," they apparently mean the fall of Troy; but their words exactly describe what their attitude will be in the third episode as Agamemnon goes step by step to his fall. "Rejoicing too soon is as foolish as mourning too soon," they say; but if they had been readier to anticipate murder they might have saved the king. (Some critics praise the chorus for courage in warning Agamemnon of his danger; I shall discuss this point later in this chapter.) The Elders wind up their reflections very much as Agamemnon (in their narrative, 217) had ended his: "May the event prove to be well." They themselves, immediately after 217, had strongly censured Agamemnon for this attitude; there is no one to censure the Elders.

Now the queen is ready at last to answer their question about the beacon and the sacrifices. Aeschylus presents the Elders' relationship to Clytemnestra with exact subtlety. The first and constant element is their deep resentment of her confidence and authority as a woman who exercises her acknowledged right (259, *dikē gar esti* . . . , "for it is your right") to deputize for her absent husband. No doubt the presence of Aegisthus in the palace intensifies both their resentment and their apprehension; but the Elders drop no hint that they are aware of it, and when Clytemnestra herself alludes to it in front of the Herald (611f.), mocking their nervousness, they change the subject at once. Their first six lines addressed to the queen allude to her resented authority, but with politeness (258–63). Clytemnestra gives her news, "Troy is taken." At first they respond with joy; then incredulity leads them at once into barely concealed scorn: "Has some dream persuaded you? Are you feeding on rumour?" The beacon speech mesmerizes them into acceptance; her second speech seems to convince them. Clytemnestra ends by repeating the prayer that the Elders have already uttered several times, "May good prevail!" (349), and thus invites them, with an irony that eludes them, to share her rejoicing. Their words of acceptance (351–54) express genuine, if temporary, belief. They cannot, however, avoid the patronizing tone of man to woman, "Your gracious words are wise, like a man's"; and their phrase, "your trustworthy evidence," seems to ring false (there are three similar phrases about "evidence" in *Eu.* 447, 662, 797—each used in an ironic context).

The relationship of the Elders to Clytemnestra will be developed further in the third episode, when these anxious men face both king and queen together; but now we must consider the first choral ode. The confidently didactic moral tone of its first two sections makes it fairly certain that we should think of the Elders at this point as convinced by Clytemnestra's news. The powerful emotion roused by the thought, "The war is won," overcomes their sense that the queen's "evidence" may not be trustworthy. They would rather believe than doubt. Though doubt withdraws only to return later, yet for the present their belief in the victory over Troy inspires a marvelous poetic statement about the divine government of the world (367–402). Then comes a description of the private and general misery caused by Helen's flight and the decision to go to war. This leads their thoughts to Agamemnon, whom they are soon to welcome home. Finally in the epode (475–87) they abruptly reject as absurd the evidence of Clytemnestra's beacons.

Page's remarks on this ode are valuable; but I cannot accept his conclusion that in the epode "the foundations of a whole stasimon are undermined . . . with sudden and total ruin." Both he and Fraenkel, in commenting on this ode, dismiss as "psychological speculation" any view which interprets as designed portraiture the lines Aeschylus wrote for his Elders. Fraenkel attributes to Aeschylus "a certain looseness" in the writing of their part; Page thinks that the poet, for "a momentary dramatic advantage," allowed "a serious flaw in the structure" at this point. There is no need to accept either explanation, or to assume that Aeschylus was incapable of psychological acumen in his portrayal of the Elders. Their sudden rejection of belief is reached by logical sequence.

The first two strophes and antistrophes need no further comment here; but their ending leads to the third strophe with its picture of "Ares the banker of bodies" and his weighing scale. The lines record how the collective anguish and anger of the families of Argos, their resentment at the folly of going to war for one runaway wife (448), directs its full force against "the contentious sons of Atreus" (451). The gods too "watch closely those who have killed many." In the parodos the chorus ascribed to Agamemnon, as his chief feature, indelible guilt; now their foreboding (456–74, an entire stanza devoted unmistakably to Agamemnon) makes them assume that, if he has indeed captured Troy, he has "succeeded without justice" (464), and is among those whom the gods will destroy (465ff.). The greater his glory, the more certain his fall (468). This logic disturbs the chorus; Troy has been punished (473f.); but hardly less dreadful is the probable fate of Troy's conqueror. Contemplating it, the Elders say, "I would not be a sacker of cities" (472). A victor should be enviable; but just as Orestes will know his victory to be "unenviable" (*azēla, Ch.* 1017), so now the Elders feel only fear for Agamemnon. And if Agamemnon were destroyed, their own prospect is dark indeed. The elation fired by the "victory message" (*A.* 10) of the beacon has turned to depression. They never more than half believed it; why had they given way to a woman's fantasies? They must have been out of their minds (479). The scornful incredulity they expressed in 274, 276, returns in a rush; they are sure that the story of the beacons was nonsense.

We can have no idea what, if anything, happened on stage in Aeschylus' production to ease the transition from the skepticism of this epode to the excited announcement that a herald is approaching the palace. The change of mood has an undoubted dramatic value; but it is certainly not an artificial change contrived merely for contrast. The Elders' dismissal of belief is amply prepared for in 456–74, and is as consonant with their character as their cheerful apology in 583f. Furthermore, the foreboding that led them to the change is a most pertinent prelude to the ambivalent elements in the Herald's report.

For the second choral ode the Elders turn their thoughts to Helen. Their attitude toward her is interesting. It is a far cry from the admiring chatter of the old men in Troy (*Il.* 3.150–60) who see Helen walking past and feel the blood stir in their veins, to the picture Euripides gives us of fifth-century Athenians using "Helen" as a name to curse by, the guilty cause of endless bloodshed. The Elders are nearer the former than the latter (their casual reference in 62, *polyanoros*, "unfaithful," is a criticism rather of the Atreidae than of Helen). They have already fixed the blame for the war, first on Paris for violating the obligations of a guest (399–402, and later 701, 748f.), and next on the folly of the Greek chieftains in marshaling the whole manhood of Greece for an unworthy object. They now speak of Helen not as a culprit (see Page's excellent note on 744ff.) but as an instrument of Fate, and their praise of her beauty and her character (*phronēma*, 739) is without malevolence. When, in their indignation after the murder, they are momentarily inclined to blame Helen (1455ff.), at Clytemnestra's rebuke they turn immediately to find a juster reason in the *daimōn* of the Atreid family, and in the ultimate responsibility of Zeus. Helen is not mentioned again in the trilogy.

In the last section of their second ode the Elders revert to the theme that dominated the first: Troy fell to ruin, not because she was prosperous (761f.) but because she supported Paris in his flagrant breach of Zeus' law. But here, as before (385–98), their account of Troy's offense is given in terms that apply no less aptly to the situation of Agamemnon:

> The impious act breeds further impieties similar to its own nature (758ff.). . . . Old *hubris* is likely to breed a younger *hubris* which resembles its parents (763–71).

The father who shed his daughter's blood will be succeeded by the son who sheds his mother's. The Elders have a clear sense that morality is based on the law of cause and effect; they know the depth and the indelible nature of Agamemnon's guilt; they know—if they would but face their own knowledge—who is the agent Zeus has appointed for his justice (see again 154f.). And they end their ode, as Agamemnon's chariot enters the orchestra, with the words (781):

> Justice . . . guides everything to its conclusion.

The chorus' first words to Agamemnon include two echoes from the end of the first stasimon, where they were driven by conviction of the king's guilt and fear of his impending punishment to a panic rejection of the beacons as evidence for the fall of Troy. They now call him *ptoliporthēs*, "sacker of cities," a title they had a little while ago deprecated in dread (472); and they explain (786) that they do not wish to be excessive in their praise of him, which recalls their belief that "to be too much praised is dangerous" (468f.). These two references show that the Elders are keenly aware of Agamemnon's peril; but they are no less alert to their own. The king has power of life and death over them (848ff.), and they are anxious to assure him of their loyalty and the genuineness of their welcome. To reinforce this assurance, they candidly confess how, ten years before, they had criticized him for going to war "for Helen's sake"; now, however, he has returned victorious, and their love is from the heart. We have already noted that here they endorse Agamemnon's belief or hope (217, "May the result be well") that the end justifies the means. The flattery in their words therefore conflicts both with their protestations of candor and with everything they have said about the finality of *hubris*, and Zeus' law of cause and effect. What makes their predicament doubly difficult is that they fear Clytemnestra as much as they fear Agamemnon. It is surely because of this that their speech does not contain one line which could imply a warning of the direction from which Agamemnon's safety is threatened—they seem rather to wish to mislead him. "You will find out by inquiry," they say, "which *of the citizens* has been loyal or disloyal." Neither Clytemnestra nor Aegisthus is a citizen.

Now the chorus are silent until the central scene is over; but they have confirmed the character already outlined: they have a clear understanding of moral and religious principles, yet in action they are guided not even by the true urgency of the moment, but by prejudice and fear.

The urgent moment comes soon enough. At Clytemnestra's command her maids spread a path of embroidered purple cloth from his chariot to the palace door, and the queen invites him to enter his palace as a victorious king should. Agamemnon shows himself fully aware of the cogent reasons why he should refuse. The Elders know these reasons equally well, and their fears are in accord with their knowledge; yet they speak no word. In *Seven Against Thebes*, when Eteocles declares that he will go to the seventh gate to encounter his brother, the chorus entreat him not to defy the gods by such impiety. In Sophocles' *Antigone*, in Euripides' *Medea*, choruses less thoughtful and enlightened than the Argive Elders speak out for restraint and for religion. But when Agamemnon says, "I will enter my palace treading on purple"—an act he has himself described, nine lines earlier, as an offense against *aidōs*, "reverence"—the Elders, who have used "the trampling of sanctities" as an image of unpardonable *hubris* (371), allow their fear of Clytemnestra to freeze their tongues, while they watch the king whom they profess to love seal his own doom in the sight of the gods. They hear Clytemnestra's shout of victory as the king's foot touches the precious cloth. Agamemnon vanishes through the door. Clytemnestra prays to Zeus for success, and then follows the king. Only when left alone on the stage do the Elders ask themselves, "Why does this foreboding persistently haunt my heart?"

In the third stasimon the Elders' thought hovers (977), chants (990), revolves (997), and smolders (1033) around a single theme: their own uneasy conscience. If their tongue was reluctant to speak without certainty, their heart —their loyalty to the king—ought to have "stepped in front" (1028) and "poured out their dread in warning." They have missed their last chance of doing their duty, and the excuse that leaps to their mind is the inevitable excuse of such failure: "It was fated to happen in any case" (1025ff.). But the excuse cannot restore their confidence (982, 994). If a man has unwisely acquired excessive wealth (1007) he can escape disaster by large offerings to the gods; but if blood has been spilled, nothing can recall it (1019ff.). They are thinking of the story they told in the parodos—their words can refer to nothing else; and they repeat yet again the theme of their earlier songs: There is no cure, no escape. Agamemnon is on the point of paying his debt. When, long ago, he made a wrong decision, he hopefully said, "May the result be well"; and now the Elders, having failed in their duty, pray hopefully (998ff.) that their foreboding may prove false.

Their scene with Cassandra, vital as it is in the design of the trilogy, adds only a few minor strokes to the portrait of the Elders. They respond to her misery with gentleness, to her courage with admiration and awe, to her vision of the immediate future with obtuseness. They hold themselves and the audience entirely under her spell. When she has gone, their questioning lines 1331–42 keep suspense unbroken until the king's death cry. Then come the notorious thirteen couplets that summarize their character in the single quality of uncertainty. They have moral principles and religious convictions, but cannot decide whether, or how, to apply them. They have evidence, but cannot decide whether to believe or disbelieve it. They have a little courage, but cannot decide whether to act or to wait. Finally they agree to "ascertain what has happened to Agamemnon."

In the scene that follows the Elders' consciousness that they have neglected their duty underlies much of what they say. They see in Agamemnon's blood the corroboration of everything they have believed about the permanence of guilt and the certainty of punishment. Yet they refuse to remember the altar at Aulis; until Clytemnestra for the fourth time reminds them of what they themselves told us in the parodos. Then at last they say, "Reproach answers reproach; it is a hard struggle to judge." They are allowed no time for a hard struggle; Aegisthus arrives, and their hatred for him and for Clytemnestra resolves the matter, revives at last some courage in them, and leaves them, for the close of the play, on the side of the defeated.

A considerable portion of the play is taken up by confrontation between the Elders and Clytemnestra. Let us conclude by asking, What precisely is the issue on which they disagree? It is surely more than personal dislike, or their general contempt for women; we may expect it rather to be a moral issue of universal application.

In the parodos the Elders, recounting the sacrifice of Iphigenia, forcefully express the fundamental emotion of indignation against wrong; and their words are certainly meant to arouse full sympathy in the audience. But what never occurs to either chorus or audience is the fact that this indignation is felt a hundred times more passionately by a person who is at no time far from their thoughts, whom the Elders have already addressed at some length (83–103): Clytemnestra. It is, and probably will remain, open to dispute whether the queen is present on stage during the narrative of the sacrifice; but it must be partly on her behalf that the story is told, since it is to provide the reference and motive for every word and act with which she, as the central character in the drama, will direct or dominate each subsequent scene. This feeling of indignation, then, is the meeting point for the queen and the Elders at the opening of the play. The point of divergence is first indicated at 255, when the chorus utter a pious wish that "for the immediate future all may turn out well"—echoing the feeble dishonesty of Agamemnon (217). For the integrity of Clytemnestra, feeling leads inseparably to action; for the Elders, feeling is a decorous and temporary indulgence, while action springs from the impulse of the moment, whether anger or fear.

The concept of heroic integrity, and its encounter with the intractable universe, seems to be, no less in Aeschylus than in his successors, an essential element of tragedy, whether shown as embodied in a person, or as an unfulfilled potential. The Elders do not possess this quality; but their degree of capacity to recognize and admire it is shown in their response to Cassandra. Cassandra herself, however, shows an integrity sharply limited by her emotional self-identification with Agamemnon, which blinds her prophetic vision to the dominant factor in her own situation—Agamemnon's crime at Aulis; and this blindness unites her with the Elders in violent abuse of Clytemnestra, whose integrity, though not without flaw, is the moral backbone of the whole drama. Clytemnestra fears neither god nor man, but obeys the human imperative of indignation. In Clytemnestra the Elders confront, but do not recognize, the sum of their own principles ratified in courageous action. Their failure shows the exact place the poet allots to them in his whole design. Three characteristics—general goodness of feeling, feebleness in action, and inability to recognize integrity—make them fairly represent ordinary humanity and the bulk of their audience. They represent the poet only in the poetic brilliance of their reflective lyrics, and not in their judgments of the moral issues that face them in the drama. The duty of the critic, the satisfaction of the reader, is not to ally himself with this chorus, but to see what they fail to see, and grasp the heroic reality which their creator designed to be beyond their reach.

9

The Libation Bearers

These women's history is briefly told in the last stanza of their parodos song (75 ff.). When the gods doomed their city to capture in war, they left their ancestral home to become slaves in the palace of Argos. It is not actually stated, but seems to be implied, that they were part of the plunder that Agamemnon brought home from Troy.

> Since we live under compulsion, our duty and necessity is to approve the actions of those who rule our lives, whether just or unjust, while we control the bitter hatred of our hearts. (78–81)

They hide under their gowns their tears for the hopeless fate of their mistress— evidently they mean Electra, who is with them; and they are "clouded with hidden sorrows."

Electra herself is kept by Clytemnestra and Aegisthus in the condition of a slave; so the devotion of these women to Electra is natural enough. Their devotion to Agamemnon is harder to understand (though it provides an illuminating echo to the devotion that Cassandra in *Agamemnon* feels for the man who has despoiled her city, her family, and her virginity). The "bitter hatred of their hearts" is hatred not of Agamemnon who has destroyed their lives, but of his enemy Clytemnestra. Their feeling for Agamemnon has grown from their sympathy with Electra, who adores her father's memory. They "revere Agamemnon's tomb as if it were an altar" (106). Agamemnon's crime, which filled the parodos of the first play, is something that this chorus, like Electra and like Orestes, have resolved never to think of. Aeschylus made his Argive Elders emphasize the sacrifice of Iphigenia as the origin of ensuing miseries; but the Libation Bearers, in the formal summary of Atreid crimes with which they close the play, omit almost ostentatiously (this will be discussed later in this chapter) that crime which Aeschylus placed at the head of the account as the immediate cause of Agamemnon's death, and substitute a remote cause, the banquet of

Thyestes, which in *Agamemnon* is not even mentioned for the first three-quarters of the play.

The prologue of *Choephori* tells us that Orestes has come from exile to mourn for his father and to kill his mother. The chorus does not yet know this; but their opening lyrics include the following passages:

> Those who live below the earth are indignant against murderers. (40)

> What rite can expiate blood once fallen on the ground? (48)

> Alas for the ruin of the house, caused by the deaths in its royal family. (50–53)

> When blood is drunk by the earth that nursed it, the guilty one is filled with disease. (66–69)

> As there is no cure for chastity violated, so for the hand foul with murder all cleansing is vain. (71–74)

In the prologue Orestes speaks of two crimes: one past, the murder of Agamemnon; and one now projected, his murder of his mother Clytemnestra. The past crime was the matter of the first play, and it is clear that in the five passages just quoted the chorus are thinking of Clytemnestra's murder of her husband. So, almost certainly, are the audience; and most subsequent readers of the play seem to have been content to look no further. But how can it fail to be obvious to those who reflect on the text that, though the chorus of slaves clearly has no second thought, the poet in writing these words was aware that they applied in every case with at least equal force to the other, and more immediately relevant, crime spoken of in the prologue, which Orestes has come to Argos to commit? and, similarly, to the earlier crime, ignored by Orestes, for which Agamemnon paid with his life. The murder that the chorus long and pray for, which they will counsel and assist to the best of their power, is subject to the same condition as that which it avenges—a condition already laid down repeatedly in *Agamemnon*: for blood once spilled there is no cure, for guilt incurred by *hubris* there is no expiation. Yet to the end of the play the Libation Bearers will remain hopeful and deluded, unaware of this truth.

This selective vision is a resolute and passionate trait; and its force is shown by the chorus' dialogue with Electra in the first episode. Electra, not having formally accepted slavery, suffers the uncertainty bred by moral tradition. At first she is not yet ready to put her hatred into decisive words, still less into action. She "is not brazen enough" to say the pious words her mother told her to say, yet not firm enough, without her friends' encouragement, to say what she herself wants to say. The chorus feel no such uncertainty. Line by line they lead her to a resolve (120ff.):

EL. Shall I pray for a judge, or for an avenger?
CH. Say simply, One who will shed blood for blood.
EL. Will the gods hold me pious, if I pray so?
CH. Why not? Evil for evil is no impiety.

So Electra accepts "evil for evil" (145f.) and prays to Hermes and to her father's spirit for the deaths of her mother and Aegisthus; and the chorus echo her prayer in a short hymn over Agamemnon's grave.

After the recognition, when Electra has welcomed her brother, and Orestes has prayed to Zeus for his help, the chorus leader speaks five lines of passionate alliance, establishing the voice of the whole group as an equal third in the long antiphony of invocation that is to follow—in fact more than equal, since the chorus speaks eleven stanzas, Orestes five, and Electra six. This confirms for the rest of the play the dominant role which the chorus assumed in their early scene with Electra. It is the chorus leader who brings the long prayer to a close (510), and then clinches Orestes' resolution by presenting, in the central symbolism of the play, Clytemnestra's dream—already hinted at in the parodos. After Orestes has accepted the omen and its meaning, it is the chorus leader who bids him proceed to the next step without further delay.

We can now begin to outline the essential character of this chorus. It is blind and resolute revenge. Blind, because their indignation is stirred only by the one crime which excites their present hatred, and not at all by the earlier crime that provoked it, or the still worse crime by which they hope it will be avenged; resolute, as their persistent goading of Orestes demonstrates. They long to see "the tyrants . . . dead, and their flesh consumed in flame" (276f.). They begin the invocation with this appeal to the Fates and Zeus (306–14):

> Justice exacts her debt, and cries aloud,
> "Let hatred be paid for hatred, word for evil word;
> For murderous blow let murderous blow be returned.
> *The doer shall suffer*":
> A law three ages old proclaims this.

This opening statement gives two different definitions of justice; but they are presented as if they were one and the same. The second, "The doer shall suffer" (*drasanti pathein*), echoes the often repeated thought of the *Agamemnon* chorus. The Elders' perception of Zeus' law, *pathein ton erxanta* (A. 1564), arose from their reflection on past events such as the punishment of Paris for his offense to Zeus Xenios. They even admit reluctantly (1561) that Zeus' law has been fulfilled in the murder of Agamemnon. It is true that the admission lasts only a few moments, until the entry of Aegisthus, and that in their rage they pray for matricide (1646ff.); but their nature is to deplore bloodshed rather than to desire it. The Libation Bearers are different: they want murder, as they have already told Electra (*Ch.* 121); now they say it again in 312. By adding immediately their echo of the Elders in 313, they imply that they are only stating what has already, as it were, been agreed upon; but in fact they go a significant step further. They are not reflecting on past calamity, but deciding on, planning for, and encouraging, future calamity.

Throughout the invocation they never relax this positive attitude. Not for a moment do they acknowledge, like the Elders, that "the issue is hard to decide," or that "reproach answers reproach." Their stanzas alternate entreaty, anger, the assurance of triumph and a happy future, with reminders of Agamemnon's murder, its indignity and shame, of the mutilation of his body, of the challenge to Orestes' loyalty. They conclude their part at line 478, with the word "victory." After that Orestes and Electra continue their appeal to their father's ghost for another thirty lines, now totally committed to their purpose. When the moment comes for describing, line by line, Clytemnestra's dream of the serpent, no word of persuasion is any longer necessary. Orestes clutches at each grisly detail with fascination, and accepts the omen as confirming Apollo's command.

The first choral ode, 585–651, begins with a general reflection on the ubiquity of violence both in the natural world and in human hearts, and more particularly in ungoverned female sexuality. Then follow four instances, each occupying a whole stanza or strophe, of the special wickedness of women—the fourth being the mass revolt of the women of Lemnos against their menfolk in legendary times; a horror used ever since as a comparison for any extraordinary crime (633f.). The text of the third instance, 623–30, is seriously corrupt ("*locus paene desperatus,*" says Murray in his *apparatus criticus*); but it undoubtedly alludes to Clytemnestra's murder of Agamemnon. And this whole section of the ode is then summarized as follows:

> Thus the female sex suffers rejection (*oichetai*), being detested by gods and dishonoured in human society. For no one honours what the gods abhor.

At this point a digression is necessary. The word I have translated as "the female sex" is simply *genos* (636). Some scholars interpret *genos* as meaning "that class of women who murder members of their families," rather than the entire female sex. There are two possible ways of arguing this point.

The first is to examine the meaning of *genos*. It can denote either a race or a class. But the word is a very common one, and in any decision based on Aeschylus' probable use of it, we must remember that we possess only one-tenth of his writings. The word is used here without any limiting adjective. It is hard to see how any number of other examples could be decisive.

The other approach is to examine the logic of the whole ode. It begins by describing the violence of the natural world; and in the second stanza gives two lines to the violence of men, and six to the violence which sexual passion arouses in females—"humans as well as beasts." The third stanza tells the story of Althaea, who by a deliberate act ended her son's life. The fourth recounts how Scylla betrayed her father to his death. The fifth recalls Clytemnestra's vengeance; the sixth, the Lemnian massacre. Then comes the summary (again the MS text is virtually untranslatable): "In misery hateful to gods, the race dishonoured among mortals is rejected." To assert at this point that "the race of women-who-murder-their-relatives is rejected" seems merely otiose. On the other hand, to say that because of notable crimes committed by a few women the entire female sex is rejected by men and gods, is not only a logical summary of the first fifty lines of the ode, but is consonant with the bitter and resentful character this chorus has borne since the first scene.

The chorus then end this main section of the ode with the question:

Is any part of my indictment unjustly urged?

This last question is in fact the unobtrusive needle that points the irony of the chorus' role throughout the play. Since the fourth strophe and antistrophe follow at once, the audience has no time to reflect on an answer to the question—and certainly the original audience, being (like Athena, *Eu.* 738) "wholly on the father's side," assumed that the question was merely rhetorical. But the poet knew that the reader has time; and at least three clear answers present themselves, each sponsored by that Mnemosyne who, as Mother of the Muses, performs equally essential service to the artist and to those who wish to understand his message.

The first answer is that the indictment they have just concluded is unjust simply because it is aimed, not at Clytemnestra in particular, but at the whole female sex. The chorus, believing themselves "hated by gods and despised by men" (635f.), adopt what many of their sex hold to be the only way of survival—they decide that men's judgment is correct, and women are indeed the curse of the race. This was not the belief of any of the three tragedians. No play dealing with the "Lemnian massacre" survives; but both Aeschylus' *Suppliants* and Euripides' *Bacchae*, though they show women in concerted and violent revolt, rejecting male oppression and asserting their freedom, evidently invite a large measure of sympathy for the female cause, without excusing the bloodshed to which their revolt leads. The attack on the female sex contained in this chorus of *Choephori* is almost a parody (similar to, and anticipating, the irrelevant execrations of Helen frequently found in Euripides, e.g., in *Andromache, Iphigenia in Tauris, Electra*) of a banal theme to be daily heard in the Agora.

The second answer is a still more obvious one. The chorus incites Orestes and Electra to kill their mother: Electra has already claimed that her revengeful spirit is inherited from Clytemnestra (420f.); Orestes has already claimed to be "in every respect a serpent" (549), and thus to be exempt from obligations of human kinship. The chorus themselves have told us that, since they live under compulsion, they have ceased to exercise rational judgment on questions of right and wrong (*dikaia kai mē dikaia . . . ainesai*, 78ff.), so that their attitudes are not moral judgments but impulses as violent as the compulsion they endure.

The third answer is to point out that, for Clytemnestra, total victory was the only alternative to total defeat. If she had welcomed her returning husband with implicit acceptance of his claim to dispose arbitrarily of her life and her daughter's life, she would have been a slave in a sense even more dishonoring than that which the chorus have accepted perforce. The submissive slave who adores her master feels a special hatred for one whose courage rejects oppression.

So when they ask, "Is any part of my indictment unjustly urged?" the unspoken answer suggested by the whole action of the trilogy is "You have indicted guilty individuals; but all this does not amount [as is implied by *ageirō*, 638] to evidence against the whole female sex." The poet places this question in its climactic position for the dramatic purpose of suggesting this answer.

We are now in a position to summarize four different conceptions of justice that Aeschylus presents in the trilogy. First, that of the Elders. This is a religious conception, a part of their belief in Zeus, and founded on observation and reflection; but they are emotionally incapable of applying it to new experience, so that when confronted with the king's murder they lapse from their civilized attitude, allowing their rage to push them back into the primitive posture which calls for matricide (1646ff.). A second conception is embodied in Clytemnestra. Hers is a personal idea of justice, based on no religious belief but on her own inner conviction of right and wrong, on indignation and a resolve that wickedness shall not destroy innocence and go unpunished and honored. Her involvement with Aegisthus is shown as having little or no part in the motivation of her justice, merely the part of an ally in its accomplishment and maintenance (*A.* 1434ff.); but in the eyes of the world it inevitably, and finally, overclouds her integrity. Third, the Libation Bearers hold a conception of justice which from the outset is frankly primitive, founded on hatred, or what is currently sometimes called gut reaction; it ignores the closest bonds of kinship, rejects *aidōs*, welcomes violence, and embraces the blind belief that bloodshed can lead to peace, cleansing, and health. Finally, there is the inspiring conception of justice contained in Athena's appointment of dikasts "who reverence their oaths" (*Eu.* 483), and elaborated in her description of a holy court where reverence, integrity, vigilance, and firmness shall prove a lasting protection for the city's life and honor. Apollo in his pleading offers prevarication, bribes, and menaces; the jurors cast their honorably divided votes; and Athena mocks them, and the city, and—if they but knew it—the audience, and her own solemn *thesmos*, with her presidential decision in 734–41. So the defeat of justice, thinly masked as the victory of Zeus Agoraios, is welcomed and hymned by a rejoicing and self-satisfied populace.

In the next scene, after Orestes has gained admission to the palace, the chorus utter an excited prayer to the earth and to Agamemnon's tomb, for his success in the plot to kill Clytemnestra and Aegisthus. They have heard Orestes allude, five times in seven lines addressed to Clytemnestra (700–706), to the fact that his purpose is, like Paris' crime, a violation of hospitality, and still profess his obligation of piety as a guest (704); and they feel no compunction. When the Nurse, weeping over the news of Orestes' death, comes from the palace on her way to fetch Aegisthus, the chorus leader, without prompting, persuades her to alter her message and tell Aegisthus to come without his armed guard. There are few passages in tragedy where a chorus takes an initiative so material to the action. The choral ode following this scene is a still more excited prayer for victory, addressed to various gods; and in the last strophe they call upon Orestes, who is now inside the palace (827–31):

> When the moment for action comes, keep your courage.
> When she cries out to you, 'My child!'
> Answer her, 'I am my father's.'
> Fulfil your dread duty, and you will be blameless.

Apollo is on their side; but we, the audience, remember also their own words, "*dikaia kai mē dikaia . . .*," "we approve both just and unjust."

Then Aegisthus comes, and the chorus lull his suspicions and send him into the palace; after which their almost hysterical lines of hope end only with his death cry. They are concentrated with rapturous anticipation upon one act: a son will kill his mother—an act whose image, for the first half of the play, enveloped Orestes himself in a horrified resolution of despair enforced by fear. The chorus feel neither horror nor despair. They are sure of success. They hate and despise their own sex, and pin their faith on the man who will crush and punish its rebellion.

When Clytemnestra appears and her son confronts her, the chorus are at last silent. Their part has been completed; Orestes will not falter now. As he follows his mother into the palace, they are sobered for a brief moment:

> I mourn even for these two. Nonetheless, now that Orestes has accomplished the culmination of many murders, it is better so, than that he, the treasure of the house, should perish.

With that unconscious echo of an earlier "treasure of the house" (*A.* 208), their humanity again retreats before the wild triumph of their deliverance. They applaud Orestes and Pylades, they applaud Apollo's command, the victory of Justice, daughter of Zeus, and its achievement by guile, they extol the power of divinity to overcome wickedness. Their total hatred of the dead is understandable; but their belief that matricide can "purge all pollution from the hearth with cleansing that banishes doom" reveals only the familiar truth that "learning by suffering" (cf. *A.* 177 et al.) is an empty theory. For their excuse, we may recall their pitiful story in the parodos.

The hectic jubilation falls silent; and Orestes comes, carrying the stained robe, the "net" in which his father died. He finds no joy in his "unenviable" victory (1017); he proclaims no ecstatic deliverance for the polluted house. The chorus weep for past crime and present misery; but still cling to the delusion that the revenge they longed for has brought freedom to Argos (1046). When the Erinyes attack, they still refuse to face moral realities, telling Orestes that what he sees is imagination, *doxai,* and his crime a victory; that as time passes his agony will diminish (1055f.). When instead they see it increasing moment by moment, they appear to recognize at last the unique dreadfulness of what he has done; and they say,

> You have one hope of cleansing: Apollo will lay his hand on you and set you free.

How mistaken they are, the next play will show.

Meanwhile, the chorus' closing lines quietly demonstrate that the blindness of their faith in revenge is incurable. At the beginning of the trilogy the dramatist stated unmistakably what act was the origin of the disasters recounted in the first two plays: the sacrifice of Iphigenia by her father. Let us recall that, when Cassandra talked with the Argive Elders, claiming to "know the past crimes of this house" (*A.* 1197), she invalidated her claim by omitting the one act that was the most direct cause of Agamemnon's death, and therefore of her own; and, as if to compensate for the omission, she dwelt at some length, three separate times, on Thyestes' banquet. The chorus of Libation Bearers, more fanatically devoted to Agamemnon than Cassandra, similarly refuse to remember the crime for which his wife killed him; and their omission of this crime, and use of the same illogical substitution, is made more self-conscious, and offered more obviously to a critical reader, by their words "first," "second," and "third" in reference to the deaths of Thyestes' sons, Agamemnon, and Clytemnestra. (When Orestes, in *Ch.* 578, spoke of the "third draught of unmixed blood," had he in mind the same enumeration?) In *Agamemnon* the Elders' indignation was too shallow to recognize integrity and justice. In *Choephori* the chorus' indignation, blinded by anger and hatred, ignores the still worse pollution they pursue. Their parting observations are designed to demonstrate, to a critical assessment, that their false faith in revenge, and their empty hope of a purified future, can be upheld only by a deliberate distortion of the truth as established by the poet.

The first two plays, then, represent in the characters of their two choruses two familiar ways in which individuals or societies react to fundamental crime such as murder within the family. The first is timid or well-meaning opportunism, a knowledge of moral principle without integrity to maintain or implement it. The second is primitive unreflecting belief in simple reprisal. The Argive Elders are on the losing side; but they succeed, despite their feebleness, in preserving throughout the action a climate of seriousness in which, desperate though their position is, hope can still survive. The Libation Bearers are apparently on the winning side; yet they escape despair only through want of perception and honest reason. Their hysterical victory song fades into silence, and the moral logic, the cause-and-effect principle which they earlier celebrated, proceeds relentlessly to fulfill itself, leaving the victor a desperate fugitive, and themselves with an empty faith in a god who commanded ultimate wickedness. The chorus of *Eumenides* will offer to solve this bankruptcy in the manner ordained by the Fates when they created man and endowed him with the elementary basis of a social morality. But by this time man, in alliance with the "younger gods," is taking Fate into his own hands with his invention of democracy; and primitive justice, developed into the hollow solemnity of a judicial system, can now be manipulated by expediency, and defeated.

10

The Furies

Aeschylus' picture of the Elders showed a familiar kind of unheroic complexity. His picture of the Libation Bearers showed a familiar kind of unhappy simplicity. His picture of the Erinyes, which at first reading seems confused and contradictory, falls into order when we recognize that it is designed to embody two different conceptions, to lead us away from a familiar one and towards the other which has been forgotten. In the end the defeated Erinyes lose their moral identity and merge into the overriding image of the victorious city. The term Erinys is used in the first two plays, with the vague meaning of "an avenger," or "spirit of destruction"; but the chorus of the third play establishes its own clear character in each of the two aspects presented.

The Latin name Furies seems to have no connection with the Greek name Erinyes. *Furia* suggests blind irrationality; and such a character has often been attributed to Aeschylus' black-robed and hideous deities. But until we are sure that the poet meant to show his chorus as blind and irrational, we should avoid both this assumption and the name that implies it. This concept of female powers dedicated to the punishment of crime was necessarily vague and variable, and subject to tendentious appropriation; the poet was free to correct or modify it at will for the purposes of his drama.

An Erinys is an avenger. A man or an animal who steals the young out of a vulture's nest is liable to be attacked by the parent birds. This is a law of nature; as the chorus says in *A.* 59, "Some god—Apollo or Pan or Zeus—sends an Erinys against the offender." In *A.* 463 "the black Erinyes" are spoken of as punishing the prosperous evildoer. In *A.* 749 Erinys is the avenging spirit sent by Zeus Xenios against the sons of Priam. In *A.* 1150 Cassandra says that since the time of Atreus and Thyestes "a company of Erinyes drunk with blood" has haunted the palace; she is thinking of the inherited propensity to hatred and crime that arises from the murder of Thyestes' children. This natural personification of revenge was the meaning that popular belief attached to the name

Erinys, as its use in *Agamemnon* shows. When a man intended to commit a revengeful murder he would say that an Erinys drove him on. And as revenge, even when carried out in the spirit of justice, may lead to uncontrolled bloodshed, so the popular image of the Erinyes moved from a necessary safeguard of good behavior to the embodiment of irrational ferocity. It even became possible to believe, as Orestes believed (*Ch.* 269–96), that the Erinyes would punish a man both for not killing his mother and for killing her. This belief some scholars have taken over from Apollo or from Orestes; not, I think, from Aeschylus.

The dramatist makes sure that his audience recognize the Erinyes unmistakably. When the Delphian Priestess, after her solemn opening speech, has entered the temple, and a moment later staggers out, gasping in terror at what she has seen, she describes creatures

> black, utterly loathsome; their vile breath
> Vents in repulsive snoring; from their eyes distils
> A filthy rheum; their garb is wickedness to wear.

The Priestess departs. The temple's interior is disclosed, with the Erinyes asleep, and Orestes and Apollo standing by the altar. Apollo promises to protect Orestes from

> these raging hunters, ancient, ageless hags
> Whose presence neither god nor man nor beast can bear;
> For the sake of evil they were born; and evil is
> The dark they dwell in, subterranean Tartarus;
> Beings abhorred by men and by Olympian gods.

There is little doubt where the sympathies of the audience will lie. It was, admittedly, terrible to see Orestes drive his mother into the palace at sword point, and later stand over her dead body. But Apollo himself had commanded revenge; she too had shed blood; and now Apollo assures the audience that the Erinyes are hateful to gods and men, and essentially evil. Orestes is seen as a young hero who has performed a painful duty; Clytemnestra is remembered as the woman who killed her husband. When Apollo says that the Erinyes "were born for the sake of evil," he does not remind us that he himself threatened to employ them in torturing Orestes to death if he failed to kill his mother. He tells Orestes that the Erinyes will continue to pursue him over land and sea, and that he must endure their attacks until he reaches the city of Athens.

When Orestes has gone, and Clytemnestra's ghost rouses the chorus from sleep, the familiar image of cruel, maddening, bloodthirsty enemies of mankind comes fully to life. In sleep they yelp like hounds dreaming of their prey. When they rise and show themselves, the terror of their presence (something not seen before in the Attic theater) is vivid. Apollo has withdrawn into his temple; the Erinyes are alone. Before them is Apollo's altar, around them all the solemnity of the Delphic scene. They know that Apollo cast a spell of sleep over them, and Orestes has escaped. But when they speak, their words are not savage cries for blood. Their tone indicates that they are shocked, appalled; they are not blind, and reason tells them that what they see is wrong. "We pursued a man who killed his mother," they say; "and Apollo, son of Zeus, not only protects and comforts him, but himself authorized the crime. If Olympian gods foster such wickedness, what hope is there for humanity?"

Their words are passionate, yet controlled; not the words of monsters, but of wise and just correctors. There must be, of course, a wise and just answer to what they say; and Apollo, who now appears at the inner door of the temple, will surely provide this answer, with a dignity appropriate to a serious issue that has been stated in serious terms. He will show the calm and sublime authority familiar to us in the central figure on the west pediment of the temple at Olympia. He will say that the crime of matricide, polluting as it is, was necessary to punish the still more serious crime of regicide; and that he himself, in this exceptional case, will purify the polluted criminal.

But Apollo says none of these things. Instead (179–97):

> Away! Out of this temple, lest you feel my arrow,
> And painfully spew forth the black foam that you suck
> From the sour flesh of murderers. What place have you
> Within these walls? Some pit of punishments, where heads
> Are severed, eyes torn out, throats cut, manhood unmanned,
> Some hell of maimings, mutilations, stonings, where
> Bodies impaled on stakes melt the mute air with groans—
> Your place is there! Such are the feasts you love, for which
> Heaven loathes you

—and more in the same vein: abuse, rhetoric, and not a word of reason.

When the angry shouting has ceased, the chorus leader says

> Lord Apollo, listen to me in turn. You are the sole cause of this dispute; you commanded Orestes to kill his mother, and now you protect him. We were appointed by Fate to punish any man who murders his mother.

"What of a wife who murders her husband?" asks Apollo. That question has some relevance, but it is nonetheless prevarication. "Our duty," the chorus leader replies, "is confined to cases of kindred blood." Whereupon Apollo makes another speech, whose pious tone disguises its perversity. He speaks of the sanctity of the marriage bond symbolized in the union of Zeus and Hera, and of the delights bestowed by Aphrodite; this bond, he says, is stronger than an oath. What marriage is he referring to? Does he cite Zeus as analogous to

Agamemnon? The chorus once again state the real issue, which is Orestes' guilt as a matricide; Apollo seeks to divert attention from Orestes' guilt to his victim's (219). In this argument, the Erinyes' tone is courteous, their method rational; Apollo's tone is derisive (209), and he declines to face the real issue.

The scene changes from Delphi to Athens. The Erinyes have pursued Orestes for perhaps a year. We see him sitting, as Apollo bade him, as a suppliant at Athena's altar. The Erinyes enter the orchestra, searching for him.

Now, in the prologue scene the poet asked his audience, or readers, to follow him in a rather subtle proceeding: he introduced the Erinyes in their recognizable image as horrible monsters, and then made them speak lines which, in contrast to Apollo's, were courteous, rational, and moral. Here in the second scene, in case some of the audience wondered whether they had misunderstood, Aeschylus repeats this process, to reassure them. When the Erinyes enter the forecourt of Athena's temple, they are once more seen as the bogeys invoked to terrify malefactors. They advance like hounds, tracing the unpunished matricide by the scent of his mother's blood; they find him again taking sanctuary at an altar. His crime is one that no punishment short of death can do justice to; and in the imagery of popular fantasy they pronounce his sentence (264f.):

> You shall, for your soul's guilt,
> Give us your blood to drink
> Red from the living limb.

After this, just as in the prologue, a subtle, unemphatic change occurs; and this time the change is permanent. The hideous masks and robes of popular belief remain; but the voice so clothed utters with authority truth at least as serious and inescapable as the pronouncements of the Argive Elders in *Agamemnon* (*Eu.* 269–75):

> Mark this: not only you,
> But every mortal soul
> Whose pride has once transgressed
> The law of reverence due
> To parent, god, or guest,
> Shall pay sin's just, inexorable toll.
> Deep in the nether sky
> Death rules the ways of man
> With stern and strong control;
> And there is none who can
> By any force or art
> Elude Death's watchful eye
> Or his recording heart.

Orestes, crouched at the altar, claims that he has been ritually cleansed from pollution, and that people have received him in their homes without suffering any harm. He appeals to Athena to come and save him, and promises as reward the perpetual alliance of Argos with Athens. But the authority the Erinyes received from Fate at the creation of the world (333, 347, 392) is far older than that of the young Olympians; and now in the first stasimon the chorus state their primeval function (312–20):

> We hold our judgement just and true:
> The man whose open hands are pure
> Anger of ours shall not pursue;
> He lives untroubled and secure.
> But when a sinner such as he,
> Burdened with blood so foully shed,
> Covers his guilty hands for shame,
> Then, bearing witness for the dead,
> We at his judgment stand to claim
> The price of blood unyieldingly.

Blood has a price. All through *Agamemnon*, all through *Choephori*, one theme was repeated: no cause is without its effect; the man who spurns justice, who treads on sanctities, cannot hope to escape. Sacrifice and other ritual may properly be offered to the gods; but there are cases where no expiation can be effectual. Unless some degree of wickedness is recognized as unpardonable, on what basis can a code of morality stand? Now Orestes claims that purgative blood offerings were made for him at Apollo's hearth; but, as has been shown in chapter 3, the text offers ample evidence that the purification, if performed, failed to have its effect.

We should notice an important point near the beginning of this statement: "The man whose hands are pure no anger from us pursues; he lives an unharmed life." This assertion, that the Erinyes pursue only the guilty, is consonant with everything else that the first and second choral odes, and the conduct of the trial, tell us: it confirms that the chorus in this ode and the next provides the sole voice in the trilogy that utters consistent and rational morality. And it has a further and more pointed significance. When Orestes was commanded at Delphi to kill his mother, the oracle (according to Orestes' account in *Ch.* 269–96) did not use arguments about justice or political necessity, but threatened that the Erinyes would torment him to death if he disobeyed. This statement by the Erinyes themselves gives the lie direct to Apollo, and thus removes the chief ground on which the matricide could be defended (see chapter 2).

This first choral ode also establishes certain truths about the gods, both Olympian and Chthonian. Here are the salient points (333–96):

Fate assigned us this portion: when guilt for kindred blood befalls a man, we pursue him to death, and even after death. (333–40)

No immortal need fear us; we do not share their feasts or attend their rituals. Our task is the overthrow of great houses; when Ares enters a home and kin murders kin, we pursue the guilty. (350–58)

We are diligent in this task, to provide immunity (*ateleian*, 361) for the [Olympian] gods, so that none of them needs to join issue with mankind on such matters. Because we bear the hateful stain of blood, Zeus disdains our company. (359–66)

The glories of men, though they tower to the sky, yet at our black-robed onset melt away and sink into dishonour. . . . Our function is lasting: resourceful, efficient, and inexorable, severed from gods, we perform our part unhonoured. (368–88)

Hear, then, and reverence our ordinance (*thesmon*), given by gods, ratified by Fate for ever. (389–96)

Nowhere in extant tragedy is there a more impressive statement of the stern basis of social morality. The Erinyes in this ode are still confident of victory and sure of their principles.

The Olympian gods are not deeply concerned with goodness. As the Argive Elders said (*A.* 182f.), there is nothing in the gods to call for our gratitude; they occupy their august throne tyrannically, *biaiōs*. Morality is concerned with what ought to be, with aspiration towards the ideal. The Olympian gods represent what is. They are eternal, unchangeable, irresistible; sometimes, not always, sublime in beauty and power; occasionally, if it suits them, beneficent. It is only Zeus who concerns himself with regard for an oath, or a suppliant, or the law of host and guest. The Erinyes differ from the Olympians; they are concerned with the values of human society. To undertake the guardianship of morality in any specific or reliable way would impair the objective grandeur, even the aesthetic autonomy, of Olympus. The Erinyes by their office provide for younger gods "exemption" from such responsibility. In the trial, of course, Athena and Apollo take part as president and pleader; but the Erinyes, who agree to accept the outcome of the trial because they trust Athena's integrity (433), have at first no cause to suspect that their trust is misplaced.

This ode sets forth two opposed kinds of value, the same that are weighed against each other in the parodos of *Agamemnon*. The primary bond of affection that stabilizes and enriches society is that of the family, and especially the bond of blood between parent and child. If humane values are to survive, any violator of this bond must be dealt with at once. The most flagrant of all violations occurs when a child destroys the life that gave him birth. To defend such violation is to destroy society and humanity. This, say the chorus, is what Apollo is attempting in his championship of Orestes. Shedding of kindred blood is a plague for which there is only one cure: the overthrowing of the house (354–59; cf. also *A.* 768ff.). This grim duty, essential to human happiness, is the task that the Erinyes have received from Fate. In performing it they preserve the basis of all humane values.

Opposed to these is another kind of value: "the august glories of men, towering to the sky" (*Eu.* 368), which tempt them to turn the sword of Ares against their own kin (356). The reference to Agamemnon could hardly be clearer. When Agamemnon contemplated sacrificing his daughter, he weighed the same two opposed values (*A.* 205–17). Aeschylus does not complicate his plot by any direct suggestion that the Erinyes took cognizance of Agamemnon's crime; but both here and at the end of the second ode their words point to the inevitable justice of his fate. These two kinds of value are referred to also as opposed *thesmoi*, "ordinances": that of the Erinyes, and that of Athena. Athena in 681 bids the people of Attica "listen to my ordinance." How she sets forth her principles in word, and how she puts them into practice, has already been shown in chapter 6. But the chorus too has called upon all citizens to respond with reverence and fear as they "listen to my ordinance" (391). The ordinance of respect for kindred blood, and of inexorable punishment for acts incurring indelible pollution, was older by an age than Athena's; and without it, as the trial will show, no judicial system, even presided over by a goddess, could preserve its integrity.

When the Erinyes first explain their case to Athena, a crucial point is left unclarified: Is the plea of provocation, of mitigating circumstance, to be admitted? The chorus state in 425 and 427 that in their view matricide is unpardonable, that no external pressure could provide a valid excuse; while Athena implies in 426 that such pressure would have to be considered. But it is also clear from the second ode that the Erinyes never accept this. For them, matricide is ultimate pollution; and Orestes himself acknowledged this in *Ch.* 438 and elsewhere. And since this view is opposed only by Athena and Apollo, whose integrity is, at best, shown to be dubious, it is fair to assume that the poet's view is the view he gives to the Erinyes.

Before the trial begins, the chorus in their second ode surmise what will happen to human society if a crime such as matricide can win acquittal in a court solemnly constituted to determine justice:

> The Furies' watchful rage shall sleep,
> No anger hunt the guilty soul;
> Murder shall flout my lost control,
> While neighbours talk of wrongs, and weep,
> And ask how flesh can more endure,

Or stem the swelling flood of ill,
Or hope for better times—while still
Each wretch commends some useless cure.

The audience will be assessors to the Areopagites; and the chorus addresses to them these reminders:

Somewhere salutary terror must remain enthroned, overseeing men's hearts. . . . What man, what city, having nothing to fear, will still reverence right? . . . I bid you reverence the altar of Justice; let no man, through sight of gain, spurn that altar with godless foot; punishment will follow. . . . The man who is willingly just, without compulsion, shall not miss his reward. But the arrogant man who defies right will be shipwrecked; he will call, and no one will answer.

That last phrase (558) has two earlier echoes. When Iphigenia was sacrificed she called upon the chiefs, and on her father by name, to show mercy; they did not listen, and Agamemnon told the attendants to gag her. In the first choral ode of *Agamemnon* (396) the Elders describe the fate of the arrogant, willful man: "None of the gods listens to his prayers." Those lines ostensibly refer to Paris, but they apply more closely to Agamemnon. He was punished with death for shedding kindred blood; now his son will be tried for shedding kindred blood, and in this ode his father's fate is recalled. Was justice done in the former case? Will it be done now?

The trial opens with trumpets and a procession. Athena, daughter of Zeus, and Apollo, son of Zeus, are in their places. Athena tells the chorus leader to open the proceedings by explaining exactly the nature of the charge. Since this has been done fully in the two choral odes, all that is needed now is a short cross-questioning of Orestes (587ff.):

CH. Did you kill your mother?
OR. Yes.
CH. How?
OR. I drew my sword and cut her throat.
CH. Who urged you to do this?
OR. Apollo.
CH. The prophet-god told you to kill your mother?
OR. Yes. She killed my father.
CH. She has paid for her act with death. You still live.
OR. Why did you not pursue her while she lived?
CH. The man she killed was not of her own blood.
OR. But I—am I of one blood with my mother?
CH. Did she not nourish you in her womb, polluted man? Do you deny your own mother's blood?

At that point Orestes hands over the defense to Apollo. He acknowledges the matricide; but asks Apollo to say whether, in his opinion, the act was just or unjust. This, of course, is strictly not the question before the court. The Erinyes hold that the guilt of matricide is absolute; but they have been maneuvered into conceding that provocation, or extenuating circumstances, may be considered; and Athena has from the beginning ignored the vital difference between matricide and homicide. Apollo now takes advantage of this position to turn the trial of Orestes, in effect, into the trial of Clytemnestra. What he does not acknowledge is that, if the plea of provocation is to be allowed to Orestes, it should in justice be allowed also to Clytemnestra. Lying always below the surface, never openly expressed, is the dangerous question: Is justice the same thing for a woman as for a man? To this Athena will in due course give a clear answer. For the present, however, the Erinyes are concerned with principles of right and wrong rather than with legal logic, and they do not take up this point.

The process of the trial in fact consists, after Apollo's first speech, of three brief questions asked by the Erinyes and Apollo's replies to them. These replies, amounting to about forty lines in all, are a remarkable mixture of prevarication, angry abuse, false logic, corrupt soliciting, and irrelevant theory. (See chapter 6.) The Erinyes can only trust the good faith and moral sense of the jurors, to whom they say simply, "You have heard what you have heard." If the Areopagites cannot see through Apollo, then indeed there is nothing but despair.

The chorus listen to Athena's two speeches, before and after the voting; but it is not the votes that decide the verdict. Democracy is after all overruled by ancient national tradition, of which Athena's words (736ff.) are the creed, and herself the symbol. When Athena announces, "Orestes wins his case," the Erinyes are shocked into silence. Their whole existence is involved with human society, with preserving the ultimate basis of a moral social order. What will now happen in a city where such a crime can hope for acquittal? The plagues which in their second ode they foresaw falling on Athens will not come from malevolence on their part, but will inevitably follow the pattern of cause and effect which is Zeus' rule for governing the world: *pathein ton erxanta*, "the doer suffers." When a city's votes decide that a guilty man shall not suffer, but be discharged honorably, it is the city that will suffer. By the time the next play about Orestes' matricide was produced (probably Euripides' *Electra*, in 418 B.C.), Athens and Hellas had already for twelve years been suffering the horrendous reality of that prophecy which here Aeschylus gives the Erinyes to utter (780ff.):

> Dishonour moves my heart to anger. I shall pour forth poison over this land, poison to match my grief, an intolerable blight upon the soil, killing plant and child, scabbing the earth's face with infectious sores.

Athena pleads with the Erinyes. The trial was quite fair, she says: "clear evidence coming from Zeus" made it impossible to condemn Orestes. Reference to *Eu.* 616–21 may be held to show that Athena's account of the trial is as false as her own betrayal of an agreed principle. The Erinyes do not reply, but repeat their lament, Athena continues to offer consolation and inducements, together with the threat of Zeus' thunderbolt.

If the terms in which that threat is conveyed carry undertones readily recognizable today, the inducements offered with it similarly invite scrutiny. What inducements does Athena in fact offer to the Erinyes to compensate them not merely for the ignominy of their judicial defeat, but still more for the loss of their peculiar and morally indispensable cosmic function?

After telling them, "You have not been defeated" (795), and speaking of "clear evidence from Zeus" (which in fact is as nonexistent as the "clear evidence" Orestes speaks of in 447; see chapter 3), Athena proceeds, with two verbal acknowledgments to justice (*pandikōs*, 804; *endikou*, 805), to that standard gesture of diplomacy, the offer of gifts. Just as Orestes and Apollo offer to Athens the alliance of Argos, so Athena now offers the Erinyes a permanent home, bright thrones, altars, and honor from the citizens. In her next speech she adds prerogatives in the rituals of birth and marriage; and promises a place beside herself in the greatest city of Hellas. She uses flattery—"You are older and wiser than I" (848f.); she invokes the divinity of Persuasion (885f.); refers again to the honor that awaits them in Athens (868, 891), and to the "justice" of her proposals.

It is clear that all the cards are now in Athena's hand; and the chorus leader capitulates:

> CH. Divine Athena, what position do you say I am to have?
> ATH. One free from all distress. Accept it.
> CH. Say I accept it: what honour remains for me?
> ATH. No house shall prosper without your favour.
> CH. You will perform this, accord me such power?
> ATH. We will give blessings to those who revere you.

Athena has won her victory—cheaply. What she has promised amounts to little in itself, and includes no restoration of the cosmic dignity she has destroyed. In this final contest, has "the good" prevailed? The guardians of social morality have abdicated, leaving the city no defense against the moral evils forecast in the second choral ode. The chorus now forget those fears, abandon a position that is no longer defensible, and promise material blessings. Athena responds with a vague pretense that their primeval moral function will still operate (930–37):

> These divinities have the disposal of all mortal destinies. . . . He who wins their enmity knows not whence come the blows of life; for the

sins of his fathers hail him before their judgement-seat; and though he cry aloud, silent destruction in anger grinds him to dust.

But Athena speaks these words ten minutes after she has demonstrated that even a confessed matricide can escape the threatened destruction; that it is not the Erinyes, nor the *dikastai*, who have the arbitrary disposal of mortal destinies, but Athena herself—in other words, the Athenian city-state, with all its traditions and immovable prejudices, and with the hidden power of Delphi at its back. The Erinyes would have ended the blood feud by destroying Orestes for his own and his father's sins; but Athena has foiled them. Now she is harsh in her mockery, as she turns to the jurors, calling them (as in 701) "the city's bodyguard" (949ff.):

Do you hear these blessings they will bring us? Great is the power of an Erinys both among immortals and among the nether gods; and it is clear how effectively, in human affairs, they dispense songs of joy to some, and to others, tears.

Having no reply to this, the Erinyes continue to chant their promise of material blessings upon Athens; and presently Athena will say that "from these fearsome faces *I see great gain (mega kerdos horō)* for my citizens"—which may, or may not, carry an ironic reference to 941, where the chorus says, "Let no one *through sight of gain (kerdos idōn)* spurn the altar of Justice." Athena sums up her triumph by saying (968–75) that Zeus Agoraios, Zeus of the law courts, has won the victory, *ekratēse*, by the art of *Peithō*, Persuasion, working through Athena's own eloquence. Is not this *Peithō* the same that the Elders in A. 385 called *talaina*, "relentless," "the intolerable child of scheming Ruin"? and is *ekratēse* (973) anything other than *biatai*? The juxtaposition of Persuasion and Force in these two passages, near the beginning and the end of the trilogy, can hardly be accidental. (See chapter 2.)

The chorus know that they are defeated, and no one will replace them. The Elders themselves in their last scene prayed for matricide (A. 1646ff.), and their wish has been granted. Victory has gone, not to the good, but to violent revenge in its most polluting aspect. Argos will have in Orestes a king unfit to perform his holy office (Eu. 654ff.). The integrity of an Athenian law court is now under question. The guardians of *aidōs* have themselves accepted bribes and abandoned their function. Henceforth they will be *eumenides*, "kindly," to those who most need the sternness for which they were once feared. In the closing lines of the trilogy they join with Athena in invoking upon the city every kind of blessing, in a hymn of joy and confidence which surely moved some in the first audience to tears. Perhaps patriotic emotion saved them from understanding that they were more likely to inherit the curse the Erinyes uttered before they were corrupted, than the blessing they pronounced after. With this unheard prophecy the poet closes his drama.

The answer, then, to the question, Who are the Erinyes? is twofold. Popular belief held that they were bloodthirsty demons who will punish you if you mis behave, and whose terrors can be used to make people act as you think they ought to act. So Apollo uses them to coerce Orestes. But the tragic poet has a profounder conception. As he presents them, the Erinyes guard the primeval, minimal basis of social morality. They recognize, and allow for, current assumptions. They do not pursue a husband-killer, because society and the male-oriented Olympian religion will provide for that, as the trial of Orestes shows; nor do they pursue the blood-guilty Agamemnon, since a society that regards women as Athens does, and has never finally condemned the exposure of infants, will easily forget Iphigenia, as everyone in the trilogy does. The Erinyes guard only those principles that are accepted *by all* (cf. *Ch.* 902, *hapantas*) as indispensable to a healthy society. In portraying these deities as inexorable in their justice the poet declares his belief that love of good is ineffective without hatred of evil.

III
Two Other Plays

I I

The Grotesque and the
Desperate: *Suppliants*

The Suppliant Women was until a generation ago thought to be the poet's earliest surviving work, written when he was thirty or less, in the decade before the battle of Marathon. This view was based on several considerations. Some of the dialogue is archaic, even stilted; only two actors are employed. The story is naive; and the impression of naiveté is strengthened by the prominence given in both lyrics and dialogue to another ancient and naive story—the story of Io, whom Zeus loved and Hera turned into a cow. All this seemed to suggest that the play was an early work. Then a fragment discovered among the Oxyrrhynchus papyri provided evidence that *Suppliants* was produced not earlier than 466 B.C., when Aeschylus was not thirty years old but nearly sixty, a mature artist and thinker already gestating the monumental trilogy of the House of Atreus. This later date has been generally confirmed by scholarly opinion.

This surprising change might have made little difference to our understanding of Aeschylus if the subject of the play had been, shall we say, the story of the *Seven Against Thebes*. But this is not only a strange story in itself, but especially strange as a story offered for the entertainment of Athenian citizens in the fifth century B.C. More than this, now that we know it was produced at a time when Aeschylus must already have been thinking about Clytemnestra, Iphigenia, and Agamemnon, we become aware of a theme, common to both works, which may well illuminate each by reference to the other.

The fifty virgin daughters of Danaus[1] fill the orchestra and stage, and sit as suppliants at altars of Zeus, Apollo, Hermes, and Poseidon. In the background we see the walls and towers of the city of Argos. The girls have landed from a ship in which they and their father have sailed from Egypt to the Peloponnese. In their opening recital, which continues for 175 lines, they tell us their story and their predicament. Their story is grotesque, their predicament is desperate; and throughout the play these two qualities, two incongruous worlds of fantasy and realism, alternate in speech and action. The play is the first of a trilogy. What happens in the second play is apparently outlined in *Prometheus* 853–69; but since both the authorship and the date of *Prometheus* are questionable, it is best, for the purposes of this chapter, to limit our argument to the text of *Suppliants*, referring occasionally to *Prometheus* "without prejudice." From the third play a single fragment supplies a tantalizing clue.

The Danaids begin by telling us that they have fled from Egypt under their father's guidance because their cousins, the sons of Aegyptus, Danaus' brother, want to marry them and intend to do so by force. The young men are now in pursuit in another ship, and will arrive in the course of the play. The Danaids make quite plain the reason why they do not want to marry their cousins. It is not because they are closely related; marriage with cousins was acceptable in Greece, and in fifth-century Athens was in certain cases required by law; while in Egyptian royal families marriage even of brother with sister was frequent. Neither should we accept the reasons that Danaus gives in 225ff., where he tells his daughters that marriage with Egyptians "would pollute your race," and that the behavior of these young men is an unpardonable crime. Both Danaus and his brother Aegyptus are descendants of Io, who five generations earlier had borne a son to Zeus in Egypt; and Danaus' daughters, like their cousins, are swarthy in complexion, which evidently implies that they are of mixed Greek and Egyptian blood. As for the young men's claim to marry their cousins whether the girls like it or not, no audience anywhere in Greece would call that a crime, since submission to a husband not of her own choice was the rule for daughters of every free family in every city.

The reason why the Danaids have fled from Egypt is simply that they do not like the manners of these young men and do not want to marry them. They also insist that it is an injustice, an affront to their dignity as free women, to be given no choice, but subjected to physical compulsion. The princes are offering proper, formal marriage—it is not casual rape that the girls are objecting to, but matrimony. To be a wife without free consent, they say, is to be a slave; they use the unequivocal word *dmōis* (335). They do not ask to be allowed to pick husbands for themselves; but they demand the right of refusal with such desperation that they will commit suicide if they are denied it. They may be only a crowd of young girls; but the simple directness and force of everything they say is entirely convincing, so that when they speak in these terms to Pelasgus king of Argos, he trembles in horror at the thought of seeing the altars of the gods of Argos polluted with dead bodies.

Desperation, then, is the first dominant note in the opening chorus:

> Hear us, you gods of marriage: let Justice triumph,
> Let wild youth not accomplish its wicked lust;
> Let pride be quelled by your abhorrence;
> Fulfil for us such wedlock as is right. . . .

And may Artemis, daughter of Zeus, lover of chastity,
In mercy respect my chaste desires;
Let her come in all her strength,
A virgin to a virgin's rescue,
And foil this lust that pursues us. . . .
And if not—then to the house the sun abhors,
To Zeus of the lower earth, lord of the dead,
We will come with our suppliant branches;
For we will hang and die by the noose
If the gods of Olympus refuse to hear us.

But the second dominant note of the play, the note of the grotesque, is equally clear in this long recital, which refers five times to the story of Io, princess of Argos, the great-great-great-grandmother of the Danaids:

Here in Argos our family began, which now claims origin
From that tormented beast . . . the Cow, mother of our race,
Made pregnant by the breathing and caress of Zeus.

The story is told with more detail in the first choral ode, an exquisite and moving poem; and it is supplemented in *Prometheus*, where Io herself tells how Zeus wooed her. The two accounts have one surprising feature in common: Zeus' wooing is not peremptory, as in his other unions—with Leda, Alcmene, Danae, Antiope; with Io Zeus is gentle. Here are Io's words (*Pr.* 645–57):

At night in my own room visions would visit me,
With gentle words persuading me: 'Most blessed maid,
Why live a virgin for so long? Love waits for you—
The greatest. Zeus, aflame with arrows of desire,
Longs to unite with you in love. Do not reject,
My child, the bed of Zeus. Go out to the deep grass
Of Lerna, where your father's sheep and cattle graze,
That the eye of Zeus may rest from longing and be satisfied.'
    By such dreams every troubled night I was beset,
Until I dared to tell my father.

And these lines from the first stasimon of *Suppliants* describe the meeting of Zeus with Io in Egypt:

Men of those days, inhabitants of Egypt,
Trembled at heart and were pale with terror.
They saw a creature at once human and brute,
Part cow, part woman, and were speechless at the prodigy.
And then—then, who was it comforted her,
Pitied the misery of her long wandering,
The pang of the whirling sting that tortured Io?
It was Zeus, who rules in sole and endless power.

> Zeus, with tender strength,
> Breathing on her the breath of godhead, brought her rest.

So, at the beginning of *Suppliants*, the fifty Danaids, harassed by arrogant and violent suitors, identify their cause with that of their ancestress Io, who suffered the cruelty of her father and of Hera, but had a gentle god for her lover.

Presently comes Pelasgus, the reigning king of Argos, to ask who they are and why they have come. Danaus keeps out of sight and leaves the chorus leader to speak. Naturally she tells of their descent from Io, and claims to be of Argive blood; but the formal and prosaic dialogue in which the well-known story is recounted lays what seems to be an altogether unnecessary emphasis on its grotesque element. It begins with a strangely modern kind of joke—in fact, two jokes. The chorus leader asks Pelasgus whether he is an Argive citizen or the king. Pelasgus then spreads himself for twenty-one lines to describe the vast extent of his dominions, and ends by saying,

> Now tell me who you are, and clearly, in few words; Argos dislikes
> long speeches.
> CH. Then, in few words, and clearly: we claim to be of Argive blood. We
> are descended from a fertile cow.
> KING Women, I find it hard to believe the story you tell me, that you are of
> Argive descent.

To convince him, the chorus leader unfolds in pedantic detail Io's metamorphosis; how Hera changed Io to a cow, Zeus turned himself into a bull, Hera set a giant with a hundred eyes to keep the bull from the cow, Hermes killed the giant, and Hera replaced him with a gadfly which drove Io in torment over some eighteen hundred miles through Asia and Syria to Egypt. Then at last Hera abandoned her jealousy; Zeus fulfilled his love for Io and gave her a son. The story is grotesque; but the emphasis laid on its grotesqueness is certainly not necessary to the plot of *Suppliants*. What then is its purpose?

When the king inquires what favor they seek, they demand that he protect them against the pursuing Egyptians. This evidently will mean undertaking a battle. The king is reluctant; the more so because, if the girls are of Argive descent, so are their cousins, and to kill them in battle is to shed kindred blood (449). But the girls, by sitting as suppliants at the altar of Zeus, have made it impossible for the king to ignore their request; and they go further. Unless the king gives his word not to hand them over to their pursuers, they will take the girdles from their gowns and hang themselves there and then in the holy place. The pollution of such an act would endanger the whole city. Is this threat a silly gesture on the part of hysterical young women? King Pelasgus does not think so; and we can see why. So far in the play the chorus has spoken considerably more than half the lines; and they have not spoken like children. Their words have force, directness, poetic power, and desperate conviction. This play is not a pantomime; it is a matter of life and death. The king, though sole ruler, cannot commit Argos to war without the citizens' consent. He promises to use all his power of persuasion to gain this; and tells Danaus too to go as suppliant to altars in the city. When they have both gone, the chorus sing their long and lovely poem telling the story of Io; and we have time to reflect upon this very unusual drama.

The description of a young woman half changed into a cow, maddened by a gadfly, and traveling all around the eastern end of the Mediterranean, to become the bride of Zeus in Egypt—this is not the only grotesque element in the play. Another is the fact that the protagonist is not one harassed virgin, but fifty. The plot, powered by the impulse for freedom and defiance of oppressors, one step from suicide, is undoubtedly a tragic plot. The tragedy—if we may rely on *Prometheus*—intensifies in the second play of the trilogy, where these girls murder their bridegrooms on the wedding night. Tragedy is an individual matter; to multiply it by fifty, or even by twelve or fifteen, is grotesque. Much has been written about the pageantry of fifty Egyptian beauties in gorgeous costume, with their fifty maids, balanced on stage by the bodyguards of Pelasgus and of Danaus, numerous enough to cope with a band of Egyptians accompanying the Herald—themselves numerous enough to attempt the forcible abduction of fifty or a hundred resolute young women—the total assembly could approach 250 persons. Yet, it is impossible to read sensitively the impassioned text of this play and still believe that pageantry was its essence. Which is truly the play—the spectacular choreography or the tragic text? Pageantry demands a certain grandeur of scale, it gains power through a perspective of repetition; but tragedy loses far more than it gains when its operation is multiplied. For a woman to hang herself before our eyes, or for a bride to kill her husband, may potently arouse pity and fear; but to present the picture in multiple must either introduce a sense of the ludicrous, or claim a different and exact significance in itself. Since the author does nothing to mitigate the antitragic effect of his crowded stage, but rather the reverse, we should look for his reason. The new dating of the play is crucial; for its author is about to become the author of the *Oresteia*. I do not believe that a poet of Aeschylus' stature tolerated the grotesqueness for the sake of the story; rather I suggest that he chose the story for the sake of its grotesqueness, because through this quality he could say something he wanted to say.

What was it, then, that he wanted to say? What he does in fact say is, in its plain meaning, something which, taken literally, seemed to the first audience even more fantastic than Io's horns. So, of course, they consigned it, along with the horns, the gadfly, and the forty-nine bridal murders, to the world of fantasy, as suitable material for a spectacular drama full of exquisite poetry and much else that could divert the mind from what was being said. But in truth what was being said was far from fantasy; it pictured a realistic situation that could arise in every home represented in the audience. Here is a group of young women claiming desperately that their personal wishes be respected in the choice of husbands. When Pelasgus points out that the cousins may have a legal right to marry them—Athenian law made similar provisions—the chorus leader roundly replies, "Whatever right they may have, may I never become subject to the rights of men"; and the word used for "rights" (*kratesin*, 393) bears also the meaning of "acts of violence."

The climax of tragedy surely came in the second play, when these young women disastrously adopt the same violence that has been used against them. "Not the same violence at all," the Athenian citizen would reasonably comment. "What they did was murder; what they were threatened with was marriage—on the same terms as every girl has to accept." What do the Danaids say about it? (787ff.)

> I would rather meet my fate in a drawn noose
> Than give my flesh to a husband I abhor,
> Or marry in despite of my heart;
> Sooner let Death possess me!

—which is exactly what Euripides' Medea said a generation later: "If you are unlucky in your husband, *thanein chreōn*, you must die." When the Egyptians are landing and Danaus is setting off to bring help, his daughters' despair is extreme: "Father, I entreat you!" (748). This chorus describes as outrageous brutality what was normal Athenian practice. It is easy to understand that a daughter's reluctance was a matter over which no citizen would admit to having problems; Aeschylus could therefore let his Danaids voice their demands explicitly, confident that the preposterous proposition would be heard and dismissed as an antique quaintness. Had it been taken seriously, it is unlikely that the play would ever have reached performance, to survive for our puzzlement. Can any reason be suggested why Aeschylus wrote it at all, unless he meant to assert against tradition and expediency the plea of the heart, the rights of free birth, the dignity of humanity? unless he meant the words of his chorus, in their tragic seriousness, to carry the weight of their simple meaning? Their appeal is, like Io's, to Zeus against Hera, to the tenderness of love against the harshness of an institution, to a justice not merely legal but humane, against the universal practice of society both Hellene and barbarian. This is why they insist that what they claim is justice; for in Greek eyes the final injustice was to treat a free person as a slave. These are unmarried daughters, the only class in the free world who have no rights; subject to a dishonor otherwise reserved for cattle—treatment, that is to say, for which the metamorphosis of Io into a cow, with all the shameful details of Hera's cruelty, is not too grotesque an image.

This view of the play accounts for some of its peculiar features; but it must also be stated that there is an opposite view. It can be maintained that in this trilogy Aeschylus is not defending, but opposing, the cause of unmarried daughters. The plight of these girls is apparently pitiful, their plea for freedom to say No sounds like a plea for justice, their courage and resolution win some respect at first; but their next move, after many Argive citizens have died in their defense, is to pretend to accept marriage after all, and then murder their bridegrooms. Such treachery, such betrayal of Argive hospitality, suggests that the Danaids' indignant appeals were hysterical or false; their shedding of kindred blood shows them irresponsible, unfit to exercise the freedom they demanded; and confirms the danger of relaxing male control over the marriage of daughters. The likelihood that after their bloody exploit they would soon be longing in vain for men who would dare to marry them seems to clinch the lesson of their female folly.

It is hard to judge which of these arguments is the more valid, or to guess which of them was more strongly presented in the two lost plays. What seems clear is that the poet wished to voice a seldom-raised question which was not confined to either Athenian or Greek society. The enormous number of tremulous virgins on stage, which in the context of suicide, or of the murder of bridegrooms, makes grotesque overtones audible, surely carries also a constructive implication. For their predicament is not individual, not national, but universal; east or west of the Aegean, no virgin could choose or reject a husband. We should note, further, that the story of the Danaids' revolt against male rule is only one of three such legends known to us, all involving entire communities of women. The Lemnian massacre is referred to in *Ch.* 631 ff. as an inevitable and frightening parallel to Clytemnestra's murder of her husband, and again in Euripides' *Hecabe* 886f., where it is coupled with the Danaids' crime; and in *The Bacchae* the mass defiance by Theban women of their husbands' authority and Pentheus' soldiers reflects even more specifically women's resentment of the increased dominance given to men by the growth of large cities and military organization. The Danaids on the one hand identify themselves with their ancestress, the desired, bullied, and defenseless Io; and on the other hand they speak for young women of every century, and especially for their counterparts in the free families of contemporary Athens, where an unmarried daughter, however loved and cherished, had no more right to the freedom of her own body than the cow grazing in the Lernaean meadow, and at the first show of independence was liable to suffer humiliation at the hands of her father and her family. We may also see meaning in the poet's insistence that the source of Io's torments was not her lover, Zeus, but Hera, goddess of marriage. It is the man-controlled institution that inevitably enlists, as the persecutors of other women, that majority of women who find their only security in total acceptance of the subordinate status that marriage allots to them.

The part played by Danaus in *Suppliants* is of great interest, but discussion of it must be omitted here as less relevant to the principal theme of this book. It only remains to mention, without detailed study, the prominence given in this play to a topic already discussed in chapter 2: the power of *Peithō*, the goddess Persuasion, and the contrasted use of *Bia*, Force. Every scene, every action, in *Suppliants* can be described in these terms. Here, however, this power is shown as allied equally to good and to evil purposes; whereas in the *Oresteia* its operation is chiefly destructive.

Thus the study of *Suppliants*, while it may not solve any of the problems of the *Oresteia*, helps to set in perspective several of the ideas around which the trilogy is built. It does not, however, include any analysis of heroic character and quality. This is a main theme of *Seven Against Thebes*, to which we turn in the next chapter.

12

The Hero under Test: *Seven Against Thebes*

Aeschylus' play *Seven Against Thebes* is not often produced on the modern stage. One reason for this is clear: it is the third play of a trilogy. To feel its dramatic movement, the audience must know the story well, as the first audience knew it. They had just watched *Laius* and *Oedipus*; their minds were full of those earlier events, and certainly they also knew, from the second play, that when the third play ends the two brothers must fulfill their father's curse by killing each other. They were aware of the sinister power of a curse, of the stark realities of war, and of the indelible pollution incurred in shedding kindred blood. An audience whose minds are so prepared can enter into the tense apprehension that belongs to this static drama, unique in the simplicity of its structure. Today such audiences do not exist; so for us the play comes to life more powerfully in the study or classroom than in the theater.

Any comment written today must take account of the admirably comprehensive and subtle study by R. P. Winnington-Ingram which appeared in *Yale Classical Studies*, 1977. The suggestions I put forward in this more limited essay do not, I feel, conflict with the view there taken, nor are they invalidated by it. All the points I raise are discussed in that article; but I think it is possible, and desirable, by simplifying the statement of the problems, to carry conclusions through to a more complete and positive interpretation, one that I believe to be close to the kind of moral argument Aeschylus worked out fully in the *Oresteia*, and probably also in the Danaid trilogy.

I propose to examine three questions: (1) How does Aeschylus present the character of Eteocles? (2) Why is no clear moral issue presented at the opening of the play? (3) At what point does Eteocles become aware of the possibility that he may confront his brother?

Winnington-Ingram writes (p. 8) of "the Eteocles of the first part and the Eteocles of the second part." I would rather say that Aeschylus has presented Eteocles in three distinct aspects.

Almost as soon as he begins to speak he indicates (4–9) that he is a man smarting under criticism, stating that if things should go wrong, Eteocles would be the one name chanted by citizens in anger and discontent. This could allude to his father's curse, which was common knowledge. But the curse, like the inheritance, belonged to both brothers. If citizens reproached Eteocles for the curse, there was an obvious answer: "My cause is just; Polyneices acts unjustly." But never, until after the fatal die is cast, does Eteocles dare to claim (667) that his cause is just. First we have his admission that he is liable to be blamed by angry citizens. Then comes the Spy's moving description of the Seven, with blood on their hands, vows on their lips, and tears in their eyes (41–51). And a few lines later (69ff.) comes the king's prayer for the safety of Thebes. After addressing Zeus, Earth, and the city's gods, he prays to "my father's curse, mighty in vengeance," not to condemn "the city at least" (*polin ge*, 71), to total destruction. We do not know until later (689ff.) that this fear haunts him; nor do we know yet whether that dread is stronger, or weaker, than another passion of which so far we are given no hint. Eteocles is at the moment responsible, controlled, courageous; but he fears criticism, and avoids claiming justice for his cause.

The chorus enters, panic-stricken, expecting havoc, rape, slavery, and death. Again and again they call on gods and goddesses, appealing to eight or more by name, to save them. They offer the usual pleas—the pious gifts they have made to temples, and the legendary connection of individual gods with their city's history. But there is one plea they do not offer, which would seem to have an obvious force. The enemy they fear is a man who attacks the place of his birth—an impiety that every god worshiped in Thebes must resent; yet the chorus do not mention it. Why is this? If Eteocles were known, to them and to the audience, to have committed some act no less impious than his brother's, no further explanation would be needed. But there is nothing in this play corresponding to Euripides, *Phoenissae* 154f., where Antigone's Tutor says to her:

> Our enemies come with a just cause; I fear lest the gods may see this all too well.

Had Aeschylus shown us that something like this lay unspoken in the minds of the chorus, and recognizable by some of the audience, both the women's panic and the king's manner of dealing with it would be fully accounted for.

Why does Aeschylus devote the king's second scene to a scolding encounter with semi-hysterical women? This could well have been replaced by some alternative dialogue more conducive to royal dignity. Here there is neither decision nor, until the very end, information. All that is attempted or achieved is the quieting of the panic by arguments and threats of a kind which a king would be wiser to depute to a subordinate (181ff.):

You intolerable creatures! I ask you, is this the way
To save us? Will this encourage our fighters on the walls—
To fling yourselves on statues of our guardian gods
And howl and shriek, to every sane person's disgust?
Women! In wartime, or amid the blessings of peace,
Save me from living with them! Give women their own way,
They're bold past bearing; but, once they're alarmed, they double
Every difficulty, in the city and in the home. . . .
Now, anyone who disregards my authority
Shall die, without appeal, stoned by the people's hands. . . .
You have no place out here; get indoors, where you can do
No harm. Do you hear or do you not? Or are you deaf?

The last line indicates that the threat has made little impact. The women fear
Capaneus, not Eteocles. He reasons with them; but furious impatience is not
far below the surface (256):

Zeus! What a gift you bestowed on us in women!

He refers again twice (223, 236) to his mistrust of the citizens' morale. When
the scene is almost over, one important piece of information comes in 282:

I will post at the gates six men, with myself as seventh.

For the rest, the scene presents him as a man deficient in authority, dignity, and
wisdom; doing his best according to his capacity; but here, as before, avoiding
reference to the justice of his cause.

When he reenters at 369 he is surrounded on the stage by six other warriors;
and the chorus, reassured, make their seemly contributions from the orchestra.
This is a different Eteocles. He is now a man among men, a model of steady
nerve and ready wit. He abhors pride, threats, and blasphemies; and admires
modest courage and piety. In preparing his forces for battle he is all that a king
should be. This is not the moment for protesting that his cause is just; nothing
matters but fighting and winning. As speech follows speech we forget misgiv-
ings felt in his earlier appearances. Aeschylus knew that it is a habit of the human mind to accept, for each individual, some single image which has been
authoritatively presented, and to let this image govern judgments of all that
person's acts, of whatever nature (this is seen with special clarity in the *Oresteia*). Eteocles is usually given credit for being, in his essential self, the person
we meet in this central episode, 369–625.

But the truth is that three different portraits are shown in three successive
contexts. The second context is the military scene, where principles are simple,
duties direct, manners formally controlled by the prime necessity of courage
and piety. In this context Eteocles can be the man his citizens wish him to be.

But earlier, facing civilians, he lacked confidence and dignity. And now, after 631, when he has left no warrior but himself to face Polyneices, suddenly the steady, responsible facade explodes, revealing what to the women of the chorus, and to the soldier who has been reporting from the city wall, can only appear as the obsession of a madman (653ff.):

> O house that gods drive mad, that gods so deeply hate,
> O house of endless tears, our house of Oedipus!
> It is his curse that now bears fruit in us his sons.
> Yet there's no time for either tears or groans, for fear
> This agony bear interest more crushing still.
> For Polyneices—truly named—we shall soon know
> What truth is in his blazon. . . .
> But neither when he escaped the darkness of the womb,
> Nor as a child, nor when he first reached manhood, nor
> When the hair of his beard grew thick, ever by word or look
> Would Justice acknowledge him. Now surely least of all,
> When his own city suffers violence at his hand,
> Does Justice stand beside him. Should she join with one
> So infatuate, Justice would herself be named a lie.
> In this faith I will go and face him—I myself.
> Who has a stronger right than I? Chief against chief
> I'll match him, brother to brother, enemy to enemy.

His care for the city has vanished; piety is scorned, pollution welcomed (690f.):

> Then let the wind of doom, Hell's tide, and Phoebus' hate
> Bear down to ruin Laius' race to the last man.

What lies behind this astonishing third phase it now remains to inquire.

My second question, Why is no clear moral issue presented? arises from the curious fact that nowhere in the text does Aeschylus tell us why the Seven came from Peloponnese to fight against Thebes. We are told simply, "There is a war; the decisive attack on the town is beginning; the battle must be won at all costs." Nothing is said about what has led to the war. Eteocles claims no justice for his cause. The play seems to assume that the brothers could rightly claim equal shares in their inheritance (727ff., 817). It is never stated which of them was the elder, or how Eteocles established himself as king, or whether there was any agreement about Polyneices' return to his city.

Clearly we should expect the answer to lie in the lost play *Oedipus*. But we can see from the summary of that play's content given by the chorus in their second ode that there can have been no room in it for the story of the brothers' quarrel to be acted out. *Oedipus* must certainly have contained the father's curse upon his sons, and clarified its terms, probably including the "Chalybian stranger, iron" (727–30). But to explain the rights and wrongs of the dispute between the brothers would have thrown the second play quite out of balance. The place for such explanations could only be in the third play; and Aeschylus has not given them. There must surely be a reason for this. In *Persians* the fatal error of Xerxes, his blind *hubris*, is referred to in the opening lyrics and reiterated in every episode. In *Suppliants* the Danaids explain their predicament and assert their right in the first ten lines, and subsequently claim justice with ever-increasing vehemence. In *Agamemnon* Aeschylus devotes the longest lyric parodos in ancient tragedy to the single act of ambitious inhumanity that begot the ensuing disasters; and in the succeeding phases of that drama persuasion, guilt, and retribution are firmly linked. It is reasonable, then, to ask why in this play alone the poet should state no moral equation, offering instead only the dying curse of an enraged and frantic parent, and the inherited temperament which is the psychological equivalent of that curse.

In the first minutes of the play (41–51), there is a passage that invites speculation and may perhaps offer a clue. These lines tell of the deep and desperate rage against Thebes and its king that fills the seven chiefs who lead the besieging army. On the morning of the attack the Spy watched them kill a bull, dip their hands in its blood, and swear in the name of War, Havoc, and bloodthirsty Terror to annihilate Thebes or die. What is the point of this "purple passage"? Of course the dramatist needed to convey from the outset that the city was in real danger; but this bull-slaying has always seemed somewhat forced and unrelated—the more so, because its point is not merely the formidable power of the attacking force, as these lines show (49ff.):

> They hung on Adrastus' chariot tokens of themselves
> To be taken home to their parents; they shed tears, but none
> Uttered a word of grief.

What the Spy's report conveys is the personal indignation of seven warriors who, being by no means certain of victory, think of death with tears, but still are resolute in their purpose. The ritual included the honorable Amphiaraus. What they seek seems to be not plunder, or revenge for injury done to themselves, but the redress of some wrong that they cannot let pass. It is hard to imagine the poet inventing that description unless he meant that his audience should recognize, in this deep indignation, the natural consequence of some act of Eteocles which he has already foreshadowed but not declared, an act which this bloody ritual now tells us has indeed been committed and has brought its necessary effect in this implacable anger.

If the account of the bull-slaying brings some such act into the third play as an operative element in Eteocles' situation, where was it first spoken of? Speculation about the content of a lost play is not a premise for argument; but we may remember too that understanding a play demands imagination. A reasonable guess is that the curse uttered by Oedipus included, in figurative, oracular language, a foreboding of some impious act; and that the third play gives us first a succession of echoes of that act, then a revelation of the source it sprang from. The echoes are those passages in the prologue and first episode which have already been discussed; the uneasiness caused by the echoes generates a tension that increases throughout the first half of the play; and the long central scene not only increases the tension but, by its pervading tone of piety and modesty, adds a shock of astonishment to the revelation in which it culminates. Eteocles' outburst (658–76), in revealing a short lifetime of hatred, illuminates the source of his fear of criticism, the reason for his lack of authority, the cause of the anger of the Seven. It tells us that the posture of modest piety was assumed and precarious and is now cast aside.

Thus my second question has involved an excursus into surmise which claims no critical cogency, but may prove suggestive when taken in conjunction with the third question: At what point does Eteocles become aware that he may confront his brother?

Kitto in his exposition of this play (*Greek Tragedy*, pp. 47–54) gives a somewhat overenthusiastic account of Eteocles as the tragic hero "alone with his fate," magnificent in his isolation. The king's decision to stand himself at one of the gates, he says, is a rational move to reassure the frightened women, but brings the possibility of fratricide sensibly nearer; there is good reason for sending other champions to the first five gates, and compelling reason for not going himself to the sixth; Eteocles does not see the approach of the curse. But if this is so, why does Eteocles, when first told of the imminent attack, specifically invoke the curse (70) that doomed him and his brother to divide their inheritance with the sword? Aeschylus, by the shape he has given to his play, has made possible a different view: that the curse sanctioned the act which Eteocles lusted to commit; that the attack of the Seven brought a welcome opportunity, and the women's panic a reasonable excuse for taking part personally in the battle.

This disturbing suspicion is strengthened when we hear the Spy's account of the champion assigned to the sixth gate. Amphiaraus hurls loud accusations, says the Spy, at Tydeus and Polyneices, the two who had chiefly induced their father-in-law Adrastus to lead the army against Thebes. (For the unsavory character elsewhere attributed to this pair, see Euripides, *Suppliants* 131–54, *Phoenissae* 409ff.). Tydeus was at the gate next to Amphiaraus; Polyneices was on the other side of the city, three gates away.[1] It was for Eteocles a natural inference that Polyneices, like Tydeus, was on the field; if so, he must be stationed at the only gate not yet named. If Eteocles had forgotten about his brother, Amphiaraus' words reminded him—as they remind the audience. Was this reminder something that Aeschylus slipped in casually, without intending it to mean anything? There was still time for Eteocles to place himself opposite Amphiaraus, and leave Lasthenes to deal with Polyneices.

But to do this has suddenly been made difficult for Eteocles, because Amphiaraus had foretold that he himself would die in this battle; so that if Eteocles decided to fight Amphiaraus, he might have appeared a coward. Yet now he knows for certain that Polyneices is at the seventh gate; and Amphiaraus' prophecy has given him, once again, the excuse he needs. To choose for himself the sixth gate is not impossible, but it seems so to Eteocles, just as Agamemnon told himself he was compelled to sacrifice Iphigenia. Such a use of words is for the passionate and willful agent, not for the tragic poet who presents him. Eteocles will clear himself of guilt only if, when he alone is left to confront Polyneices, he accuses the gods of beguiling his innocent valor with cruel stealth, if he convincingly protests that he is unwilling to shed kindred blood. But his words, already quoted above, include no such expression.

Instead, Eteocles reveals hatred of his brother as a lifelong obsession. "When the gods give evil no man can escape it," he asserts; but he has forfeited credibility. It is no longer necessary to ask what unjust act he had committed against Polyneices. It is now clear why he did not claim justice, why he feared criticism and lacked authority. When the chorus tells him (694) that to shed his brother's blood is unlawful, *ou themistou*, he answers, "It was my own father who cursed me with a shameful curse"; and this implies (*gar*, 695) that his father's unnatural act justifies his own unnatural act. The simple consequence of denying responsibility in this way is the frantic desire for death (697, 703f.); and for this he once again (709) blames his father's curse. "Such blood cannot be cleansed; the stain of it never grows old," says the Spy (or perhaps the chorus; the assignment of lines here is uncertain). But the thought of pollution, which agonized Agamemnon (*A.* 207–10) and appalled Orestes (*Ch.* 438), appears to make no impact on Eteocles. He speaks (689–719) like a man released at last into the welcome madness of hate. His earlier praise of modesty and piety (409f., 554, 610) now rings false; even more so his reference to "the justice of kindred blood" (*Dikē homaimōn*, 415). Eteocles is still, in this play, a man who can pass for a hero with the audience; the dramatic force of the play moves also our modern sensibility with a lively sense of doom and fate which wins a measure of pity for the desperate man. Yet the drama demands more than pity; its severity lies in its omissions, which call for the exercise of judgment. The poet denies Eteocles not only piety but candor; what remains is the courage of frantic guilt. His reflections about Amphiaraus (597–608) as the good man allied with the ungodly, are an inverted diagram of himself as the reckless and impious man allied with six modest and upright champions.

The ode that follows Eteocles' departure tells the story of three generations: Laius' disobedience; Oedipus' parricide and incest; and now the lust of the sons to fulfill their father's curse. The fascination of the saga that they summarize here makes them forget for the moment their fear of what may issue from the fighting, and they tell their tale clearly and with insight. But, though the events of the first two plays are marshaled in a plain pattern of cause and effect, no such rationale is offered for the third play. Two words in 785f. would perhaps have given the reason why Oedipus cursed his sons—if the text had been clear; but it is not. Nowhere is any cause suggested for the brothers' mutual hatred, except the fact that they were co-heirs of Oedipus. This is surely as deliberate as Eteocles' silence about the justice of his cause. For fratricide, the poet implies, there can be no cause, reason, or excuse. There is an ultimate wickedness, about which all that need be known is the plain fact. It is worth noting that this ode, both in certain thoughts and phrases (e.g., 743ff., 769ff.) and in its general feeling, foreshadows the *Oresteia*—a work in which the theme of irretrievable pollution by kindred blood is pursued in similar detail, and carried further by the arguments used in the trial of Orestes. With the death of Eteocles the long and heavy account is closed (766f., *bareai katallagai*). The chorus recognize the *daimōn* of Oedipus' race; yet they insist in the same sentence (827–31) that both the brothers "perished through impious wilfulness," *asebei dianoiai*. That once said, the rest of their song is wonder and pity, without further severity.

The antiphonal lament of the two sisters[2] similarly balances an emphasis on the powerful curse of Oedipus with a clear statement of his sons' wickedness (989–92):

ANT. You [Polyneices] know that you transgressed—
ISM. You too [Eteocles] know it, since the same moment—
ANT. —When you [Polyneices] returned to Thebes.
ISM. —When you [Eteocles] raised your spear against him.

Thus the question of Eteocles' moral guilt, unobtrusively but persistently presented throughout the play, is kept in mind by the chorus and by the sisters in the closing lamentation. It is dismissed only in the last few words (1002–4):

ANT. In what place of earth shall we lay them?
ISM. Where their honour shall be greatest.
ANT. Let them rest beside their father, to his grief.

In the famous dispute in Aristophanes' *Frogs* between Aeschylus and Euripides the author of *Seven Against Thebes* claims (1021) that he wrote "a drama full of martial spirit," *Areōs meston*, one that "would make any man crave to be a warrior." We may assume that we have here the average citizen's view of the play. That such a view is more or less the opposite of that suggested by a careful study of the poet's actual words is not surprising; the degree of percipience a tragic poet could expect from most of his audience is indicated not unfairly in the enchantingly fatuous figure of Aristophanes' Dionysus. Aristophanes himself, in the whole of that scene, is probably using an irony similar to that which both Aeschylus and Euripides employed for the purposes of tragedy (see *Ironic Drama*, p. 11). Modern interpretation has improved somewhat on Aristophanes, or at least on Dionysus; and no longer judges it probable that Aeschylus should concern himself rather with blind Fate than with keen-eyed Justice, and find the potency of pity and terror in man's helplessness and state of tutelage rather than in the crises of his independent moral nature. I believe that interpretation of Aeschylus ought to begin with the assumption that we can share with the poet his conception of what is honest, dignified, courageous, and above all "sound-minded," *sōphrōn*. If we cannot, interpretation is a wild goose chase. If we can, then we know from very near the beginning of the play that Eteocles may be only the shadow of a hero. There is honesty in the chorus, piety in the Spy, dignity in the mourning for the dead; and Eteocles was doubtless a brave fighter; but more is required of a son of Oedipus. The poet allows him no other heroic virtues, least of all the virtue of honesty. The play is not called "Eteocles." The tragic quality of the play belongs to him not in his own right, but rather in virtue of the pity felt for him; and chiefly it belongs to that one refuge for our harrowed sympathy—the bereaved, torn, but surviving city.

IV

Euripides' Commentary on the *Oresteia*

13

Counterfeit Nobility:
Electra

From 418 to 408 B.C. four more plays chiefly or largely concerned with the murder of Clytemnestra by her son Orestes were produced in Athens. These were Euripides, *Electra*; Sophocles, *Electra*; Euripides, *Iphigenia in Tauris* and *Orestes*. It is evident that this theme of the matricide was acceptable to the Athenian public; and each of these plays inevitably bears its relation to the work of Aeschylus. The relationship in the case of Euripides, however, seems to me to be especially close, as if the poet were trying to make clear to his audience by a more direct, realistic, even homely treatment, the ironic and tragic force which Athenians had declined to recognize in the epic stateliness of the *Oresteia*.

There is no record of any play dealing with the matricide during the forty years following the death of Aeschylus; and in view of the veneration with which the *Trilogy* was regarded this is not surprising. Then between 420 and 410 we have the two plays called "Electra," by Euripides and Sophocles. There is no decisive evidence to tell us which was the earlier. For the purpose of the present argument I accept the view that places Euripides' play in 419 or 418 and Sophocles' about five years later. Should proof of Sophocles' priority suddenly appear, what I have to say would in fact be little affected. The dating of these plays depends on questions of style, structure, treatment of common elements, or references to known events. On literary grounds I judge that Sophocles' play is an intelligible response to Euripides', but Euripides' play is less intelligible as a response to Sophocles'. My discussion of detail in this chapter will in part explain my reasons for this opinion.

No one knows why Euripides decided after so many years to break the awed abstention of poets from the matricide theme; but the effort of conjecture may be fruitful. The interpretation of Aeschylus' trilogy that I have put forward suggests two possibilities.

First, since in my own experience it is the study of Euripides' work that has led me to recognize the implications of the *Oresteia*, I cannot but believe that Euripides was among the few who perceived the connection between the narrative in the *Agamemnon* parodos and Clytemnestra's arraignment of the "sacrificer" in the final scene; who recognized in the trilogy's successive crises the victory of the expedient over the good; who saw the issue joined between *aidōs* and *dikē*; who heard in Athena's decisive speech the divine echo of Agamemnon's mortal *hubris*, and knew that the surrender of the Erinyes symbolized not only the defeat of woman but the defeat of morality. The poet's message was a living one; yet the trilogy, its surface splendor lauded, its heart unperceived, had now become a fossil—a revered classic, recited, quoted, unassailable as a poetic monument. Athenians saw Orestes as Athena saw him, "pure, harmless, blameless"; they saw Clytemnestra as Cassandra saw her, a vile and ravening monster; they saw Agamemnon as a "king and martyr," and Athena and Apollo radiant in the glory with which official religion clothed them. Something drastic was needed to shake this superficial edifice created by the many who looked to the poet only for the reassurance of their own conventions.

Second, the forty years' interval had seen Aeschylus' prophecy fulfilled. If matricide was a symbol of that ultimate wrongdoing which rejects *aidōs*, disowning the prime source of moral feeling, then the predictions that the Erinyes uttered in their second choral ode, and in their outcry after the verdict, have by the year 418 become felt and visible realities. Athens, permanently weakened by the plague of 430–429, has been at war for twelve years, with calamitous losses of life, of prosperity, of prestige. She has experienced the still profounder loss of moral confidence, sharing in the general collapse of standards of behavior, the growing falsity of speech and thought, that had poisoned the life of Greek cities ever since the atrocities in Corcyra. Aeschylus' irony had been too gentle even for his time. Athenians now were coarser, and needed a more obvious demonstration that evil was evil, whatever evasions *dikē* might provide. Euripides designed something that was not only a new kind of play in its own right, but would urge its audience to look again at the *Oresteia*, and question its meaning more closely.

Euripides, whatever his expectations from his audience, assumes in his *Electra* the same moral position that Aeschylus took in *Choephori*; but, since *Choephori* failed to make its message understood, Euripides uses a more transparent irony and a more direct statement. The world of the old story is presented in realistic terms of the modern world to which the play is addressed. In choosing this method Euripides certainly intended that his play, for all its realism and black comedy, should be still the work of a poet rather than a propagandist; but here he perhaps came nearer than in any other play to doing what he has often been perversely accused of—weakening his drama to point his message. This is a play packed with interest, incident, and subtlety; but it is unique in not containing one character with whom we can feel any degree of real sympathy, except the Peasant, whose place in the action is peripheral. *Electra* therefore has not the true tragic quality, or any touch of sublimity. In place of this, the play makes an incisive plea for criticism of received opinions on what is noble and heroic and what is not, and for a moral sense based on individual *aidōs*, proof against social coercion and divine authority.

The idea of the heroic, the concept of nobility, is central in the Homeric poems. In the sixth century, when aristocratic families dominated Athenian social life, and the text of Homer was established as the basis of a citizen's education, it is probable that the recognition of this concept was rarely questioned. When in the fifth century democracy began to diminish the prestige of inherited greatness, tragedy could still present sublime mortal figures and rely on a general understanding of the morality they recalled. Thus it is not surprising that, when Aeschylus showed his imperious Agamemnon and his devout Orestes, the claim of these royal figures to nobility was allowed in spite of the weakness and perverted judgment with which their author characterized them. Their crimes were overlooked, their noble airs assumed to be virtues; the painful questions posed by their deeds were barely heard. The spectator was ready to recognize *to gennaion*, nobility, by name and costume, being now less sure of any other criterion.

Euripides' attempt to counter the falsification that Aeschylus' play had suffered consists largely in an analysis of the concept of nobility, first in Orestes, then in Electra. Nobility is a virtue sometimes more clearly apprehended from below ("No man is a hero to his valet"); and some key passages in Euripides' study come from the Peasant and the Old Man. First, 404−7:

> EL. You know how bare your house is. These two guests
> Are far above your level. Then why ask them in?
> PEAS. Why not? If they're as noble as they look, they'll be
> Equally at home in a cottage or anywhere else.

The Peasant invited the strangers indoors before he had heard Orestes speak a word. Since then Orestes has delivered a speech of embarrassing banality about humble goodness, of which the Peasant has probably understood little; but in the next scene we shall learn whether or not the prince knows how to behave when he is a guest of the poor. He and Pylades come out onto the stage (550−55):

> O. M. (*aside*). They have nobility; but it may be counterfeit.
> Many who are nobly born belie it. None the less—
> (*to Or. and Pyl.*) My courteous greeting to our guests!
> OR.   Greeting, old man.—
> Electra, whose friend is this antique relic here?

> EL. This man, Sir, was my father's guardian when a child. . . .
>   Orestes, if he still lives, owes his life to him.

A moment later the Old Man's image of "counterfeit" nobility is unconsciously reinforced by Orestes himself:

> Why does he stare at me, like a man examining
> The stamp on a silver coin?

Euripides' dialogue urges his audience to examine the portraits, so familiar in Aeschylus' trilogy, of the noble Agamemnon and Orestes, in exactly the same way—to see if their nobility is counterfeit. In his first talk with Electra Orestes has already shown himself slow to recognize generosity in others. Though Electra has told him that her husband is "generous (*gennaion*) and respectful towards me" (253), Orestes three times (256, 258, 260) imputes unworthy feelings to the Peasant; and when at last he acknowledges that the man is generous, he instinctively cancels his admission with "We must reward him." His tendency to moralize (strong even for a tragic hero), and his unconsciousness of his own patronizing superficiality, are first shown briefly in 294ff.:

> For sympathy comes with perception; a brutal man
> Has none; while the perceptive pay a certain price
> For their too keen perception, in their own distress;

but presently with a fulsome articulateness (368ff.):

> There's no clear sign to tell the quality of a man;
> Nature and place turn vice and virtue upside down.
> I've seen a noble father breed a worthless son,
> And good sons come of evil parents; a starved soul
> Housed in a wealthy palace, a great heart dressed in rags. . . .
> This man is not a leading Argive citizen;
> He's not a well-known member of a famous house;
> He's one of the many; yet he's a true nobleman. . . .

These words, and more that follow, perhaps suitable to a man of age and experience but absurd in the mouth of a stripling, show merely a callow sententiousness. The line, "I've seen a noble father breed a worthless son," touches a theme that Euripides illustrates repeatedly, in *Heracleidae, Phoenissae, Orestes*; here its application is to the speaker himself. After this we have first Orestes' plotting, prompted by the Old Man, to kill Aegisthus while present as his guest at a sacrifice; then later his words encouraging Electra to throw Aegisthus' body to the dogs and birds. So far the portrait has been simple. Then Orestes sees Clytemnestra approaching, and at last recognizes his moment of truth. An aspect of his awareness hitherto obscured now appears, to complete the portrait.

In *Choephori* Orestes had considered the claim of *aidōs* in a single line (899):

Pylades, what shall I do? Shall I recognize *aidōs* and spare my mother?

and then dismissed it when Pylades asserted that Apollo's external authority was paramount. But Euripides' Orestes has the virtue, as well as the faults, of the unheroic. In Electra's disturbed mind her brother's problem, at this moment, does not exist (959–64):

> EL. Men, take his body indoors and put it out of sight.
>   My mother must not see it before her throat is cut.
> OR. Wait. There are other things we must decide.
> EL.   What now?
>   What do I see? An armed force from Mycenae?
> OR.   No.
>   It is my mother, she who gave me birth.

Then in eight successive replies to Electra's ruthless resolution Orestes struggles with his "internal authority." Eight times she defeats his appeal for *aidōs*; and Orestes yields to a wickedness for which he knows there is no excuse.

This is the point where we see most clearly what Euripides, as inheritor of both the dramatic tradition and the national function of Aeschylus, wishes to add to what Aeschylus had said forty years earlier. Those years, and especially the thirteen years of war with Sparta, have made urgent for Athenian citizens the question, Is there room any longer for the recognition of *aidōs* in a man's decisions about his own conduct? In violent political struggle, or in combat by land or sea, is there now anything a man should shrink from? Or do religion and patriotism provide new meanings for words (see Thucydides 3.82), to cover every crime? Is the disintegration that began in Corcyra eight years ago now to be accepted as normal? The feeling expressed by Orestes in 985–87, of being forced by circumstances into wickedness, was likely to be shared, if never spoken of, by many in the first audience. In Sophocles' play, Electra is more articulately aware of the way circumstances compel evildoing (see, e.g., *El.* 307–9); and the true nobility of her nature makes the recognition tragic. But in Euripides' play the ignoble nature of Orestes makes his struggle and capitulation less tragic than pathetic. And the realism of pathos was more likely than sublimity to convey a clear message to the unheroic audience for which Euripides wrote.

The first and second stasima are also both relevant to the characterization of Orestes. If we recognize that the first episode is largely devoted to exposing the counterfeit nobility of the young man who has come to Argos to kill his mother, the ode that follows (432–86) assumes a pointed meaning. It tells the story of Achilles, who died fighting for the sons of Atreus (451) and whose nobility bears no suspicion of being spurious. On the rim of Achilles' shield was depicted (458–63) another noble hero, Perseus, who like Orestes had Hermes (*Ch.* 1, 812) for his guide, when he came to sever the head of the Gorgon. Here too the analogy of detail points to the contrast of character. The second stasimon narrates the crime of Thyestes in seducing Atreus' wife; and the implied conclusion is, If the outrage—common enough—of adultery caused Zeus to reverse the sun's course, what will happen as the consequence of matricide? A clue to interpretation is given in the first line, *atalas hupo matros . . .* , "a mother and her lamb in Argos . . . ," where the phrase recalls the last time Clytemnestra saw her son, an infant in her arms (cf. *IT* 229–35). Another subtle point occurs in the last four lines of the ode, 745–46:

> But frightening tales are a benefit to mortals, inducing them to revere the gods. It was because you did not remember such tales that you killed your husband, [O sister of famous brothers, *or*] O mother of a famous brother and sister.

Sungeneteira, which occurs only here, would be assumed—apart from irony—to mean "sister," and *kleinōn adelphōn* would then refer to the Dioskouroi. But *geneteira* is known to mean "mother"; and in 536 we have *adelphoin* used of Orestes and Electra. If the latter alternative is the correct translation, *kleinōn* is ironic and means "notorious," and the irony includes the thought that "frightening tales," which should have deterred the wife from killing her husband, must convey an even sterner warning to the matricides.

The nature of nobility is examined similarly in Electra's words and actions. When she speaks over Aegisthus' body the "evil words" (913) she had wanted to utter to his face, she contrasts, by implication, her own noble nature with Aegisthus' meanness (941–42), just as Electra in *Orestes* 126–27 contrasts her own nobility with the evil nature she imputes to Helen. Before beginning the speech in which she vilifies Aegisthus, she hesitates (900–902):

> I am ashamed to insult the dead, yet I want to speak.

She asserts that a sense of shame (*aischunomai*, 900) still influences her; "shameful" is her word (932) for Aegisthus' subordination to Clytemnestra; she knows what is unsuitable for an unmarried woman to utter (945); yet feels no shame at what she is plotting. The line just quoted marks her tirade as a conscious indulgence in malevolence; just as, a little later, Orestes' recognition of the wickedness of Apollo's command (971) marks his matricide as a conscious crime which he could have shunned. There is no doubt that it is natural for Electra, being Agamemnon's daughter, to assume that her own nature is noble; and it is natural for her, being Clytemnestra's victim, to feel resentful of the wrongs she suffers. But a disinherited life, which has made Orestes foolish and weak but has not finally destroyed his moral sense, has had a different effect on Electra: she has become neurotically addicted to grievance and self-pity, wildly inconsistent in her attitudes, and ruthless in her thirst for revenge. The falseness of her nobility is exposed when she says (911–13):

> So now, being free, I'll pay my debt—those evil words
> I longed to say to you when you were still alive.

That was not the Hellenic tradition of "free" behavior.

Electra's addiction to grievance and self-pity is described in 126 by the words, "a pleasure of many tears." She complains of her life in the cottage, 303–10: "Never a feast on holy days, never a dance"—though the chorus, her neighbors, have begged her (169ff.) to come with them to a feast of Hera, and offered to lend her a gown with a gold clasp. She tells Orestes that her marriage is *thanasimon*, "a living death"; though in 67–76 her picture of life with the Peasant is far from disagreeable, and she honors him "like a god." She longs for Orestes to come; but when the Old Man recognizes him she is reluctant to be convinced, and her greeting to her brother extends to some seven words in all, 578–80. At no point does she show, in speaking of the plot to murder Clytemnestra, any compunction about shedding a mother's blood; and for Orestes' anguished hesitation she has not a moment's sympathy—as the chorus later recalls, 1204–5.

The full revelation of Electra's warped character comes in the speech over Aegisthus' dead body. Her earlier brief account of his behavior, spoken to Orestes in 318–31, is unconvincing though excusable in view of the way her stepfather treated her. But her address to his corpse is decisive. Her just reproaches are contained in three and a half lines, 914–17. The thirty-eight lines that follow are unmixed malignity—a series of assertions unrelated to anything else in the play, and supported only by Electra's vindictive word.

> You were a fool to think my mother would not be unfaithful to you, as she was to my father. Each of you, being evil, obtained the other's evil destiny. You too were unfaithful to her, using your royal position to indulge promiscuity with women. You were always subordinate to my mother in character and in social quality. You believed that your wealth made you a great man.

Such invective, devoid of nobility or even common dignity, is relevant only to her own miserable and deprived life.

The portrait is not yet complete: Electra has still to confront her mother. This scene, from Clytemnestra's entry to the appearance of the Dioskouroi, is masterly. It achieves two purposes, both closely related to the *Oresteia*. First, it makes explicit, for a coarsened audience that could not be expected to understand Aeschylus' implications, the total condemnation of Orestes and of the rejection of *aidōs* which he represents. Second, it relates the whole sequence of events to what had now for thirty-seven years been Euripides' principal and recurrent theme, the fate of woman in Greek society.

The scene first shows unmistakably to the audience of 418 the truth which Aeschylus had firmly but unobtrusively offered to the Athenians of 458, and which they had ignored: that their popular hero Orestes, asserting the superior value of the male at whatever cost to truth, humanity, and social health, was less a hero than a pitiful product of an outworn tradition that not only divided the human race into two hostile camps (see particularly *Ch.* 585−638), but perpetuated in civilized communities the tyrannical practices of barbarism. The sole virtue of this second Orestes is that he still has enough native moral sense to repent in agony. This gives him almost a unique place in Greek drama. Xerxes in *Persae*, Creon in *Antigone*, admitted error; *aidōs* made Neoptolemus reverse, and Admetus repent, a wrong decision; but the anguished acknowledgment of wickedness shown in this scene of *Electra* has only faint parallels, such as the dying speech of Polyneices in *Phoenician Women* 1440−53.

Here, surely, we should look for an answer to the question, Why was Orestes' act a recurrent theme in tragedy? Since we have no reason to suppose that matricide was a prevalent crime in Athens, this legend must have borne a symbolic meaning; and it is hard to find any other symbolic meaning than that which the Erinyes express in *Eumenides*, where matricide is the ultimate crime: the rejection of that inner moral authority with which Zeus and Moira endowed man to distinguish him from beasts. The human condition that this crime symbolized is pictured in Thucydides' history of a city which progresses from a passion for freedom to the exercise of tyranny, from a reverence for truth to expertise in falsehood, from respect for mercy to ruthlessness. This progress Euripides later, in *Phoenician Women*, imaged as a growing insanity. In that play insanity led to disaster, but the city survived. In *Orestes*, a year later, insanity is rampant, and the hope of recovery is gone; for insanity is, as fifty years earlier in *Choephori*, the inevitable result of matricide. A pattern of matricide appears also at the close of *Phoenician Women*. Thus we can see, below the dramatic surface, the portrait of a generation which has destroyed the land that bore it, and incurs the natural consequence.

A second purpose is achieved in this scene of *Electra*. Euripides' attitude to the status of woman was close to that which Aeschylus expresses in his treatment of the story of Clytemnestra—her defeat at Aulis, her revenge and victory, her death, and the final defeat of her cause in *Eumenides*. Euripides' first play, *The Daughters of Pelias*, was produced three years after the *Oresteia*; and it began a long series of works, known to us only by fragments, that set forth with stark clarity both the wrongs inflicted on women and the faults that reflect and occasion those wrongs but do not excuse them. Because Euripides like Aeschylus was a dramatist rather than a propagandist, his meaning has b own day often been missed, the passion of his irony ignored, by a world in which the observation that "mourning becomes Electra" supplies a fatalistic seal of approval to a serviceable social order; and this was no less the case in fifth-century Athens. I cannot doubt that Euripides himself understood the full implications of Aeschylus' work. In *Electra*, his most direct comment on the *Oresteia*, he has, through three-quarters of the action, little to say about the position of women; but in Clytemnestra's scene, 988–1146, this topic suddenly becomes central.

First the scene shows how intractable the whole problem of woman is. Man's treatment of woman begets anger that explodes in violence (1109–10); when the fire burns itself out in one generation (1105–6) it revives in the next with a coarser and crueller quality. Here, as in the *Oresteia*, the single origin of this particular complex is shown as the scene opens. Clytemnestra is obsessed with a memory; as she steps from her carriage a Trojan girl holds her hand, and she recalls the daughter who loved her, seventeen years dead (1002–3); and immediately after, states the truth exactly as Aeschylus had stated it (1011–12):

> Your father brought all this on you by his wicked treachery to one he should have loved.

By a subtle turn Euripides shows the hopelessness of the problem even more realistically than Aeschylus. The great Clytemnestra referred (*A.* 1446–47) to Cassandra's death merely as an extra satisfaction added to her revenge for Iphigenia; Euripides' Clytemnestra, demoralized by the emotion that rises as she recalls her daughter, lapses first into conventional vulgarity ("I could forgive him for Iphigenia but not for Cassandra"), then into argumentative nonsense. When she ends with "Prove to me that your father's death was not justified," we know that years of fear, remorse, and unpopularity have destroyed the formidable champion of woman whose axe quelled the "king of men." But Electra, destroyed herself, does not see that her mother is no longer worth killing.

The chorus' comment on Clytemnestra's speech (1051–54) contains a point not usually noticed:

> Your words are just; yet in your 'justice' there remains
> Something repellent. A wife ought in all things to accept
> Her husband's judgement, if she is wise. Those who will not
> Admit this, fall outside my scope of argument.

The first remark wins full acceptance; the second means "Agamemnon had a perfect right to sacrifice his daughter," and thus morally invalidates the first. The problem grows more hopeless than ever.

Electra's reply begins with yet another reference to *Choephori*. Aeschylus' Electra, before meeting Orestes, prayed (140–41) "to be purer in heart and more pious in act than her mother." This desire was soon swept away by the flood of revenge; but it was uttered. Euripides' Electra begins differently (1060–61): "I wish that you, mother, had a better character." She accuses her mother of frivolity and lasciviousness. The charge, coming from a source already so clearly characterized, carries its own refutation. In 1063–64, 1083, Electra joins the company of vicious or foolish persons in Euripides who vilify Helen. In 1076–78 her statement that

> If ever Troy gained a victory, you rejoiced, but if Troy lost a battle your eyes were clouded

is the same worthless argument that marks a vicious speaker in *Women of Troy* 1004–7. Most noticeable of all is her complete indifference to the sacrifice of her sister, whom she refers to twice as "your daughter"; her own fate, she says, is crueller than Iphigenia's. She ends by saying (1096), "If it was just for you to kill Agamemnon, it is also just for me and your son to kill you." She is unaware that the argument works both ways.

The dialogue following the speech, a sinister exchange of "dramatic ironies," leads to Electra's request that her mother will enter the cottage to perform the tenth-day sacrifice for the birth of a child. Clytemnestra will die, then, as Aegisthus died—engaged in a religious ritual; Aegisthus was killed by a guest, she will die as a guest in her daughter's house. When she has gone in, the chorus' reflections on Agamemnon's death include this cry (1160–61):

> Alas! Her husband is to be pitied, however grievous was the wrong she suffered—

words that suggest to the listener, what the speaker does not think of, the more immediate truth, that the mother is to be pitied, however grievous the wrongs the daughter suffered. But the daughter's bloody act will purge her poison, as murder has purged her mother's; and her long penance will remit her punishment.

The closing tableau of *Electra* shows brother and sister overwhelmed by self-loathing. They do not need to name, or to reason about, *aidōs*; even in the despairing struggle of 962–87 Orestes does not utter the word. He sees the truth unmistakable before his eyes, and the convention of "justice" backed by religious sanction is exploded. It becomes clear that in this play Euripides is for once not concerned to show woman's lot as harder than man's. The motive power which ensures the accomplishment of the crime is Electra's; Orestes is guilty through weakness; yet Electra departs with Pylades to a quiet domesticity, away from the scene of her wretchedness and crime, while Orestes must face the Erinyes and years of wandering. So at the close of the drama the fundamental moral question is not obscured by an irrelevant social issue. It is directly answered in the murderers' self-condemnation, which is so heartfelt that even in his reproach to Apollo (1190–93) Orestes does not attempt to lighten his own burden of guilt, while Electra twice (1182, 1303–4) accepts her own responsibility. This provides, from one point of view, a less despairing conclusion than Orestes' complacent departure in *Eumenides*. It is Castor, not the two matricides, who takes the more legalistic view and passes on the blame to Apollo. The play is addressed to Athenians engrossed in the war, and it asserts that the time is past for inconclusive judgments, that crime must be acknowledged as crime, whatever its provocation, and irrespective of punishment or pardon. The censure of Apollo is coupled with recognition that the instinct of mankind also has authority. Orestes asks (1196–97):

> What pious man will dare to look at me—a son who has killed his mother?

Here he specifically gives the right and unexpected answer to the alternative stated by Pylades in *Ch.* 902,

> Think all men your enemies, rather than the gods.

(See chapter 2.) Euripides' play lacks the majesty of the *Oresteia*, but its realism had a chance of reaching a sobered, if unsubtle, audience. The poet speaks to a generation which, like the guilty brother and sister, has lost its foothold in the moral world; but the comfort he offers is that even in Electra *aidōs* is, after all, not dead.

The role of Clytemnestra exhibits the aftermath of successful revenge. Her crime as shown in *Agamemnon* is the most—is the only—magnificent crime in extant Greek tragedy. Euripides acknowledges, as it were, the immortal Aeschylean creation when his chorus says in 1162–63,

> Like a lioness from the mountains
> Roaming through meadows and orchards
> She carried out her purpose.

That was once, and is no longer, the woman we have just seen enter the Peasant's cottage. Courage has turned to fear, clarity to confusion. The first half of her speech 1011–50 suggests the genuine sorrow that has not healed in seventeen years; then she becomes first irrational, and soon silly. Her memory of time sequence is as subjective as her daughter's (1035–38):

> Well, women are frail, I grant you. But when, knowing this,

> A husband looks elsewhere, and slights his lawful wife,
> She'll copy him, and find herself another friend.

This is not meant to be any more credible than Electra's (1069–71)

> Before your daughter's sacrifice was decided on,
> When Agamemnon still was scarcely out of sight,
> You were before your mirror, smoothing out your hair.

But this sad and confused Clytemnestra speaks four lines which make her role creative. Her response to Electra's tirade of hatred is to speak of love (1102–5):

> My child, your nature has always been to love your father.
> It is natural; some children love their fathers best,
> And some their mothers. I'll forgive you. I do not,
> In fact, exult unduly over what I did.

Doubtless the words infuriate Electra even more; but there is another side to their meaning. They recall the moment when news reached Argos that the ceremony at Aulis had been not a wedding but a sacrifice. The daughter who "loved her mother best" was gone; and the mother's indignation roused in the other daughter only the resolve to defend her father at any cost. The mutual hatred of mother and daughter has lasted long; and for the aging Clytemnestra the blood of Iphigenia, as of Agamemnon, has become a *gerōn phonos*, an "old blood guilt" which "should no longer beget its kind" (*Ch.* 806). It is characteristic of Euripides that the word "forgive" should be uttered by the person from whom we least expect it. To a speech like Electra's this is a surprising answer. Yet it is the only answer; nor is there, among the many scenes of anger and recrimination in Greek drama, any reply comparable with these lines of Clytemnestra for quiet, honest, conciliatory good sense. To interpret the whole scene in the light of these lines is to do no more than justice to their singular quality. They direct us to discount the foolish excuses and arguments of 1035–48, and to respect the grief and indignation of 1018–29. Finally, they complete Euripides' moral comment on *Choephori*. Clytemnestra was the one person in Aeschylus' trilogy whose indignation was both courageous and—until tainted by jealousy of Cassandra—pure; and here Euripides gives to her the enunciation of a new moral concept, *sungnōmē*, "pardon," which had become current a generation after Aeschylus' death. Euripides explored this concept in a number of plays, notably *Hippolytus*. The persons of Sophocles' *Electra* are unaware of it; but Euripides touched on it again when he continued the "Oresteian dialogue" in *Iphigenia in Tauris*.

For further comment on the relation of *Electra* to *Choephori* I refer the reader to my introduction to the Penguin translation ("*Medea*" *and Other*

Plays, 1963), especially p. 14, where the use of the "tokens" for recognition is discussed. The argument of this chapter has, I hope, confirmed the view that sees Euripides as sharing some of Aeschylus' central concerns and convictions, while keenly aware of the changed character and circumstances of his audience. The two poets, I conclude, are fundamentally at one in their view of their material, and of their function as admonishers of their fellow citizens.

14

The Survivors and Their Home: *Iphigenia in Tauris*

The central theme of this play is human sacrifice—the whole grisly syndrome of fear and blood. Since the play was written in a critical period of the Peloponnesian war, it is reasonable to assume that the various aspects of this syndrome were meant to bear their full implication. The action springs from an event of twenty years before, the sacrifice of Iphigenia by her father: an experience that has haunted and obsessed the victim ever since the moment when, she tells us, as the knife was raised to her throat, the goddess Artemis snatched her away.

The scene is a barbarous coast remote from Athens and Hellas, to which Artemis transported Iphigenia when she rescued her from the altar; and a background theme throughout the play is the nostalgic thought of home, of the love and security of family life. This theme gives its own direction to many features; for example, when Iphigenia believes that her last link with home has been severed by Orestes' death, she hardens her heart to savor revenge on the two captured Greeks. It is also clearly related to the story of the three Atreid murders, which were all violations of the home, of family love. The chorus too, in exile, long for their own families, and the odes poignantly recall the music and dancing, all the beauty, comfort, and stability of social and domestic life in the Hellas of tradition, before the war came to disrupt everything (1106–22). The place of woman as maker and preserver of a happy home is assumed at every point. The development moves from the remembered sacrifice of a daughter by her father to the discovery that the Greek stranger, whose noble bearing symbolizes the health, joy, and beauty associated with Hellas and home—all that the exile longed for—that this young man is himself guilty of his mother's blood and burdened with insanity; and successive scenes reveal the disasters that the Trojan war has inflicted upon one family. The enigmatic epilogue leaves the audience to answer for themselves the question, Is anything of value now retrievable?

A play about Iphigenia was overdue. It was forty-five years (the date is not exactly known; I assume it to be about 413 B.C.) since the inhumanity of the sacrifice had been set forth by the chorus at the opening of *Agamemnon*. In *Iphigenia in Tauris* Euripides takes his audience back to that scene, whose familiarity has blunted its edge; ungags the victim and lets her speak not only of that moment but of the complex emotional pattern that has over twenty years developed from that public act of callous disregard.

This play, like others, is designed for a double purpose: to entertain the average spectator, and to speak for the poet to those who will look more closely for his implicit meaning. The barbaric yet solemn setting, the noble behavior of the two friends, the recognition, the comic King, the escape, and the "happy ending," together form a romantic unity which, provided the sacrifice can be accepted as a holy and beautiful tableau, and the epilogue made credible, ensures popularity for the play. A recent scholarly analysis of it, by A. P. Burnett in *Catastrophe Survived* (pp. 47–72), accepts this view, maintaining that the drama shows benevolent divine purpose overruling human error. The facts of the text, however, are as follows. In the first eight hundred lines there are only two brief passages where the emotion ceases to be somber or anguished: one is the delight of the Herdsman that the Greek strangers are to be sacrificed, the other is Iphigenia's suggestion that only one of them, after all, need be killed. All the rest is either recounting, or mourning for, deaths past, present, and future. Then comes the recognition, for which twenty-two lines of rejoicing are allowed before anguish descends again in 850f. In the second half the deception of Thoas and the bogus procession provide relief between the cumulative disasters of the Atreid family and the combined malevolence of Apollo, Artemis, and Poseidon in frustrating the plan for escape. At every point the presence of Iphigenia recalls attention to the hideous performance at Aulis and to its immediate causal connection with the horrors that ensued, including Orestes' fit of insanity as witnessed and described by the Herdsman. Iphigenia had been sacrificed to further a military expedition; and the appearance on stage of two young men destined for an altar of the same goddess can have borne only one significance for the members of an audience in which few had not lost young men from their own family during eighteen years of war. The first choral ode opens with the romance of distant travel, but then turns to a prayer for slaughter, followed by heart-rending nostalgia; and this last theme continues even more poignantly in the second ode. Romantic interest embellishes the play; but the stuff of it is tragedy.

Iphigenia and Orestes are presented as two surviving victims of the Trojan war. The sacrifice of Orestes on the Taurian altar, though not carried out, provides a stage symbol of the protracted suffering that the war has inflicted on him—exile, a hideous and mistaken duty, endless wandering, and insanity. All this Orestes describes in the prologue, 77ff. Iphigenia has already told us how Artemis saved her from death at the altar only to condemn her to twenty years of living death—to exile, enforced virginity, and the task of preparing human victims for slaughter. Iphigenia comforts herself, as a Greek, by ascribing the bloodthirsty local custom to Taurian barbarity (389–90), forgetting that her words similarly condemn her father and his fellow Greeks as murderers and their act as sordid, *phaulon*. So, all through the play, characters and chorus meeting in this barbaric spot speak longingly of the noble and civilized quality of life in Hellas, while every new report that comes from their beloved home is of war, death, murder, and misery. This irony, felt at many points in the play, is epitomized in Iphigenia's words as she mourns for her brother (377–78):

> Unhappy Orestes, what nobility of life is lost to you if you are dead!
> What splendour of inheritance!

Yet, though this play is ironic—and its irony includes the "happy ending"— and in spite of its pessimistic attitude towards events, it contains in its detailed portrait of Iphigenia a rare, indeed a unique, instance of a heart obsessed with anger struggling to free itself from that bondage. The opening speech tells first (26–27) of a monstrous and unforgettable wrong done to the speaker in child-hood by a beloved father. It continues with the dream (44–55) which she inter-prets to mean that her brother has died. In mourning for her only brother she retells indignantly her father's crime and the treachery with which it was con-trived (177, 211), and alludes again and again to scenes and symbols of family life and affection (173–74, 204–6, 221–24, 231–35). Her lament ends with the picture of Orestes as she last saw him, a child tenderly nursed in Clytem-nestra's arms; and is followed by the Herdsman's picture of a young man still noble and brave, but afflicted with horrifying insanity. While she waits for the prisoners to be brought, Iphigenia speaks to the chorus. All pity, she says, is gone from her heart; now that her home has lost its hope, the strangers will find her cruel. Her anger against her father includes all Greeks. She has already mentioned Calchas and Odysseus, and now adds Helen and Menelaus—in this and the next scene she wishes death upon them all by name. In telling yet again the story of her father's cruelty she remembers the home she had left, where "my mother and my friends were singing the wedding song for me."

> At home, I hid my face in my fine wedding-veil,
> And would not take my brother in my arms—and he
> Is dead now; and I would not kiss my sister's lips,
> For I was hot with blushes, going to the house
> Of Achilles. I would see Argos again one day,
> I said; and I would keep my kisses until then.

Suddenly the bitter resentment against fellow Greeks that charged the beginning of this soliloquy is melted away by these thoughts of home. Iphigenia quite illogically persuades herself that it is only barbarians who are cruel, not Greeks; she acquits Artemis, forgets her father's crime, and after the choral ode receives the captives with tender sympathy (472ff.):

> You were once little children [she says]. Who was your mother then?
> Your father? Had you a sister?

Her questioning leads soon to Argos and Troy. Then bitterness returns, and she curses her enemies. She asks (543),

> What of the general, fortunate in his victory?

"The one I know was not fortunate," Orestes replies, and is reluctant to answer further. This is a hint that Agamemnon has met a deserved fate; and Iphigenia presses her question:

> Don't refuse; tell me—it will give me pleasure.

A few lines earlier it gave her pleasure to learn of Calchas' death. But when she hears that Agamemnon is dead, the news does not after all give her pleasure, but sorrow. When she learns further who killed him, she says,

> Oh! Tears and more tears for her who killed, and for him who—
> killed!

She would have said, "Him who died"; and one MS gives *ho thanōn*. But Iphigenia knows—of course—the motive of Clytemnestra's bloody act, and she says "killed." She is the only person in Greek tragedy who has tears for Clytemnestra. A moment later, learning of the matricide, she looks from yet another angle, and "applauds the evil deed because it was just." Next (563) Iphigenia asks,

> Is there any word of his daughter who was sacrificed?
> OR. No, except that she is dead.
> IPH. I weep for her, and for her father who killed her.

Twice in a dozen lines she has felt pity for her father; and pity liberates her from bitterness. The indignation she has felt against him is different from Electra's indignation against Clytemnestra in Euripides' *Electra*, which sprang from cold hate. Iphigenia's bitterness reflects her outraged love. Pity overcomes outrage; and presently she says (992–93),

> I want to feel no anger against him for killing me.

The voluntary replacing of justified anger with pardon is a theme peculiar to Euripides. It is unknown in Aeschylus; the various words for anger ring incessantly through the *Oresteia*, and when the Erinyes renounce anger they do so partly by compulsion and partly for advantage. In Sophocles we find the noble exercise of moderation, *sōphrosunē*, which is a cooler concept. But Euripides in a number of plays explores the notion of pardon, *sungnōmē*, a word that came into use in this sense only from about 440 B.C.; and the occurrence here of the same notion—though the word *sungnōmē* is not used—sounds a rare note of hopefulness in the grim Atreid saga.

As Iphigenia achieves freedom from anger, her despondency changes to elation; and when the stranger tells her that Orestes is alive—which, obviously, only means he was alive some months ago when the man left home—she at once concludes, with a consistent want of logic, that last night's dream was a false portent. Her conclusion elicits from Orestes a speech of some significance, 570–75:

> IPH. False dreams, away with you! You are worth nothing.
> OR. You are right; the gods themselves, even those we call prophetic,
>   Are no more trustworthy than fleeting dreams. The world
>   Of gods is as chaotic as our mortal world.
>   What galls one is, that while still of sound mind, he should,
>   By heeding the words of prophets, plunge himself into
>   A depth of ruin known only to those who suffer it.

We may note that, if the date of production was 412, the allusion to Nicias' fatal delay in escaping from Syracuse is obvious. Apart from this, there is no need to take this passage, rather than others, as expressing the poet's own belief about the Olympian religion, since Orestes after the recognition scene changes his mind (1015–16); but it is clear that the words raise, in regard to events treated in the play, first a question of particular reference, and secondly the most radical general question of all: What is the function of religion in human life?

The particular reference is to the act of matricide, which Orestes by heeding the oracle undertook "while still of sound mind." In other words, he now regards his obedience as not the act of a sane man; nor does he regard himself even now as a fully sane man, though at present his mind is lucid. With that act Orestes, like his father, had "put on the bridle of necessity"; and now he feels himself led by necessity toward a fate he cannot foresee. In this he represents the fighting generations of Hellenes on both sides of the struggle who, committed to the tradition of endless retaliation, backed by Delphic authority, and excused by the compulsions of patriotism, were pursuing the fated pattern of the war to their own physical and moral destruction. Now from the bleak isolation of the Tauric coast Orestes looks back, with a judgment matured by suffering, on his own past act; and can hardly believe that it was he who precipitated himself into his present predicament. He recalls that, after the crime that destroyed his humanity, he could at first look forward to trial, absolution, and release; but he will recount later (939ff.) how trial and formal absolution did not in fact lead to release, since a quorum of Erinyes continued to persecute him. Thus he will add one more to the list of lies that Apollo has told him; and his rational conclusion that "the world of gods is as chaotic as our mortal world" links his experience vividly with that of the war-exhausted audience as they recall every enthusiastic blunder Athens has made from the betrayal of Plataea to the Sicilian venture.

The second and profounder question raised in this pregnant speech of Orestes, a question not confined to any period ancient or modern, lies in the phrase *polus taragmos* (572), "utter confusion in the world of gods." This is, of course, a fair description of the two immoral injunctions laid by divine agency on Agamemnon and on Orestes. The words "in the world of gods" include both "the conduct of gods" and "religious matters," "men's thoughts about gods." So, to the general question, What is the function of religion? the reference of these lines to the events of the play implies an answer which is consistent with the attitude shown in Euripides' work as a whole. Religion, the poet would say, unites the feelings of a community on public or domestic occasions, with a sense of reverence, order, and stability; and such occasions this play speaks of repeatedly (e.g., 221–24, 1143ff.). But most people add to this a second and different function, regarding gods no less as those to whom the individual appeals for help and protection in trouble, and for moral guidance in perplexity. The warning that the world of gods is chaotic is pertinent to both these beliefs.

First, the successive prayers addressed in this play to Apollo and Artemis are all ignored; finally Poseidon joins in frustrating the escape. This is congruous with the Homeric picture. In the *Iliad* a prayer for victory is always worth trying; the uncertainty of response never inhibits the instinctive cry. In a more sophisticated age Euripides writes also for those who try to discern fact from fancy: a man's well-being depends on natural, not on supernatural circumstances. His city may protect him, as Athena in the epilogue intervenes to prevent the depressing conclusion which the plot and the Messenger's speech have made factually inevitable. But to supply divine help to pious mortals is not to be assumed, in the last phase of the Peloponnesian war, as one of the functions of religion.

And the second popular belief, that religion should guide men in moral decisions, is no less strongly opposed. Forty years earlier, in the *Oresteia*, once Agamemnon is dead, Clytemnestra's is the sole voice that dares criticize him for the sacrifice authorized in the name of Artemis. Everyone else preserves an obstinate silence about it, and accords his memory the reverence due to a god. Now at last in Euripides' play Orestes breaks the silence. He echoes Iphigenia's indignation:

> How could my father bear to do it? [he asks.]
> I picture that pitiful sight as if I had been there.

Yet the idea that Agamemnon is to be censured is so unfamiliar and so unwelcome that when Iphigenia asks,

> And what was her reason for killing him?

the obvious answer, which she is surely expecting, does not occur to Orestes, who replies instead with a dark hint about Aegisthus, which for the audience was traditional, but in this play ought to be surprising. The killing of Agamemnon too meets unexpected treatment in this play. Iphigenia—naturally—can only see her mother's violent act as an inevitable and agonizing retribution for her own sacrifice. When we come to the third crime, the matricide, we find that, though Iphigenia in 559 admits that it was just, she also calls it evil, *kakon*, and shares with Orestes the full sense of its polluting horror (557, 693–94, 711–15, 924–28, 940, etc.). To reinforce this sense, Iphigenia's words constantly recreate the image of Clytemnestra as a young wife and mother in the home which her husband first abandoned and then desolated. This thought is expressed eight times in the first half of the play.

Iphigenia in Tauris, then, unobtrusively suggests a reversal of the usual judgment on the three crimes. The killing of Agamemnon, traditionally execrated as inexcusable, is here credited with the justice that Clytemnestra claimed, and is thus felt to be, though not excused, at least freed from the total condemnation awarded elsewhere; while the other two crimes are unreservedly denounced as violations of kindred blood, attacks upon the most gentle, vulnerable, and precious of human institutions, the family. The old judgment based on and vindicating the superior value of the male is repudiated, and replaced by the sounder criterion of humanity. When Iphigenia, still defying logic, refuses to believe that any god is evil, she rightly implies that her own judgment on divine acts is valid. The two crimes here condemned as violations of the bond of blood were both the result of guidance by a god; while the crime she pities and in part excuses is that of Clytemnestra, who consulted no oracle but her own indignation.

This moral perception on the part of Iphigenia is paralleled by Orestes when he relates the upshot of his trial. He was, as everyone knew, formally discharged; but he adds that, when the seemly agreement had been reached, he was still a man plagued and pursued by the avengers of unnatural crime; bearing a pollution that Apollo could not cleanse, and the Areopagus could not cancel. Legal discharge could not allay the poison in his soul. He must win his freedom by a desperate attempt to set right the original wrong committed by his father, which hitherto everyone had been content to forget: he must restore Iphigenia to her home, and with her reestablish the torn bond of family love. If these are the "threads drawing together" that Orestes speaks of in 1015, perhaps we should allow Apollo a modicum of credit for making the suggestion— though this could not explain his incompetence in seeing it through. In any case the poet's lesson becomes clear: that the function of religion is not to save men and women from the necessity of making their own moral decisions. The objective reality of gods is self-evident in the physical universe, in the dynamic forces of society, and in the mysterious fires of human nature. The subjective realities of right and wrong man can only discover for himself by the practice of *aidōs*, his sense of respect for intangible values.

So far in this inquiry we have seen how Euripides uses the story of Iphigenia to develop that broader theme of the relation between man and woman which was already discernible in the *Oresteia* as the field of reference in which the crucial issue of Orestes' matricide questioned the assumptions of Athenian society. His psychological study of Iphigenia is one of the most sensitive of all his studies of women; and at this point in the action an unprecedented gesture from the chorus opens another aspect of the play's theme (576–77). After brother and sister have recognized each other, the chorus leader asks:

> And what of us? Do we not know what sorrow is?
> Our parents too were dear to us; where are they now?
> And living, or not living? Who can tell us this?

These lines have sometimes been remarked for their gentle pathos; it is less often observed that Iphigenia does not remark them at all. Throughout the play the women of the chorus embody one of its main themes, the exile's longing for home, and the nostalgia of a besieged city for the happy days before the war began. They also have a close relationship with Iphigenia. She must share with them her grief for Orestes; they echo her hate as well as her love. When the plan for escape is laid, Iphigenia makes a personal appeal to each of them for help; they promise, and later keep their promise, knowing the risk. When the Messenger's story shows that their lives are in danger, their only thought is for Iphigenia and Orestes. They are not impersonal onlookers, but deeply involved, sharing exile, affection, and terror. At this one point only do they ask a moment's sympathy for their own suffering. Iphigenia's reply begins with "Listen, I have thought of a plan. Success most often follows when the same undertaking suits everyone." But by "everyone" Iphigenia means herself, Orestes, and Pylades; the plan she has thought of does not include the captive women. In fact, in this passage as elsewhere (e.g., 1005–6), Iphigenia shows that, though indignant at her own wrongs, she thinks of women in general according to the male convention, as negligible or expendable. She does not address one word to the chorus until at the end of this long scene she discovers that she needs their help (1056–74). Then she calls them "dearest friends," clasps their hands, touches their cheeks, kneels to them and entreats them, in the name of their own dear ones whom they have not seen for many years—with an improbable promise of coming back later to rescue them.

And this insensitive behavior is not an isolated feature of a character warped by cruelty suffered in childhood; selfishness is matched by vindictiveness. When Iphigenia asks the unknown Orestes for news of Greeks she had known, she mentions first four people she hates, whose deaths she rejoices at or prays for. Only after that does she ask about her family. What is the point of this embarrassing portrait? It is the contrast with the attractive picture given in 372–77—I have already quoted it—of the young girl at home, preparing for her marriage, before her introduction to the world. The whole pattern is accordant with the theme of many plays belonging to Euripides' early period, such as *Protesilaus*, *Cretan Women*, *Danae*, *Alope*, all depicting men's cruelty to their daughters. So Iphigenia's loneliness and bitter memories are reflected in this palpable and saddening loss of the nobility she should have inherited. This loss is emphasized by the fact that immediately afterwards Orestes and Pylades both show a nobility unimpaired by misfortune, to which Iphigenia warmly responds. The kind of suffering that comes to men can be survived; but to endure a woman's lot corrodes the soul.

The second and third choral odes—the one tragic in tone, the other elegantly satiric—echo the allusions to Orestes' infancy by recounting the infancy of Apollo and Artemis.

> Bird of the sharp sea-cliffs,
> Halcyon, chanting your mournful note . . .
> I match with yours my wingless song of sorrow,
> Longing for the festivals of Hellas
> Where the people of my country gather;
> Longing for an Artemis whose worship is joy,
> Who has her temple by the Cynthian hill
> Where soft-haired palm and shapely laurel grow,
> And the silver-green of the holy olive
> Which sheltered Leto in her labour;
> The round lake where pools slowly turn,
> Where the swan's chant honours the Muses.

Popular festivals, joyful gatherings amidst the natural beauty of grove and lake—this, says the poet, is true religion; it is linked with seasons of the earth and of human life, and celebrates undisputed and unalterable truths. In the second ode this simple idyll is rudely shattered by a scene of war; and in the third there is a satiric hint of corruption by monopoly of influence and increase of wealth. The play shows, on the mortal plane, a shy loving girl (372–77) grown embittered and selfish, and an innocent babe grown to a hunted and haunted criminal; and on the immortal plane, a god and goddess who, once the dogs of war are let loose, bid a father kill his child and a son his mother. This corrupted and corrupting religion is what the third ode ironically celebrates, recalling, like the Priestess in *Eumenides*, Themis and the authority of human social custom, established before the younger gods were born. Both these poems reinforce the lesson that the proper function of religion is to give grace, form, and social unity to natural joy and sorrow, but not to replace human judgment in directing moral or practical decisions.

The deception of Thoas and the bogus procession are pure relief. The tone has been somber and intense; even the hopes of escape are not free from the shadows of insanity and guilt; while the idealized Hellas remembered so lovingly by the chorus and by Iphigenia, being represented by the sick Orestes and his bloodstained family, shows a grim affinity with the Hellas in which the audience are living. Iphigenia prays to Artemis, 1086ff.,

> Be gracious; come with us out of this savage land
> To Athens. Here is no fit place to make your home;
> There a city of gladness waits to welcome you.

Athens in 413 B.C. was a city of intense anxiety; in 412 the anxiety was succeeded by shock and despair. A chance to laugh at Thoas was the more necessary because of the implications of the Messenger's speech that followed. The ending of the play is, let us admit, on the surface happy; and Athena's speech contains one short passage that relates seriously to the theme of the play, 1458–61:

> Give them this law: when my people hold festival
> The priest shall with his sword touch a man's throat, and draw
> One drop of blood, as ransom for your blood now spared,
> To accord due reverence and awe to Artemis.

That is to say, the power of the sacrifice ritual may be recalled, by an appropriate symbol, on religious or civic occasions, as a reminder that men are not beasts, and that civilized society demands in the name of Athena the repudiation, not the glorification, of the sordid elements in heroic saga. Apart from this one sentence, Athena's epilogue speech has little, or contradictory, connection with the facts of the play, whose inevitable and horrendous conclusion is shown as ensured by the indifference of gods and the cruelty of man. Athena is the author's recognition of his audience's judgment about what is artistically and theatrically tolerable. The gods themselves bow to this necessity (1486).

The unfulfilled catastrophe carries the play's lesson: Seeking moral guidance from gods instead of from your own judgment puts you at the mercy of their indifference.

The purpose of this play, then, can be summarized as twofold. First, the poet restores at last to its proper place in the whole Atreid legend the original crime from which the other two followed; and this is, of course, the place Aeschylus gave it. The sacrifice of Iphigenia was the act of a man, a king, and a father, performed on behalf of men in pursuit of a war, and symbolizing the subjection and expendability of woman. Here at last Orestes, having learned from his sufferings to condemn his own obedience to Apollo, is ready also to condemn his father's acceptance of Artemis' condition. Iphigenia too demonstrates the authority of instinctive human judgment. She burns with indignation at the immeasurable wrong her father did her, and returns to it again and again; yet she loves her father because she is his own flesh and blood, and she pities him and lays aside her resentment. The play also connects the first crime closely with the third, both being committed against women, and both authorized by gods; and in some degree mitigates the guilt of the second crime, hitherto execrated as the most heinous of all. This too recognizes the design first created by Aeschylus.

Second, Euripides presents Iphigenia and Orestes as two lives destroyed by the war their father undertook; the one a victim, the other guilty, of unnatural crime, of kin murder. The most distressing feature of the Peloponnesian war was the fact that, since many cities in the Spartan alliance contained a democratic minority, and many in the Athenian alliance an oligarchic minority, in every community the struggle partook of the nature of civil war. Faction divided families; each city had its list of dissident citizens in exile, and its list of alien citizens in temporary residence. The possibility of betrayal by a man's own kin was always present: as Thucydides records, "Blood became a weaker bond than party" (3.82.6). Thus the Atreid revenges provided an all too clear symbol of the course of the war. Euripides in *Iphigenia in Tauris* continues Sophocles' use of the story as an analogue of the moral tensions induced by the conflict, but shifts emphasis from personal moral standards to the disruption of families; and he adds an element missing in Sophocles, the sense of a mental and emotional disease following on the violent rejection of those natural ties that bind together a city and base a city's strength on the loyal cohesion of each family group.

The uncertain end of this play leaves open the question whether at this late stage escape is still possible from the barbarism that has overtaken a noble tradition; that is, whether the political insanity of Hellas is curable. Euripides posed the question still more urgently two or three years later in *The Phoeni-*

cian Women, where the choice between Dionysus the life-giver and Ares the bringer of death is placed before two brothers fighting for the throne of Thebes; and their death leaves the city shattered but still living. Two years after that, in *Orestes*, the last play Euripides himself presented in Athens, the time for choice has gone by; there insanity is plainly incurable, and destruction the only prospect.

15

The Ultimate Casualty:
Orestes

Euripides composed this play for the fiftieth anniversary of Aeschylus' *Oresteia*. It is a pessimistic play. Its theme is deterioration; the son of Agamemnon is shown as a worse man than his father. Orestes and Pylades here are in painful contrast to the two friends we meet in *Iphigenia in Tauris*, written five years earlier. In the play's action—in Orestes, in Electra, and in the chorus—virtue vanishes before our eyes.

In 408 B.C. Athens had been at war with Sparta for twenty-three years. It was nearly five years since two large Athenian fleets and two large armies had been totally lost in Sicily. Few citizens can have had any doubt that final defeat must come; but the prospect was so incredible that the Assembly was still in a mood to reject terms of peace; and the war was continued for a further four years. The audience to which *Orestes* was presented had for three years been virtually under siege. Euripides' play of the previous year, *The Phoenician Women*, had opened with a grimly realistic scene on the walls of a besieged city, with two characters gazing out at the enemy army and identifying by face the chiefs of many states who had gathered for the attack.

The whole of that play had been about war; and its choral odes had presented the story, not as an issue between the besieged city and its enemies, but as an issue between two modes of existence, figured as two gods with opposite claims on men's worship: Dionysus the life-giver and Ares the destroyer. In *Orestes* there is no fighting. The action begins six days after the deed of blood, the murder of Clytemnestra, and just before the passing of the death sentence on Orestes, who throughout the play is a sick man waiting for death. The image has changed from a besieged city to a condemned man; from the curse of Labdacus to the curse of Tantalus; but the theme is still Athens.

Within a few months after the production of *Orestes* the poet had left his home and settled in Macedon. When writing this play he may well have guessed, or known, that he was preparing the last direct address he would ever offer to his fellow Athenians. Why did he choose this theme? What question is resolved in this play, what act accomplished? Kitto in his *Greek Tragedy* says it is a melodramatic *tour de force* designed to hold interest by surprise and violence. Wesley D. Smith, in an article in *Hermes* (1967), interprets it as a thoroughly worked out study of disease. Each of these views is true, as far as it goes; but neither explains what the play is about and why it was written.

Let me begin with an outline of the action. In the prologue Electra tells us that Orestes has been lying ill for six days since he killed his mother, unconscious most of the time, but occasionally waking to remorse and despair, or to fits of raging insanity. She refers, in terms of violent hatred, to Helen, who during the previous night came back with Menelaus after seventeen years' absence. Presently Helen comes in, and she and Electra have a short conversation, which later I shall discuss in detail. The chorus of Argive women arrive to sympathize with Electra. Orestes wakes, and Electra tells him that Menelaus and Helen have come. They both hope that Menelaus may somehow be able to save them from the death sentence which the Argive Assembly is likely to pass this same day. As soon as he begins to talk of Helen, Orestes falls into a fit of violent insanity which lasts several minutes. It passes; and after a short, tender passage in which brother and sister comfort each other, he collapses again on his couch, and the chorus pray to the Furies to have mercy on him.

In the second episode Menelaus arrives from the harbor; and Orestes kneels to him and begs for his help. What Orestes wants him to do is to bring up to the city whatever men he has with him and use their armed force to make the Assembly of Argos acquit him and Electra. A third figure appears, Clytemnestra's father Tyndareos, who does not share Menelaus' sympathy with Orestes. It is made clear that the Argos of this play is a fully organized fifth-century democratic state, in which the proper course for Orestes would have been, not to murder Clytemnestra, but to indict her in legal form before the Assembly, which had the same power to deal with her as it is now exercising to deal with her murderer. Now, Menelaus was never king of Argos, but of Sparta; and he has been away from Peloponnese for seventeen years, so that to the new generation of citizens he means nothing. His connection with Argos is that his brother the king was murdered there seven years ago, and the city had clearly accepted that as a *fait accompli*. Menelaus has every reason therefore to be cautious—indeed apprehensive. He listens sympathetically to Orestes—which in itself incurs the risk of pollution; and then promises to go to the Assembly and use tact and persuasion to oppose a death sentence. Orestes replies to this offer with a volley of abuse, calling Menelaus coward and traitor.

Then Pylades arrives, and Orestes welcomes him as a true friend. Pylades encourages Orestes to go with him to the Assembly and speak in his own defense. When they have gone, the chorus of Argive women, who in their first ode had prayed to the Furies to spare Orestes, and lamented the overthrow of the house of Tantalus, now state the moral issue of the play in unequivocal terms. They have listened to the debate in the previous scene, and heard Orestes' defense of his action; and they pity Orestes but cannot acquit him. Above all, they dismiss as irrelevant the oracle that commanded matricide; and they reinforce the view that Apollo's command was a crucial moral test for brother and sister, whose obedience to it was their irretrievable moral failure. Electra saw this clearly in her first exchange with the chorus:

> EL. Apollo made our lives a sacrifice when he laid upon us this unnatural,
>   this heart-rending deed, to kill our mother, who killed our father.
> CH. Just it may have been.
> EL. Right it was not.

Orestes saw the truth in his first scene:

> I believe my father, had I asked him face to face
> Whether I ought to kill her, would have gripped my hand
> And begged, implored me not to lift the sword against
> My mother.

Menelaus and Tyndareos both see it; and now the chorus, in their second ode, state the truth forcibly:

> That noble deed was not noble. . . .
> 'Crime in a just cause' is an impious sophistry,
> An insanity breeding in evil hearts.

In the third episode a messenger comes to report that the Assembly has condemned Orestes and Electra; the only concession is that instead of being publicly stoned they are to take their own lives. Pylades is in almost as desperate a position, since his father has exiled him as polluted by the murder in which he had shared. Here, then, we have a trio of condemned murderers hemmed in on all sides by indignant enemies. Their earlier recognition of their own guilt has vanished from the minds of Orestes and Electra. It is replaced partly by a sense of the tragedy that has overtaken a once glorious house—this Electra voices in her monody:

> Here is pity, here is indignation
> For the fate of those who will die,
> Who once were leaders of the armies of Hellas.
> Lost, lost and vanished,
> Gone is the race of Pelops, root and branch,
> The prosperous home that was the world's envy. . . .
> In the length of mortal life there is no permanence.

But stronger than the sense of tragedy is the furious resentment against a world that has condemned them. Brother and sister unite in again calling Menelaus a coward and traitor. If Menelaus had still any intention, after the insults that his offer of help had evoked, of speaking for Orestes at the trial, it would have evaporated when he heard the incredibly stupid speech that Orestes made in his own defense before the Assembly. From the Messenger's report of this performance we can recognize again the half-insane tone of Orestes' arguments with Menelaus and Tyndareos—here is a sample of his address to the citizens:

> For if wives may kill husbands
> And not be guilty, you had all best lose no time,
> But die today, before your wives make slaves of you. . . .
>   If you now kill me,
> The law is void; the sooner a man dies the better,
> Since wives lack but encouragement, not enterprise.

Plainly Orestes had disgusted the Assembly. His resentment at being condemned directs itself against Menelaus, who is out of his reach. What does a criminal do when cornered? He has a friend at hand who knows his mind exactly. Pylades says to him:

> Let's put heads together, since we're going to die,
> To ensure a share of suffering for Menelaus.
> OR. Friend! I could die contented, if I saw that done.
> PY. Let's kill Helen. That will really hurt Menelaus.
> OR. How can we do it? I'm ready, if the plan will work.

The next hundred lines offer the most concentrated essence of depraved nastiness to be found in Euripides; its climax is Electra's proposal that they should seize Hermione as a hostage and, if Menelaus won't help them to escape, cut her throat. The scene ends with another parody of the conspiracy scene in *Choephori*, the invocation of Agamemnon's spirit; and the two men enter the palace with swords drawn.

But meanwhile another significant thing has happened. While the men of Argos were in the Assembly listening to speeches for and against Orestes, and voting to condemn him, a representative group of their wives was on stage as the chorus, echoing their husbands' judgment in other terms. They were present to sympathize with the sick Orestes as victim of a divine command which was hideously wrong. "That noble deed was not noble." This was their sober judgment; the duty of piety was to disobey Delphi. Then came news of the death sentence, and Electra's lament for the past glories of a great house; followed by Orestes' gloomy despair, his passionate and morbid duet of farewell with his sister, and the emotional exchange between the two men which echoes, and debases, a similar scene from *Iphigenia in Tauris*; and finally Pylades' proposal to commit one more murder before they die—not because it has any chance of saving them, but out of jealousy, revenge, and lust for blood. The sudden change from passive gloom to positive action, joined with the impact of Pylades' personality, which is courageous, decisive, impudent, and totally unscrupulous—all this throws the chorus off their balance. Those women of Argos now forget their earlier judgment; and, hearing Pylades and Orestes propose to murder Helen to pay out Menelaus, they comment simply:

> The daughter of Tyndareos, who disgraced her sex,
> Deserves the loathing of all women everywhere.

Clytemnestra and Helen were both daughters of Tyndareos. One left her husband, the other murdered her husband; but the chorus do not now ask themselves which was the worse crime. They are caught up in the hysteria induced by Pylades. When the men have gone indoors to do the murder, the chorus accept Electra's instructions, and stand on guard enthusiastically to give warning if Menelaus should return to rescue his wife. They illustrate exactly the demoralization of civilian communities in times of violence that Thucydides described in his famous chapters in Book 3. They hear without a qualm Helen's death shriek, and the terrible lines with which Electra greets it in an ecstasy of hate—"Kill, kill, kill!" Electra next addresses the chorus as "her dearest friends," O *philtatai gynaikes*; and they express a vivid desire to "see Helen's dead body lie in blood on the palace floor." This horrifying transformation of a chorus is unparalleled in extant Greek tragedy.

Hermione comes. "Go indoors," says Electra, "and beg Helen to plead for my life and for Orestes'"—and Hermione agrees at once. Inside the door we hear her scream as Orestes grabs her. The Phrygian slave comes out to escape Orestes' sword and to report Helen's murder. He had been her slave, and Menelaus had destroyed his country; but this Phrygian slave is sane, not revengeful, and he sees the murder for what it is—a pitiful and disgusting brutality. Orestes comes out, holds his sword at the slave's throat, and gives a demonstration of violent lunacy. Then he goes in, and soon appears again with Pylades on the palace wall, with his sword at Hermione's throat. Menelaus comes, parleys with the madman from below, but is uncertain how to deal with him; when at last Apollo appears above, and stops the action. We will discuss Apollo presently; we have spent long enough in outlining what happens in the play, and it is time to ask, What on earth is it all about?

Kitto speaks of the contrast between the mutual affection and tenderness of brother and sister and their inherited criminality, and rightly sees this as an element in the play's tragic quality. But to write of the poet's "firm control of dramatic rhythm" in this "spectacular portrayal of insane behaviour" is to describe the play without explaining anything. The same applies to analysis of the sickness imagery. A. P. Burnett, who devotes two chapters of *Catastrophe Survived* to this play, believes the essence of its meaning lies in a serious, face-value interpretation of the epilogue. That is to say, the Delphic command to kill Clytemnestra was divine and righteous; Orestes' insanity was due to his loss of faith in the god he obeyed, and his sanity and his faith are now mercifully restored by a personal epiphany of Apollo. This view of Apollo as a revelation of truth seems to me to contradict not only the evidence of our eyes and ears, but—more important—to contradict every serious moral perception expressed in the play.

Let us ask, then, what justification there is for the suggestion I have already made, that in the figure of the sick and insane Orestes, Euripides was offering to his audience a personification of their own city of Athens, and in the whole play a statement that the sickness is now past cure. For an interpretation of this nature, proof is out of the question; but probability, confirmed by dramatic development, can be strong.

The previous year's play, *The Phoenician Women*, presented a much more obvious analogy, with its setting of a besieged city, its vivid portrait of Eteocles so exactly like the Athenian spokesman in the Melian Dialogue, and the constantly repeated image of two fighting beasts—an image that settled itself clearly on Eteocles and Polyneices, making them transparent analogues of Athens and Sparta. In the downfall of the royal house of Thebes, at least the city itself survived, with its walls intact and its population still capable of political life under Creon's kingship. In *Orestes* the prologue gives us again the history of a once glorious house now threatened, after successive generations of violence, with final extinction. Just as in *Phoenissae* the mutual slaughter of the two combatants caused the death of their mother, so in *Orestes* the young generation, by adherence to an outworn tradition of bloody reprisal backed by religious sanction, have killed their mother. Athens, like Thebes, claimed that her race was born from the soil of Hellas. In other words, the generation of Hellenes that has destroyed Hellas with war is guilty of matricide. In the first choral ode the Argive women, standing by the prostrate Orestes, ask, "What is this pitiful, bloodthirsty struggle, *agōn*, which drives you to frenzy?" They continue:

> The greatest happiness is not permanent
> In the world of men;
> But the storms of God rise against it,
> Like a light sailing-ship they shatter it,
> Terrors and disasters roll around it,
> Till crashing waves close over death.
> And this was the House of Tantalus,
> Born from the marriage of gods—

> A house that claims my reverence
> More than any house I have known.

It seems unlikely that thoughtful Athenians who saw their city's defeat coming nearer month by month did not understand what was being said; or that the smaller number who knew that the poet was speaking to them for the last time did not hear in this chorus ending his farewell to the city that had been his home and claimed his reverence for seventy-three years.

There is much more, and of intense interest, that demands study in this last of the "matricide plays"; in particular, the part played in the drama by Helen, and the symbolic implication of her murder by Orestes and Pylades. To pursue the inquiry beyond this point, however, into the complex action of the play's second half, would not be relevant here. (A full analysis of *Orestes* will be found in chapter 3 of my *Ironic Drama*.) In brief, I believe that the true character of Helen in this play represents those gentle, noble, and personal values in social life which most men and women recognize—when they are not driven by violent passion—as containing the essence of human happiness. Orestes and Pylades represent the generation of Greek fighters who in their lust for bloodshed and revenge had despised and attacked those values, and thus had destroyed the life of the land that gave them birth.

It is true that at the time when this play was first acted one of the most perfect examples of the Athenian love of beauty, the Erechtheion, was nearing completion in spite of the ominous direction the war was taking. But what Helen symbolized was more than the beauty of art. She was not a statue, but a woman, full of the warmth, truth, and simplicity that Euripides depicted in her single short scene in *Orestes*. These are the qualities and values that Thucydides in his famous comment, already referred to, on the Corcyrean revolution, described as poisoned and destroyed by the strains and passions of war.

It was this human quality that alone could make life in a tragic world endurable for men and women—a quality which, as desperation closed in on Athens, Euripides saw diminished, perhaps dying. Up to the previous year, the year of *The Phoenician Women*, there had still been a possibility of choice between Dionysus and Ares, life and death. Now, the poet felt, the choice had been made; Athens had committed herself to the leadership of Ares. The vestiges of truth, visible in Orestes and Electra in their first scene, vanish; and the ultimate casualty of their cult of hatred and revenge is the woman who embodies that quality for love of which Athens, above all cities, had been revered. This view may have been pessimistic; but it is the view that this farewell play expresses. In the most ironic of all epilogues Helen appears, silent, beyond reach of a world that is no longer fit to house either perfect beauty or the Muse of Euripides.

Notes

All quotations from the plays of Aeschylus and Euripides are from the author's published translations of these plays or are newly rendered for this book.

Chapter 1

1. Some discussion of the method and significance of the voting (*Eu.* 707–53) will be found in chapter 6.

2. Praxithea's speech from *Erechtheus* is referred to again in chapter 5. Here it is in full:

> A generous act is the more welcome when performed
> With noble readiness. Those who act, but act only
> After delay, fall short, I think, in nobleness.
> I, then, will give my daughter to be killed. My thought
> Offers me many reasons. First, no one could find
> Another city of more precious worth than this.
> We are a race not gathered out of foreign lands,
> But born from this soil—unlike other cities which
> Are composite of different elements brought in,
> As if by a game of chance, from various origins.
> The man who from another city settles here
> Resembles an ill-fitting mortice in a beam—
> A citizen in name, in fact an alien.
> Secondly, we bear children to this end, that we
> May rescue the altars of the gods and our home-land.
> An entire city has one name, but many souls
> Live in her: is it right I should destroy the many
> When I can give, for all their lives, one girl to die?
> If I can count, and tell the greater from the less,
> The fall of one man's house is not of greater moment
> Than a whole city's fall, nor even equal. If
> The children I have raised were boys instead of girls,
> And flames of war enclosed us, would I then refuse,
> In fear for my sons' lives, to send them out to war?
> No; I would wish to have children who will fight and take
> Their glorious place as soldiers, not mere ciphers who
> People the city with their uselessness. Mothers

Who shed tears as their sons go forth to war destroy
Their manhood. I hate women who choose for their sons
Life before glory, and train them up to cowardice.
When soldiers die in battle flanked by all their peers,
The city gives them their reward, an honoured grave
And fame; and when my daughter gives her single life
To save this city, she alone shall win the crown.
She shall preserve her mother, you, her two sisters;
Why, then, is it not noble to receive this gift?
I will give up this girl, who is mine only by birth,
To be offered for her country. Should this city of ours
Be captured, what joy in my children have I then?
What power I have shall not betray our common cause;
The part of others is to govern; mine, to save.
Our city's health will prosper by this firm resolve:
That no man living shall, with my consent, ever
Annul the ancient customs of our ancestors;
Nor shall Eumolpus and his Thracian troops set up
Their trident decked with garlands on the city's steps
To oust Athena's olive and the Gorgon's gold
And leave the Maiden's shrine unhonoured. Citizens,
Take for your use the child I bore! Deliverance
And victory be yours; for I shall never shrink,
To spare one life, from saving Athens. O my land,
Would that each soul within you loved you as I do!
Then we should live at ease, and you be safe from harm.

For more detailed discussion of all the fragments of *Erechtheus*, see my *Ironic Drama*, pp. 193 ff.

3. E.g., C. P. Segal, "The Two Worlds of Euripides' *Helen*"; J. J. Peradotto, "The Omen of the Eagles and the Ēthos of Agamemnon."

4. "Morals and Politics in the *Oresteia*," ad fin.

5. *Catastrophe Survived*, pp. 183 ff.

6. *Sophocles*, trans. H. and D. Harvey, p. 197.

Chapter 2

This chapter appeared previously as "Aeschylus' Orestes," in vol. 77, no. 3 of *The Classical World*, pp. 145–57. It is reprinted by permission.

1. See also Dodds, "Morals and Politics in the *Oresteia*," p. 30, where he describes Orestes as taking upon himself "the necessary guilt of human action."

2. Notably that of Lebeck, Zeitlin, and Peradotto (see References).

3. It is possible that this notion originated with Mazon's misleading translation of *mētrothen* as "sortant de sa mère."

Chapter 3

1. The grim or rueful tone of this phrase is echoed in Sophocles *Electra* 1425: *kalōs, Apollōn ei kalōs ethespisen*, "if Apollo did well to command matricide."

2. To pass on an embarrassing suppliant to someone else, offering politeness, promises, and good wishes instead of the help needed, is a routine memorably illustrated in Euripides' *Heracleidae*.

Chapter 5

1. The first two utterances of the refrain (121, 139) are occasioned by pity for the hare; the third (159), by pity not only for the death of Iphigenia but also for the sorrows which must follow it, canceling the "great advantages" (156) of the victory over Troy.

2. Aeschylus' Elders have an interesting parallel in Shakespeare's Prospero. In both cases we have *a voice* speaking at times profound prophetic truth, linked with *action* that displays self-deception and false judgment.

3. The personal nature of many such reactions illustrates the uniqueness of Aeschylus' achievement in the creation of character. The only precedent to such creation was the very different achievement of Homer in the principal portraits of the *Iliad* and *Odyssey*.

Chapter 6

1. The close of Athena's speech may recall a moment in *Hamlet*:

HAMLET.   If she should break it now . . . !
QUEEN.   The lady doth protest too much, methinks.

Chapter 11

1. Did the chorus of Danaids number fifty? Nothing in the text states this directly; but in 321 it is mentioned that Aegyptus, brother of Danaus, has fifty sons; and these are the young men who wish to marry the Danaids, and who reach the Argive shore in several ships halfway through the play. It may well be that this single reference to the number known to tradition was felt by the dramatist to be sufficient indication that a chorus of twelve or fifteen was to be accepted as representing the full legendary complement. See Taplin, the chapter on *Suppliants*.

Chapter 12

This chapter appeared previously as "Aeschylus' *Seven Against Thebes*," in vol. 73, no. 4 of *The Classical World*, pp. 211–19. It is reprinted by permission.

1. See the diagram supplied in Tucker's edition of *Suppliants*.

2. It is not relevant to the purpose of this chapter to discuss at what point the genuine text ends and the spurious begins.

References

Burnett, A. P. *Catastrophe Survived*. Oxford: Oxford University Press, 1971.

Devereux, G. *Dreams in Greek Tragedy*. Oxford: Blackwell, 1976.

Dodds, E. R. "Morals and Politics in the *Oresteia*." *Proceedings of the Cambridge Philological Society*, 1960.

Dover, K. J. "Some Neglected Aspects of Agamemnon's Dilemma." *Journal of Hellenic Studies* 93 (1973): 58–69.

Fraenkel, E., ed. *Agamemnon*. Oxford: Oxford University Press, 1950.

Kitto, H. D. F. *Greek Tragedy*. 3d ed. London: Methuen, 1961.

———. *Form and Meaning in Drama*. 2d ed. London: Methuen, 1964.

Lebeck, A. *The Oresteia: A Study in Language and Structure*. Cambridge, Mass.: Harvard University Press, 1971.

Mazon, P. *L'Orestie d'Eschyle*. Paris: Fontemoing, 1903.

Page, D., ed. *Agamemnon*. Oxford: Oxford University Press, 1957.

Peradotto, J. J. "Some Patterns of Nature Imagery in the Oresteia." *American Journal of Philology* 85 (1964).

———. "The Omen of the Eagles and the Ēthos of Agamemnon." *Phoenix* 23 (1969).

Pope, M. W. M. "Merciful Heavens? A Question in Aeschylus' *Agamemnon*." *Journal of Hellenic Studies* 94 (1974): 100–113.

Reinhardt, K. *Sophocles*. Translated by H. and D. Harvey. Oxford: Blackwell, 1979.

Segal, C. P. "The Two Worlds of Euripides' *Helen*." *Transactions of the American Philological Association* 102 (1971).

Smith, W. D. "Disease in Euripides' *Orestes*." *Hermes* 95 (1967).

Taplin, O. *The Stagecraft of Aeschylus*. Oxford: Oxford University Press, 1977.

Tucker, T. *The "Supplices" of Aeschylus*. Cambridge: Cambridge University Press, 1908.

Vellacott, P. *Ironic Drama: A Study of Euripides' Method and Meaning*. Cambridge: Cambridge University Press, 1975.

Whallon, W. "The Serpent at the Breast." *Transactions of the American Philological Association* 89 (1958).

Whitman, C. H. *Homer and the Heroic Tradition*. Cambridge, Mass.: Harvard University Press, 1958.

Winnington-Ingram, R. P. "Septem Contra Thebas." *Yale Classical Studies* 25 (1977): 1–46.

Zeitlin, F. "The Motif of the Corrupted Sacrifice in Aeschylus' *Oresteia*." *Transactions of the American Philological Association* 96 (1965).

Addendum. I would also like to mention an article by D. S. Carne-Ross, "The Beastly House of Atreus" (*The Kenyon Review*, n.s. 3 [1981]: 20–60). This lively and stimulating article was kindly brought to my notice by Mr. Reynolds Smith after the manuscript of this book was completed.

Index of Subjects and Persons

This index does not include items that can be more readily traced by referring to chapter headings or to the Index of Passages in the *Oresteia*.

Index of Passages in
the *Oresteia*

This index includes passages referred to in chapters 1–10. Line numbers are italic, page numbers are roman.

657–61, 42, 81–82
667–73, 35, 82
681–710, 82–83
710, 22

736–41, 29
762, 82
850, 44
970–73, 35